Science and Christianity:
CONFLICT OR COHERENCE?

D1082277

Henry F. Schaefer

The University of Georgia

Printed in the United States of America
by the University of Georgia Printing Department, Athens, Georgia.
Design and illustrations by William Reeves

Library of Congress Cataloging-in-Publication Data

Schaefer, Henry F., 1944-
Science and Christianity: Conflict or Coherence? / Henry F. Schaefer,

All correspondence should be addressed to:
Professor Henry F. Schaefer
Center for Computational Chemistry
University of Georgia
Athens, Georgia 30602

ISBN 0-9742975-0-X

www.ccc.uga.edu

Science and Christianity: CONFLICT OR COHERENCE?

HENRY F. SCHAEFER

Contents

Appendices

Preface

The present book developed from a series of university lectures given over the past twenty years. There are advantages and disadvantages to such an evolutionary process. On the positive side, the lectures have been given sufficiently many times (in so many different stages of development) that one hopes the most egregious errors have been identified and removed. There is a small amount of overlap between some chapters to maintain the integrity of each lecture. In addition, the public lectures have provided opportunities for a great many helpful people to present me with pieces of valuable information that were subsequently incorporated into the lectures and now the book. I am grateful to all who contributed in this way, and I apologize for not recording each name at the time the help was rendered.

On the negative side, for at least the first decade in which the lectures were given, I did not consider it probable that a book might be forthcoming. Audio and video tapes of the lectures were recorded and distributed, and I was happy with those means of communication. My audiences of university students and faculty were expecting "popular" rather than "technical" lectures, so citation records were maintained casually if at all. This means that the citations in the book are drastically less complete than would be required for an original scholarly piece of research, the sort of paper I would publish in the *Journal of Chemical Physics*. I have used the writings of some authors so frequently (for example, Hugh Ross on cosmology, Dean Kenyon on origin of life, and Faye Ann Crowell on C.S. Lewis) that it would have been impossible not to mention their work. However, I am sure that many others have not been given proper credit here. For all who fall in that category and recognize my sins of omission, I would ask that you write to me, providing detailed citation documentation. Should a second edition of the book be forthcoming, I intend to be much more careful in this regard.

My wife Karen, the desire of my eyes (Ezekiel 24:21), has endured each of these lectures, some many times. For a person with a degree in Art History from Stanford University, this has been cruel and unusual punishment. Not surprisingly, her favorite of the lectures is "The Ten Questions." Karen has also carefully proofread most of this manuscript. She has my undying love and appreciation. Special thanks go to Dr. Theodore Lewis, Blum-Iwry Professor of Near Eastern Studies at Johns Hopkins University, for mercilessly insisting that the lectures be turned into a book. Those who constructively criticized all or part of the manuscript include Dr. Howard Abney (Athens), Attorney Todd Bair (Atlanta), Professor William Bordeaux (Huntington College), Professor Tucker Carrington (Montreal), Professor Christopher Cornwell (Athens), Virgil Early (Jekyll Island), Dr. Paul Hartman (Athens), Professor Thomas Lessl (Athens), Professor Frederic Merkt (Zürich), Professor William H. Miller (Berkeley), Vincent Nelson (Walnut Creek, California), and Professor Martin Quack (Zürich). I thank Professor Phillip Johnson (Berkeley) for 25 years of friendship and for countless discussions on subjects broached in this book. I thank the University of Georgia freshman (15-18 gifted students each year for the past five years) who have listened to and commented on many (but not all) of these lectures, as a part of a first semester course with the same title as the book. Finally, I thank my peerless senior administrative secretary, Mrs. Linda Rowe, who has cheerfully labored through the past 15 years, during which this book was very slowly coming to fruition. Of course, all errors and oversights are my sole responsibility.

Introduction 1

first began teaching freshman chemistry at Berkeley in January of 1984. The physical sciences lecture hall at Berkeley holds about 550 persons. On the first day of class one could squeeze in 680 students, which we had on that particular morning. It was a very full auditorium. Those of you who have had freshman chemistry at a large university will know that many have mixed feelings about such courses. I had never addressed a group of 680 people before and was a bit concerned about it. But I had a fantastic demonstration prepared for them.

At Berkeley in the physical sciences lecture hall, the stage is divided into three parts. It rotates around, so you can go to your part of the stage and work for two hours before your lecture, getting everything ready. My assistant, Lonny Martin, who still does the undergraduate chemistry demonstrations at Berkeley, was behind the stage in the process of setting up ten moles of a large number of common chemical quantities. Ten moles of benzene, iron, mercury, ethyl alcohol, water, etc. At just the right time, at the grand crescendo of this lecture, Lonny was going to press the stage button, and he would unexpectedly rotate into view and show the students the ten moles of various items. The students would have a moment of enlightenment as they realized that each displayed quantity of these chemical substances had the same number of molecules, namely ten times Avogadro's number.

It was going to be wonderful. We got to the critical point in the lecture and I said, "Lonny, come around and show us the moles." Nothing happened—the stage did not move an inch. Lonny was not ready with the moles. This was very embarrassing. I went out in front of the 680 students and was really at a complete loss of what to say, so I made some unprepared remarks. I said, "While we're waiting for the moles, let me tell you what happened to me in church yesterday morning." I was desperate. There was great silence among those 680 students. They had come with all manner of anticipations about freshman chemistry, but stories about church were not among them!

At least as surprised as the students, I continued, "Let me tell you what my Sunday School teacher said yesterday." The students became very quiet. "I was hoping the group at church would give me some support, moral, spiritual, or whatever, for dealing with this large class, but I received none. In fact, the Sunday School teacher first told anecdotes about his own freshman chemistry instructor, who kicked the dog, beat his wife, and so on. Then he asked the class, in honor of me:"

> *"What is the difference between a dead dog lying in the middle of the road and a dead chemistry professor lying in the middle of the road?"*

The class was excited about this and I hadn't even gotten to the punch line. They roared with laughter. The very concept of a dead chemistry professor lying in the middle of the street was hilarious to them. I'm sure some of them began to think, "If this guy were to become a dead chemistry professor very close to the final exam, we probably wouldn't have to take the final exam. Berkeley would probably give us all passing grades, and this would be wonderful."

Then I told the students that my Sunday school teacher had said that the difference between a dead dog lying in the middle of the road and a dead chemistry professor lying in the middle of the road is that there are skid marks in front of the dead dog. It was a new joke at the time, and the class thought it was outstanding! Just as they settled down, I pressed the button and around came Lonny with the moles. It was an extraordinary beginning to my career as a freshman chemistry lecturer.

About 50 students came down to the front of the auditorium at the end of class. About half had the usual questions like "Which dot do I punch out of this registration card?" There is always some of that. But about half of these students had related questions. Basically they wanted to know "What were you doing in church yesterday?" One in particular said, "The person I have most admired in my life to date was my high school chemistry teacher last year. He told me with great certainty that it was impossible to be a practicing chemist and a Christian. What do you think about that?" I responded briefly, but we didn't have time for a lengthy discussion. However, some of the other students who were listening in asked me if I would give a public lecture on this topic. That was the origin of the present essay.

I gave this talk in Berkeley, at Stanford University, and in the San Francisco Bay Area a number of times. The lectures were well attended and mildly controversial. One of the local newspapers ran a substantial story (April 19, 1986) on the Stanford lecture, given at an American Scientific Affiliation symposium "God and Modern Science: Who Shapes Whom?" The author of this particular story titled it "Science and Religion: Chemist an Exception." As you will see if you read on, this conclusion was quite the opposite of the picture I had attempted to draw in my lecture. The lecture was also given to a modest audience at Brown University (1985), to a large audience at the University of Canterbury, Christchurch, New Zealand (1986), and to an audience of five brave souls at the University of Kansas (1986; a return trip to the University of Kansas drew an audience of 200 in April, 2000).

When I moved to the University of Georgia in late 1987, the level of interest in these lectures increased dramatically. In large part this was because some faculty members complained to the University of Georgia administration. It was an interesting chapter in my life. The *Atlanta Journal and Constitution*, the largest newspaper in the southeastern United States, ran a front page story on October 23 entitled "UGA Science Prof's Lectures Prove Volatile Brew." These hostile faculty members were of the opinion that it was unconstitutional for anyone to use a vacant university classroom to discuss the relationship between science and religion. A few days later my sister-in-law called from Seattle, saying that she had heard on the radio that I was being fired for preaching in the classroom! In fact, I had yet to teach my first class at the University of Georgia. Moreover, the President of the University of Georgia, Dr. Charles B. Knapp, swiftly came to my defense. Dr. Knapp stated to the press "This kind of intellectual ferment is good for the place. I think it's an exercise of his freedom of speech." And on Saturday morning October 31, the *Atlanta Journal and Constitution* published an editorial supporting me. The *AJC* stated "Fanatics are demanding rigorous control over the dissemination of ideas . . . . University officials have had the good sense—and the courage—to resist. They must continue to do so." The Athens, Georgia (a city of 100,000) newspapers also came to my defense and a "street poll" conducted by the media indicated that virtually all the students on the University of Georgia campus viewed the issue as a matter of freedom of speech.

Lesser headlines followed, the most creative appearing in the January 10, 1988 edition of the *Savannah Morning News/Evening Press*: "Chemistry Prof's Bible Lectures Explosive."

Scientists and Their Gods

2

Many educated people are of the opinion that there has been a terrible warfare between science and Christianity. Let us attempt to put this question of the relationship between science and Christianity in the broadest, most reasonable perspective possible. We begin by noting that the rapprochement between science and other intellectual pursuits has not always been easy. For example, the recent book *Literature* by Susan Gallagher and Roger Lundin states: "Because in recent history, literature has often found itself in opposition to science, to understand modern views about literature, we must recognize the dominance of science in our culture. For several centuries, scientists have set the standards of truth for Western culture. And their undeniable usefulness in helping us organize, analyze, and manipulate facts has given them an unprecedented importance in modern society."

For example, John Keats, the great English romantic poet, did not like Isaac Newton's view of reality. He said it threatened to destroy all the beauty in the universe. He feared that a world in which myths and poetic visions had vanished would become a barren and uninviting place. In his poem *Lamia* he talks about this destructive power. In this poem, he calls "science" "philosophy," so I will try to replace the word "philosophy" with "science" so as not to confuse the 21st century reader:

> "*Do not all charms fly*
> *At the mere touch of cold science?*
> *There was an awful rainbow once in heaven.*
> *We knew her woof, her texture.*
> *She is given in the dull catalog of common things.*
> *Science will clip an angel's wings,*
> *Conquer all mysteries by rule and line,*
> *Empty the haunted air and gnomed mine,*
> *Unweave a rainbow.*"

My point is that there has been friction between science and virtually every other intellectual endeavor since the appearance of modern science as a newcomer on the scene around 1600. So it would be surprising if there were not some heated exchanges between science and Christianity. What I am describing is called "The new kid on the block" syndrome in colloquial North American English.

Has Science Disproved God?

Nevertheless, the position is commonly stated that "science has disproved God." C. S. Lewis says, in the autobiography of his early life, *Surprised by Joy*, that he believed the above statement. He talks about the atheism of his early years on the faculty at Oxford University and credits it to science. Lewis writes: "You will understand that my (atheism) was inevitably based on what I believed to be the findings of the sciences; and those findings, not being a scientist, I had to take on trust, in fact, on authority." What Lewis is saying is that somebody told him that science had disproved God; and he believed it, even though he knew nothing about science.

A more balanced view of this question was given by one of my scientific heroes, Erwin Schrödinger (1887-1961). He was perhaps the most important of the founders of wave mechanics and the originator of what is now the most important equation in science, Schrödinger's Equation. Schrödinger declares: "I'm very astonished that the scientific picture of the real world is very deficient. It gives a lot of factual information, puts all our experience in a magnificently consistent order, but it is ghastly silent about all and sundry that is really near to our heart, that really matters to us. It cannot tell us a word about red and blue, bitter and sweet, physical pain and physical delight, knows nothing of beautiful and ugly, good or bad, God and eternity. Science sometimes pretends to answer questions in these domains, but the answers are very often so silly that we are not inclined to take them seriously." From *Nature and the Greeks*, Cambridge University Press, 1954.

Scientists do tell some interesting stories about religion. A good one is from *Chemistry in Britain*, which is something like the *Time* magazine of the chemical profession in England. Talking about the release of a new book on science policy, *Chemistry in Britain* (July, 1989) explores an interesting idea: "If God applied to the government for a research grant for the development of a heaven and an earth, He would be turned down on the following grounds:

- His project is too ambitious;
- He has no previous track record;
- His only publication is a book, not a paper in a refereed journal;
- He refuses to collaborate with his biggest competitor;
- His proposal for a heaven and an earth is all up in the air."

Some Alternatives to Belief in the Sovereign God of the Universe

I present here two examples of notable atheists. The first is Lev Landau, the most brilliant Soviet physicist of the twentieth century. Landau received the 1962 Nobel Prize in Physics for his research on liquid helium. Moreover, Landau was named a Hero of Socialist Labor by the Soviet government. He was also the author of many famous physics textbooks with his coworker E. M. Lifshitz. I used some of these books as an undergraduate at M.I.T. A story about Landau by his good friend and biographer I.M. Khalatnikov appeared in the May 1989 issue of *Physics Today*. Khalatnikov writes: "The last time I saw Landau was in 1968 after he had undergone an operation. His health had greatly deteriorated. Lifshitz and I were summoned by the hospital. We were informed that there was practically no chance he could be saved. When I entered his ward, Landau was lying on his side, his face turned to the wall. He heard my steps, turned his head, and said, 'Khalat, please save me.' Those were the last words I heard from Landau. He died that night."

The second example is Subrahmanyan Chandrasekhar, the famous astrophysicist who won the Nobel Prize in Physics in 1983. He was a faculty member at the University of Chicago for most of his life. At the back of his biography is an unusual interview. Chandrasekhar begins the dialogue, saying: "In fact, I consider myself an atheist. But I have a feeling of disappointment because the hope for contentment and a peaceful outlook on life as the result of pursuing a goal has remained largely unfulfilled."

His biographer, K. C. Wali, is astonished and responds: "What?! I don't understand. You mean, single-minded pursuit of science, understanding parts of nature and comprehending nature with such enormous success still leaves you with a feeling of discontentment?" Chandrasekhar continues in a serious way, saying: "I don't really have a sense of fulfillment. All I have done seems to not be very much."

The biographer seeks to lighten up the discussion a little, saying that everybody has the same sort of feelings. But Chandrasekhar will not let him escape, saying: "Well it may be. But the fact that other people experience it doesn't change the fact that one is experiencing it. It doesn't become less personal on that account." And Chandrasekhar's final statement, which I urge every potential young scientist to ponder, reads: "What is true from my own personal case is that I simply don't have that sense of harmony which I had hoped for when I was young. And I have persevered in science for over fifty years. The time I have devoted to other things is minuscule."

From K. C. Wali, *Chandra: A Biography of S. Chandrasekhar* (University of Chicago Press, 1991).

Is it Possible to be a Scientist and a Christian?

So the question I want to explore is the one that I was asked by that young man after my first freshman chemistry class at Berkeley, "Is it possible to be a scientist and a Christian?" The student and his high school chemistry teacher obviously thought it was not possible.

Let me begin from what some might call neutral ground by quoting two people with no particular theistic inclinations. The first individual is C. P. Snow (1905-1980). C. P. Snow remains well known in intellectual circles as the author of an essay titled *The Two Cultures and the Scientific Revolution.* C. P. Snow was a physical chemist, actually a spectroscopist, at Cambridge University. He discovered about halfway through his career that he also was a gifted writer, and Snow began writing novels. One in particular about university life at Cambridge or Oxford is called *The Masters*, and I would recommend it. C. P. Snow became quite comfortable with the royalties from his novels and was able to sit in a unique position between the world of the sciences and the world of literature. From this perspective, Snow wrote: "Statistically, I suppose, slightly more scientists are in religious terms unbelievers, compared with the rest of the intellectual world, though there are plenty who are religious, and that seems to be increasingly so among the young." So, is it possible to be a scientist and a Christian? C.P. Snow answered in the affirmative.

> **"Indeed, contrary to popular myth, scientists appear to have the same range of attitudes about religious matters as does the general public."**
>
> **— Alan Lightman**

Richard Feynman (1918-1998), Nobel Prize in Physics in 1965, was a most remarkable person. Perhaps some of my readers have seen his book of anecdotes *Surely You're Joking, Mr. Feynman.* He said some nine years before receiving the Nobel Prize, "Many scientists do believe in both science and God, the God of revelation, in a perfectly consistent way." So is it possible to be a scientist and a Christian? Yes, according to Richard Feynman, an outspoken atheist.

A good summary statement in this regard is by Alan Lightman, who has written a very well received book called *Origins: the Lives and Worlds of Modern Cosmologists.* Dr. Lightman is an M.I.T. professor who has published this seminal work with the Harvard University Press. A critical paragraph of the book states: "References to God or divine purpose continued in the scientific literature until the middle to late 1800s. It seems likely that the studied lack of religious references after this time resulted more from a change in social and professional convention among scientists rather than from any change in underlying thought. Indeed, contrary to popular myth, scientists appear to have the same range of attitudes about religious matters as does the general public."

Now someone could regard the above statement as strictly anecdotal. Many Americans like statistics better than anecdotes. So let me present the results of a poll of the members of the scientific professional society Sigma Xi. Three thousand three hundred scientists responded to the survey, and the conclusions are undoubtedly beyond statistical uncertainty. The description of the survey in the November 7, 1988 issue of *Chemical and Engineering News* reads "Scientists are anchored in the U. S. mainstream." The article states that half of the scientists polled participate in religious activities regularly. Looking at the poll more carefully, one sees that something like 41% of Ph.D. scientists are in church on a typical Sunday. In the general American public, perhaps 42% are in church on a typical Sunday. A less exhaustive but more recent (*The Scientist*, May 19, 2003) survey finds 52% of biologists identifying themselves as Christians. So it seems that whatever it is that causes people to adopt religious inclinations is unrelated to having an advanced degree in science.

Let us go a little deeper with a statement from Michael Polanyi (1891-1976), professor of chemistry and later of philosophy at the University of Manchester. His son John Polanyi won the Nobel Prize in 1986. I think that it may be true that when John Polanyi's scientific accomplishments, which have been truly magnificent, have been mostly forgotten, the impact of his father's work will continue.

Michael Polanyi was a great physical chemist at the University of Manchester. About halfway through his career, he switched over to philosophy, and particularly the philosophy of science. He was equally distinguished there. His books, the most influential of which is called *Personal Knowledge*, are not easy to read, but are very worthwhile. He was of Jewish physical descent, raised in Budapest, Hungary. About the same time that he began the switch from chemistry to philosophy, he joined the Roman Catholic Church. A typical Michael Polanyi statement reads: "I shall reexamine here the suppositions underlying our belief in science and propose to show that they are more extensive than is usually thought. They will appear to coextend with the entire spiritual foundations of man, and to go to the very root of his social existence. Hence I will urge our belief in science should be regarded as a token of much wider convictions."

If you read further, you will probably come to the same

conclusion that I draw. Polanyi points out that the observer is always there in the laboratory. He or she always makes conclusions. He or she is never neutral. Every scientist brings presuppositions to his or her work. A scientist, for example, never questions the basic soundness of the scientific method. This faith of the scientist arose historically from the Christian belief that God the father created a perfectly orderly universe. Now I must provide some concrete evidence for the latter conclusion.

Why Might a Scientist Become a Christian?

I will ask this question several times in the course of the present essay. Physics Nobelist Eugene Wigner (1902-1995) once noted "the unreasonable effectiveness of mathematics" and remarked that "the miracle of the appropriateness of the language of mathematics for the formulation of the laws of physics is a wonderful gift that we neither understand nor deserve." Interestingly, Wigner (like Polanyi) was a man of Jewish origin who found his way into nominal Christendom, in Wigner's case Protestantism. Indirectly, Wigner is hinting that the intelligibility of the universe points to a sovereign creator God. Thus mathematical physics can be an answer to the question we pose in this section. The laws of nature look just as if they have been selected as the most simple and elegant principles of intelligible change by a wise creator. Belief in the intelligibility of nature strongly suggests the existence of a cosmic mind, who can construct nature in accordance with rational laws. Dr. Keith Ward, Regius Professor at Oxford University, well stated in April 1999:

"Thus appeal to the general intelligibility of nature, its structuring in accordance with mathematical principles which can be understood by the human mind, suggests the existence of a creative mind, a mind of vast wisdom and power. Science is not likely to get started if one thinks that the universe is just a chaos of arbitrary events, or if one thinks there are many competing gods, or perhaps a god who is not concerned with elegance or rational structure. If one believes those things, one will not expect to find general rational laws, and so one will probably not look for them. It is perhaps no accident that modern science really began with the clear realization that the Christian God was a rational creator, not an arbitrary personal agent."

I need to be clear that it is not only persons with Christian sympathies who acknowledge the remarkable intelligibility of the universe. For example, Sheldon Glashow (Nobel Prize in Physics, 1979) stated in 1990: "Many scientists are deeply religious in one way or another, but all of them have a certain rather peculiar faith—they have a faith in the underlying simplicity of nature; a belief that nature is, after all, comprehensible and that one should strive to understand it as much as we can." However, without a belief in the sovereign God of the universe, one may project such general observations in questionable directions. For example, Glashow continues: "Now this faith in simplicity, that there are simple rules—a few elementary particles, a few quantum rules to explain the structure of the world—is completely irrational and completely unjustifiable."

Science Developed in a Christian Environment

I like to begin with an outrageous statement that always causes reaction. This is a statement from a British scientist, Robert Clark, and it will at least make you think. Clark states in his book *Christian Belief and Science*: "However we may interpret the fact, scientific development has only occurred in a Christian culture. The ancients had brains as good as ours. In all civilizations— Babylonia, Egypt, Greece, India, Rome, Persia, China and so on—science developed to a certain point and then stopped. It is easy to argue speculatively that, perhaps, science might have been able to develop in the absence of Christianity, but in fact, it never did. And no wonder. For the non-Christian world believed that there was something ethically wrong about science. In Greece, this conviction was enshrined in the legend of Prometheus, the fire-bearer and prototype scientist who stole fire from heaven, thus incurring the wrath of the gods."

I would prefer if Dr. Clark had said "sustained" scientific development in the first sentence quoted above. I think he went a little too far here, but his words certainly give people something to cogitate.

A frequent objection to Clark's statement is that science made significant progress in the Middle East under Islam during the Middle Ages. This is of course true, but why did these early scientific contributions fail to be "sustained"? In his important 2002 book Professor Bernard Lewis of Princeton University has addressed this critical question. Lewis's book is appropriately titled *What Went Wrong? The Clash between Islam and Modernity in the Middle East.* The inability of science to continue under Islam is perhaps best illustrated by the fate of the great observatory built in Galata, in Istanbul, in 1577. This observatory gave every promise of being comparable to that of the Danish scientist Tycho Brahe (1546-1601), who revolutionized astronomy. In *What Went Wrong?* Lewis relates that the observatory at Galata was razed to the ground by an elite corps of Turkish troops, by order of the sultan, on the recommendation of the Chief Mufti (Islamic leader) of Istanbul. For the next 300 years there was no modern observatory in the Islamic world.

Let us explore the idea involved in the statements that Polanyi, Ward, and Clark made; i.e., that modern science grew up in a Christian environment. I was taught in my childhood that Francis Bacon (1561-1626) discovered the scientific method. The higher critics have now gotten into the history of science and some claim that Bacon stole the scientific method from a multitude of others and just popularized it. We must leave that dilemma to the science historians to settle. One of Francis Bacon's most frequently quoted statements is called the "Two Books" manifesto. These words of Bacon have been highly influential and the subject of a magnificent recent essay by Professor Thomas Lessl. Francis Bacon said: "Let no one think or maintain that a person can search too far or be too well studied in either the book of God's word or the book of God's works." Bacon is talking about the Bible as the book of God's words and nature as the book of God's works. He is encouraging us to learn as much as possible about both. So, right here in the earliest days of the scientific method, we have a statement of the compatibility of science with the 66 books of the Hebrew Bible and New Testament. I have taken Bacon's advice personally, having read through the Bible more than a dozen times since I became a Christian in 1973.

Johannes Kepler (1571-1630) was a brilliant mathematician, physicist, and astronomer. Kepler posited the idea of elliptical orbits for planets and is considered the discoverer of the laws of planetary motion. He was a devout Lutheran Christian. When he was asked the question "Why do you engage in science?" Kepler answered that he desired in his scientific research "to obtain a sample test of the delight of the Divine Creator in His work and to partake of His joy." This has been re-stated in many ways by other people, to think God's thoughts after him, to know the mind of God, and so on. Kepler might be mistakenly considered a Deist based on this first statement alone. But he elsewhere clarified: "I believe only and alone in the service of Jesus Christ. In him is all refuge and solace."

Blaise Pascal (1623-1662) was a magnificent scientist. He is the father of the mathematical theory of probability and combinatorial analysis. He provided the essential link between the mechanics of fluids and the mechanics of rigid bodies. And he is in my opinion the only physical scientist to make profound contributions to Christian thinking. Many of these thoughts are found in the little book, the *Pensees*, which I was required to read as a sophomore at M.I.T. They were trying to civilize us geeks, but a few years later M.I.T. decided that it was not working; so current students are not required to take as many humanities courses.

Pascal's theology was centered on the person of Jesus Christ as Savior and based on personal experience. He stated that God makes people "conscious of their inward wretchedness (which the Bible calls sin) and his infinite mercy, unites Himself to their inmost soul, fills it with humility and joy, with confidence and love, renders them incapable of any other end than Himself. Jesus Christ is the end of all and the center to which all tends."

Robert Boyle (1627-1691) was perhaps the first chemist. He gave the first operational definition of an element, demonstrating enormous ingenuity in constructing experiments in support of the atomistic hypothesis. Many of my freshman chemistry students remember Boyle's law. I typically return to Berkeley for a week or two every year, and every once in a while I will meet one of my former chemistry students on the campus. They typically ask "Didn't you used to be Professor Schaefer?" I ask them in return "What do you remember from my freshman chemistry course?" Occasionally they will say: "pV = nRT." In such cases, I know that my teaching was fabulously successful. This of course is the ideal gas law, of which Boyle's law is a critical part. Robert Boyle was a busy person. He wrote many books, one of which is *Some*

Considerations Touching the Style of the Holy Scriptures. He personally endowed an annual lectureship promoted to the defense of Christianity against indifferentism and atheism. He was a good friend of Richard Baxter, one of the great Puritan theologians. He was governor of the Corporation for the Spread of the Gospel of Jesus Christ in New England.

Although I disagree with the finding, a recent poll concerning the most important person in history gave that honor to Sir Isaac Newton (1642-1727). Newton was a mathematician, physicist, co-discoverer with Liebnitz of calculus, and the founder of classical physics. He was the first of the three great theoretical physicists to date. He also investigated many other subjects. Newton tried very hard to do chemistry, but was less than successful. He wrote more words about theology than science. Still in print is his book about the return of Jesus Christ, entitled *Observations on the Prophecy of Daniel and the Revelation of St. John.* One of Newton's most frequently quoted statements is: "This most beautiful system of the sun, planets and comets could only proceed from the counsel and dominion of an intelligent and powerful Being." One might assume from the above statement that Newton was a deist (the system of natural religion that affirms God's existence but denies revelation). However, typical Newton statements like the following show that this is not true: "There are more sure marks of authenticity in the Bible than in any profane history."

> **"This most beautiful system of the sun, planets and comets could only proceed from the counsel and dominion of an intelligent and powerful Being."**
>
> **—Sir Isaac Newton**

In fact, one may more reasonably conclude that Newton was a Biblical literalist than a Deist. Edward B. Davis (*Science and Christian Belief,* pages 103-117, October 1991) writes that for Newton it was not enough that an article of faith could be deduced from Scripture: "It must be expressed in the very form of sound words in which it was delivered by the Apostles. For men are apt to run into partings about deductions. All the old heresies lay in deductions. The true faith was in the Biblical texts."

George Trevelyan, the distinguished secular historian, summarized the contributions I have been discussing as follows (*English Social History*, 1942): "Robert Boyle, Isaac Newton and the early members of the Royal Society were religious men, who repudiated the skeptical doctrines of Thomas Hobbes. But they familiarized the minds of their countrymen with the idea of law in the universe and with scientific methods of inquiry to discover truth. It was believed that these methods would never lead to any conclusions inconsistent with Biblical history and miraculous religion. Newton lived and died in that faith."

Beyond the 18th Century

My very favorite among these legendary figures and probably the greatest experimental scientist of all time is Michael Faraday (1791-1867). The two hundredth birthday of Michael Faraday's birth was celebrated in 1991 at the Royal Institution (the multi-disciplinary scientific research laboratory in London, of which Faraday was the Director). There was an interesting article published in this context by my friend Sir John Meurig Thomas, who said if Michael Faraday had lived into the era of the Nobel prize, he would have been worthy of *eight* Nobel Prizes. Faraday discovered benzene and electromagnetic induction, invented the generator, and was the main architect of the classical field theory of electromagnetism.

Let me contrast the end of Faraday's life with the end of Lev Landau's life, previously described. As Faraday lay on his death-bed, a friend and well-wisher came by and said, "Sir Michael, what speculations have you now?" This friend was trying to introduce some cheer into the situation. Of course the passion of Faraday's career had consisted of making "speculations" about science and then dashing into the laboratory to either prove or disprove them. It was a reasonable thing for a friend to say in a difficult situation. Faraday took the question very seriously. He replied: "Speculations, man, I have none! I have certainties. I thank God that I don't rest my dying head upon speculations for I know whom I have believed and am persuaded that he is able to keep that which I have committed unto him against that day."

The first time I used this statement in a public setting (nearly 20 years ago) a bright eyed and bushy-tailed young person in the front row of the audience burst out "I've heard that before, and I am delighted to know that it was Michael Faraday who first spoke those words." As gently as possible, I informed him that the words were first penned by St. Paul some 1800 years earlier to express his confidence in Jesus Christ. Michael Faraday had a firm grasp of the New Testament.

The second of the three great theoretical physicists of all time would certainly have to be James Clerk Maxwell (1831-1879). Trevor Williams (*Biographical Dictionary of Scientists*, 1982) has summarized Maxwell's career this way: "Maxwell possessed all the gifts necessary for revolutionary advances in theoretical physics: a profound grasp of physical reality, great mathematical ability, total absence of preconceived notions, a creative imagination of the highest order. He possessed also the gift to recognize the right task for this genius—the mathematical interpretation of Faraday's concept of electromagnetic field. Maxwell's successful completion of this task, resulting in the mathematical [field] equations bearing his name, constituted one of the great achievements of the human intellect." Those who have thought deeply about the history and philosophy of science (e.g., Michael Polanyi and Thomas Kuhn) would disagree with one statement made above. If Maxwell indeed had a "total absence of preconceived notions," he would have accomplished a total absence of science.

Although Maxwell's Equations are indeed one of the great achievements of the human intellect, as a member of the M.I.T. sophomore physics class during the 1963-1964 academic year, I probably would have described them in different language at the time. However, just before our first examination in electromagnetism, one of the members of our class had a brilliant idea. This entrepreneurial wag had 900 tee-shirts printed with Maxwell's Equations embossed in large script. The entire class showed up to the first exam dressed in this unusual garb. Maxwell's Equations were plainly visible from every seat in the auditorium. Our class averaged 95% on the first electromagnetism exam! Regrettably, the professor was distinctly unhappy. The average on his second exam, despite our awesome tee-shirts, was 15%. Never mess with a professor.

On June 23, 1864 James Clerk Maxwell wrote: "Think what God has determined to do to all those who submit themselves to his righteousness and are willing to receive his gift [the gift of eternal life in Jesus Christ]. They are to be conformed to the image of His Son, and when that is fulfilled, and God sees they are conformed to the image of Christ, there can be no more condemnation."

Maxwell and Charles Darwin were contemporaries. Many wondered what a committed Christian such as Maxwell thought of Darwin's ideas. In fact, Maxwell once was invited to attend a meeting on the Italian Riviera in February to discuss new developments in science and the Bible. If you have ever spent time in Cambridge, England, you know it is very gloomy in the wintertime. If I had been a member of the Cambridge faculty, I would have taken every opportunity to go to the Italian Riviera at this time of the year. However, Maxwell turned down the invitation, explaining in his letter of declination: "The rate of change of scientific hypotheses is naturally much more rapid than that of Biblical interpretation. So if an interpretation is founded on such a hypothesis, it may help to keep the hypothesis above ground long after it ought to be buried and forgotten."

This is sage advice. An example of just this is the steady state theory, which was popularized by Fred Hoyle and others. It was for decades one of the two competing theories of the origin of the universe. The steady state hypothesis basically says that what you see is what was always there. It became less tenable in 1965 with the observation of the microwave background radiation by Arno Penzias and Robert Wilson (much more on this in the "Big Bang" chapter). There are not many cosmologists left who believe in the steady state hypothesis. But it is amusing to go back to about 1960, find Biblical commentaries on the book of Genesis, and see the ways in which an unfortunate few explain how the steady state hypothesis can be reconciled with the first chapter of Genesis. Any reasonable person can see that the Genesis account is describing a creation from nothing (*ex nihilo*), so it takes a vivid imagination to reconcile a beginning in space, time, and history with the now discredited steady state hypothesis. By the second half of the twenty-first century, should planet earth still be here, the steady state hypothesis will be dead and nearly forgotten. These commentaries will probably still be available in libraries, but few people will be able to understand them. This is an excellent example of the important point made by James Clerk Maxwell well more than a century ago.

One of my favorite cartoons was published by Sidney Harris a few years ago in *The American Scientist*. Two distinguished elderly scientists are staring unhappily at an obscure equation on a blackboard. One of them delivers the punch line: "What is most depressing is the realization that everything we believe will be disproved in a few years." I hope that is not true of my students' research in quantum chemistry. I don't think it will be the case, but there is an important element of reality to this, in that science is inherently a tentative activity. As scientists we come to understandings that are always subject, at the very least, to further refinements.

Of course, not all biographers of these pioneers of modern physical science spoke positively of their Christian convictions. For example, James Crowther states in his biography of Faraday and Maxwell: "The religious decisions of Faraday and Maxwell were inelegant, but effective evasions of social problems that distracted and destroyed the qualities of the works of many of their ablest contemporaries." In context, what Crowther is saying is that because they were Christians, Maxwell and Faraday did not become alcoholics, womanizers, or social climbers, to enumerate the disabling sins of a number of gifted scientists of the same era.

I need to insert a little organic chemistry here, so that my colleagues on the organic side will know that I paid some attention to them. William Henry Perkin (1838-1907) was perhaps the first great synthetic organic chemist. Perkin was the discoverer of the first synthetic dye, known as Perkin's mauve or aniline purple. Prior to Perkin's discovery, the use of the color purple had been extremely expensive and often limited to persons of royal descent. He is the person for whom an important journal, the *Perkin Transactions of the Royal Society of Chemistry (London)*, was named. In the year 1873, at the age of 35, Perkin sold his highly profitable business and retired to private research and church missionary ventures. One of the more humorous responses to the present lecture was a suggestion from the audience a few years back that I follow William Henry Perkin's example in this particular respect.

Perkin was carrying out research on unsaturated acids three days prior to his death, brought on by the sudden onset of appendicitis and double pneumonia. The following account is given in

Simon Garfield's 2001 biography of Perkin. On his deathbed, William Henry Perkin stated "The children are in Sunday School. Give them my love, and tell them always to trust Jesus." He then sang the first verse of the magisterial Isaac Watts' hymn "When I Survey the Wondrous Cross." When he reached the last line, which reads "And pour contempt on all my pride," Perkin declared "Proud? Who could be proud?"

One can find the name of George Stokes (1819-1903) in any issue of the *Journal of Chemical Physics*, the most prestigious journal in my field. In recent years, Coherent Anti-Stokes Raman Spectroscopy (CARS) has been a subject of much scholarly investigation. Stokes was one of the great pioneers of spectroscopy, fluorescence, and the study of fluids. He held one of the most distinguished chairs in the academic world for more than fifty years, the Lucasian Professorship of Mathematics at Cambridge University. This was the position held by Sir Isaac Newton and is the chair currently occupied by Stephen Hawking, subject of the third chapter in this book. Stokes was also the president of the Royal Society of London.

Stokes wrote on a range of matters beyond chemistry and physics. Concerning the question of miracles, Stokes wrote in his book *Natural Theology*, published in 1891: "Admit the existence of God, of a personal God, and the possibility of miracles follows at once. If the laws of nature are carried out in accordance with His will, He who willed them may will their suspension. And if any difficulty should be felt as to their suspension, we are not even obliged to suppose that they have been suspended."

William Thomson (1824-1907) was later known as Lord Kelvin. Lord Kelvin was recognized as the leading physical scientist and the greatest science teacher of his time. His early papers on electromagnetism and his papers on heat provide enduring proof of his scientific genius. He was a Christian with a strong faith in God and the Bible. In a speech to University College in 1903 Kelvin stated: "Do not be afraid of being free thinkers. If you think strongly enough, you will be forced by science to the belief in God."

In 1897, J. J. Thomson (1856-1940) identified and character-ized the electron, one of the most profound discoveries in the history of science. J. J. Thomson was for many years the Cavendish Professor of Physics at Cambridge University. The old Cavendish Laboratory still sits in the middle of the beautiful Cambridge campus. So many remarkable discoveries were made in the old Cavendish that it has essentially become a museum. A total of something like a dozen Nobel prizes resulted from research done in that laboratory. When the old Cavendish was opened by James Clerk Maxwell in 1874, he had a Latin phrase from Psalm 111 carved over the front door. Perhaps ten years ago I had my daughter Charlotte, who subsequently graduated from Stanford University in classics, translate this phrase for me. Then we walked out into the Cambridge countryside, where the shiny new Cavendish Laboratory was dedicated in 1973. Placed over the front door is the very same phrase, but this time in English: "The works of the LORD are great, sought out of all them that have pleasure therein." Cavendish Professor J. J. Thomson made this statement in *Nature* (a journal in which I have actually published): "In the distance tower still higher [scientific] peaks which will yield to those who ascend them still wider prospects, and deepen the feeling whose truth is emphasized by every advance in science, that 'Great are the works of the Lord'" (*Nature*, Volume 81, page 257, 1909). For the brilliant J. J. Thomson, the bottom line in science was that the works of the Lord are magnificent.

Those who know my research will not be surprised that this essay must include at least one theoretical chemist. Let's make it three in this paragraph. Charles Coulson (1910-1974) was one of the three principal architects of the molecular orbital theory. I had the privilege of meeting Coulson just once, at the Canadian Theoretical Chemistry Conference in Vancouver in 1971. He probably would have received the Nobel Prize, but he did not pass the usual first test. This typical first hurdle to getting the Nobel Prize is to live to be 65 years old—a wonderful excuse for those of us comfortably below that threshold who have not made the trip to Stockholm. The second test, far more challenging, is to have done something very important when you were 30-40 years old. Coulson indeed did profoundly significant work when he was in his thirties, but he died at 64, thus disqualifying himself from the Nobel Prize. Coulson, a professor of mathematics and theoretical chemistry at Oxford University for many years, was also a Methodist lay minister. Norman March (a good friend), successor to the renamed Coulson Chair of Theoretical Chemistry, was also a Methodist lay minister. Alas, upon the retirement of Professor March a few years ago, a suitable Methodist lay minister could not be found for the Coulson Chair at Oxford. So the university settled for an Anglican Christian, Professor Mark Child (also a friend). Charles Coulson was a spokesman for Christians in academic science and the originator of the term "god of the gaps," now widely used in philosophical circles.

From the biographical memoirs (1974) of the Royal Society of London, following Charles Coulson's death, we read Coulson's own description of his conversion to faith in Jesus Christ in 1930 as a 20 year old student at Cambridge University: "There were some ten of us and together we sought for God and together we found Him. I learned for the first time in my life that God was my friend. God became real to me, utterly real. I knew Him and I could talk with Him as I never imagined it possible before. And these prayers were the most glorious moment of the day. Life had a purpose and that purpose coloured everything."

Coulson's experience was fairly similar to my own, 43 years later, as a young professor at Berkeley. It would be arresting if I could say that there was a thunderclap from heaven, God spoke to me in audible terms, and hence I became a Christian. However, it did not happen that way. The apostle Paul's Damascus Road encounter with Jesus was the exception rather than the rule. But I did (and still do, some 30 years later) experience the same perception that Coulson described. My life has a purpose in Jesus Christ, and that purpose colors everything.

The "Why" Question

Before we move on exclusively to contemporary scientists, let us explore some of the reasons for the pattern I have described thus far. Namely, why did sustained scientific development occur first in a Christian environment? The best answers I have seen to this question were very recently (2003) formulated by my University of Georgia chemistry colleague Dr. Wesley Allen. His (slightly modified) five answers to this question are as follows:

(1)   If Christianity is true, the universe is real, not illusory. The universe is thus the product of a God whose character is

immutable, at variance with pantheistic notions which place inherent distrust in sensory experience in a mercurial world.

(2)   If Christianity is true, the universe, being divinely created, is of inherent value and thus worthy of study. This conclusion supplants any *Zeitgeist* which would view science as a mere intellectual pastime.

(3)   If Christianity is true, nature itself is not divine, and thus humanity may probe it free of fear. This was an important realization in early eras dominated by superstitions about the natural environment. Worship and ultimate reverence is reserved for the Creator, not the creation, nor humans as creatures therein.

(4)   If Christianity is true, mankind, formed in the image of God, can discover order in the universe by rational interpretation. That is, the codes of nature can be unveiled and read. Without such faith, science might never have developed, because it might have appeared impossible in principle.

(5)   If Christianity is true, the form of nature is not inherent within nature, but rather a divine command imposed from outside nature. Thus, the details of the world must be uncovered by observation rather than by mere rational musing, because God is free to create according to His own purposes. In this way science was liberated from Aristotelian rationalism, whereby the Creator was subjected to the dictates of reason constructed by humans. Such gnosticism, which transformed speculation into dogma, undermined the open-endedness of science. To be sure, Christianity holds that God is a perfectly rational being who cannot act inconsistently with His character. But this principle only places partial constraints on His creative activity, which science must be free to discover in all its diversity.

Contemporary Scientists

Robert Griffiths (1937-), a member of the U.S. National Academy of Sciences, is the Otto Stern Professor of Physics at Carnegie-Mellon University. He received one of the most coveted awards of the American Physical Society in 1984 for his work on statistical mechanics and thermodynamics. The magazine *Physics Today* reported that Griffiths is an evangelical Christian who is an amateur theologian and who helps teach a course at Carnegie-Mellon on Christianity and science. I find this to be particularly intriguing, since for the last five years I have taught a freshman seminar at the University of Georgia on the same subject. In the April 3, 1987 issue of *Christianity Today* Professor Griffiths made the interesting statement: "If we need an atheist for a debate, I go to the philosophy department. The physics department isn't much use."

At the University of California at Berkeley, where I was a professor for 18 years, we had 50 chemistry professors. But for many years there was only one who was willing to publicly identify himself as an atheist, my good friend Robert Harris, with whom I still have occasional discussions about spiritual things, usually during my annual summer week back on the Berkeley campus. After one such discussion perhaps 20 years ago, Bob told me he might have to rethink his position and become an agnostic. I thought to myself "OK, Bob, one step at a time." But Bob came back to me a week later, firmly reinstalled in the atheist camp. A more recent addition to the Berkeley chemistry faculty is a second open atheist, Richard Saykally. Rich is also a close friend, soundly disproving the notion that disagreements about ultimate questions necessarily lead to personal rancor.

For many years, Richard Bube (1927-) was the chairman of the Department of Materials Science at Stanford University. No less than 56 Stanford graduate students received their Ph.D. degrees under Professor Bube's direction. Bube has carried out foundational research in solid state physics concerning semiconductors, the photoelectronic properties of materials, photovoltaic devices (solar cells), and amorphous materials. He seconds Robert Griffiths' above statement, noting: "There are proportionately as many atheistic truck drivers as atheistic scientists." Richard Bube has long been a spokesperson for evangelical

Christians in academic life, serving for many years as editor of the journal *Perspectives on Science and the Christian Faith*, published by the American Scientific Affiliation, of which I am a Fellow. Bube teaches a second year undergraduate course at Stanford entitled "Issues in Science and Christianity."

Another member of the U.S. National Academy of Sciences is John Suppe, noted professor of geology at Princeton University. John is an outstanding scholar in the area of plate tectonics, the deformation of the earth's crust. Vaguely aware of his own spiritual needs, he began attending services in the Princeton chapel, then reading the Bible and other Christian books. He eventually committed himself to Christ and, remarkably, had his first real experience of Christian fellowship in Taiwan, where he was on a prestigious Guggenheim Fellowship. I have spoken before the Christian faculty forum at the National Taiwan University in Taipei, so I know personally that they are a good group.

Suppe makes some interesting comments concerning the evolution controversies: "Some non-scientist Christians, when they meet a scientist, feel called on to debate evolution. That is definitely the wrong thing to do. If you know scientists and the kinds of problems they have in their lives: pride, selfish ambition, jealousy; that's exactly the kind of thing Jesus talked about, and which he came to resolve (by His death on the cross). Science is full of people with very strong egos who get into conflicts with each other . . . . . The gospel is the same for scientists as for anyone. Evolution is basically a red herring. If scientists are looking for meaning in their lives, it won't be found in evolution." Although I will have more to say about evolution, and especially the origin of life, in a later chapter, John Suppe certainly provides a good practical starting point.

My candidate for the outstanding experimental scientist of the twentieth century is Charles Townes (1915-), who received the 1964 Nobel Prize in Physics for his discovery of the laser. However, I must confess to some possible bias, since Professor Townes is the only plausible candidate for scientist of the century that I know personally. But the laser is a discovery that has significantly impacted the life of every person who reads these words. Dr. Townes almost received a second Nobel Prize for his observation of the first interstellar molecule. The study of interstellar molecules has subsequently become a major part of astrophysics, affecting even my own research. I will have more to say about this in the "Big Bang" chapter. Charles Townes was the Provost at M.I.T. when I was an undergraduate, and later a colleague (but in the physics department) during my 18 years on the faculty at Berkeley.

At Berkeley every Ph.D. oral examination requires four faculty members from the candidate's own department and a fifth committee member from an outside department. In chemical physics, which is actually a part of the chemistry department at Berkeley, the "outside" committee member is almost inevitably a physics faculty member. This puts a significant strain on some of the physics faculty, since only a few of them are sufficiently knowledgeable about chemistry to serve on such committees, of which about 30 must be constituted each year. So it was not unusual for this particular subset of the physics faculty to come up with highly original reasons why they were unavailable for such two-hour ordeals. But Charlie Townes was never such a one. He always served the chemistry department cheerfully, although his duties in Washington and elsewhere were legion. And his demeanor on these committees was always gentlemanly to a tee. His questions to the chemistry Ph.D. students were almost inevitably thoughtful, and designed to bring out the very best in a quaking student.

Dr. Townes has written an autobiography entitled *Making Waves*, a pun referring to the wavelike phenomena that scientifically describe lasers. The book was published in 1995 by the American Institute of Physics, and I recommend it. Charlie makes reference to his church involvement and then provides the statement: "You may well ask, 'Just where does God come into this?' Perhaps my account may give you some answer, but to me that's almost a pointless question. If you believe in God at all, there is no particular 'where'. He's always there—everywhere. He's involved in all of these things. To me, God is personal yet omnipresent—a great source of strength, Who has made an enormous difference to me."

Arthur Schawlow (1921-2000) won the Nobel Prize in Physics in 1981 for his work in laser spectroscopy. Artie Schawlow served until his recent death as a professor at Stanford and was a truly beloved figure in the physics community. He did not hesitate to identify himself as a Protestant Christian. And he makes this unusual statement, which I suspect might only be made by a scientist: "We are fortunate to have the Bible, and especially the New Testament, which tells so much about God in widely accessible human terms." I know that Arthur Schawlow believed that his experimental studies of molecular spectroscopy were also telling him something about God's creative powers. The contrast with the New Testament accounts of the life of Jesus was that Schawlow did not think that his scientific research was providing information about God in "widely accessible human terms."

John Polkinghorne (1930-) was the chaired Professor of Mathematical Physics at Cambridge University from 1968 to 1979. This is the "other" chair of theoretical physics at Cambridge, in addition to that held by Stephen Hawking. In 1979 Polkinghorne made an abrupt career switch, enrolling in theological studies before becoming an Anglican priest. Then in 1986, Polkinghorne returned to Cambridge, first as Dean of Trinity Hall and later becoming President of Queen's College. Queen's College sits just next to St. Catherine's College, where I stay in Cambridge during my frequent visits to my longtime scientific collaborator and close friend, theoretical chemistry Professor Nicholas Handy, also an Anglican. Perhaps needless to say, John Polkinghorne has been outspoken about spiritual matters: "I take God very seriously indeed. I am a Christian believer, and I believe that God exists and has made Himself known in Jesus Christ."

My essay on cosmology follows later, but I would like to make one particular point here as it relates to biology, and to a more general question. The world's greatest living observational cosmologist is Allan Sandage (1926-), an astronomer at the Carnegie Institution in Pasadena, California. Sandage was called the "Grand Old Man of Cosmology" by the *New York Times* when he won the highly lucrative 1991 Crafoord Prize, given by the Royal Swedish Academy of Sciences. This prize is given to a cosmologist every sixth year and is viewed by the Swedish Academy as equivalent to the Nobel Prize. Allan Sandage committed his life to Jesus Christ at the age of 50. In the Alan Lightman book noted above, Dr. Sandage was asked the old question "Can a person be a scientist and also be a Christian?" Sandage's affirmative response is expected, but he provides a surprising focus: "The world is too complicated in all its parts and interconnections to be due to chance alone. I am convinced that the existence of life with all its order in each of its organisms is simply too well put together."

Sandage is the person responsible for the best current scientific estimate of the age of the universe, perhaps 14 billion years. Yet when this brilliant astrophysicist is asked to explain how one can be a scientist and a Christian, he turns not to cosmology but biology. Which brings me full circle to the question I addressed earlier from the perspective of mathematical physics and the intelligibility of the universe: Why might a scientist become a Christian? The answer from biology is that the extraordinary complexity and high information content of even the simplest living thing (the simplest self-replicating biochemical system) points to a sovereign creator God.

As mentioned earlier, a typically important ingredient to receiving the Nobel Prize in Chemistry is the attainment of age 65. For example, my good friend John Pople, a serious Methodist Christian, received the Prize in quantum chemistry at the age of 73 in 1988. He shared the prize with Walter Kohn, who was 75 at the time. However, the Physics Nobel is often given to much younger individuals. William Phillips (1949-) received the Nobel Prize in Physics at the age of 48 for the development of methods to cool and trap atoms with laser light. On the announcement date, October 15, 1997, Phillips was participating in a conference on high-powered telescopes in Long Beach, California. At the mandatory press conference William Phillips spoke the words: "God has given us an incredibly fascinating world to live in and explore."

Phillips formed and sings in the gospel choir of the Fairhaven United Methodist Church, a multi-racial congregation of about 300 in Gaithersburg, Maryland. He also teaches Sunday School and leads Bible studies. If you took the time to delve further into the October 1997 media reports, you could find out that on Saturday afternoons, William Phillips and his wife often drive into central Washington, D.C. to pick up a blind, elderly African-American woman to take her grocery shopping and then to dinner.

Allow me just once more to ask the critical question "Why might a scientist become a Christian?" My third answer is the remarkable fine-tuning of the universe. The formidable anthropic constraints will be treated in more detail in the "Big Bang" essay but let me draw a picture by citing three persons with no obvious theistic inclinations. Paul Davies, an excellent popularizer of science, states: "The present arrangement of matter indicates a very special choice of initial conditions." Now, if language means anything, a special choice implies that someone or some thing is doing the choosing. Stephen Hawking elaborates: "In fact, if one considers the possible constants and laws that could have emerged, the odds against a universe that has produced life like ours are immense."

> **"The present arrangement of matter indicates a very special choice of initial conditions."**
>
> **—Paul Davies**

The always-quotable Fred Hoyle adds: "A common sense interpretation of the facts suggests that a super intellect has monkeyed with physics, as well as with chemistry and biology, and that there are no blind forces worth speaking about in nature." My own view is that all three of these skeptics, in their own unique ways, are unintentionally supporting the position put forth by St. Paul nearly two millennia earlier: "For since the creation of the world God's invisible qualities—His eternal power and divine nature—have been clearly seen, being understood from what has been made." Romans 1:20.

Two Common Questions

Prior to my concluding remarks, I would like to respond to two questions that are frequently raised following this lecture. The first is "Given the evidence you present, why do so many persist in the belief that it is not possible to be a scientist and a Christian?" Although I am about as far from being a conspiracy theorist as possible, I conclude that part of the problem is indeed misrepresentation. The respected British science historian Colin Russell has described T. H. Huxley's important role in these developments in his scholarly account in the April 1989 issue of *Science and Christian Belief*, the quarterly publication of the Victoria Institute, of which I have been a member for the past fifteen years. Here, rather, I would like to focus on a famous book published in 1896, entitled *The History of the Warfare of Science with Theology*. Of course, given the origins of modern science, such a title sounds rather silly. The author of this polemic was Andrew Dickson White, the first President of Cornell University, the first North American university founded on purely secular terms. The most famous passage in White's book reads: "[John] Calvin took the lead in his *Commentary on Genesis*, by condemning all who asserted that the earth is not the center of the universe. He clinched the matter by the usual reference to the first verse of the 93rd Psalm and asked, 'Who will venture to place the authority of Copernicus above that of the Holy Spirit?'"

Perhaps needless to say, this is not making John Calvin look good. Nor was that Andrew Dickson White's intention. However, the truth of this matter has recently been brought forth by Dr. Alister McGrath, Professor of Historical Theology at Oxford University. In his definitive 1990 biography of Calvin, McGrath writes: "This assertion (by White) is slavishly repeated by virtually every writer on the theme 'religion and science,' such as Bertrand Russell in his *History of Western Philosophy*. Yet it may be stated categorically that Calvin wrote no such words (in his Genesis commentary) and expressed no such sentiments in any of his known writings. The assertion that he did is to be found, characteristically unsubstantiated, in the writings of the nineteenth century Anglican dean of Canterbury, Frederick William Farrar (1831-1903)."

It would be fair to ask what Calvin really thought of Copernicus' heliocentric theory of the solar system. The honest answer is that we do not know. Calvin was probably not familiar with the work of Copernicus, who was hardly a household word in France or Switzerland during the former's lifetime. But in his preface to his friend Pierre Olivetan's translation (1534) of the New Testament into French, Calvin wrote: "The whole point of Scripture is to bring us to a knowledge of Jesus Christ. And having come to know Him (with all that this implies), we should come to a halt and not expect to learn more."

A second frequently asked question following this lecture is "OK, OK, but how does it change your science?" Having first heard this question at Stanford University 15 years ago, I have had plenty of time to develop a good response. But I must confess that I cannot qualitatively improve on the answer given by the brilliant Notre Dame historian George Marsden in his 1997 Oxford University Press book *The Outrageous Idea of Christian Scholarship*. My answer modifies Marsden's only slightly. In science, Christian faith can have a significant bearing on scholarship in at least four ways:

(1)   One's Christian faith may be a factor in motivating a scientist to do his or her work well. This is not to deny that some atheist or agnostic scholars may be just as motivated to work with just as much integrity. For any particular scholar, however, Christianity may be an important motivator.

(2)   One's Christian faith may help determine the applications one sees for his or her scholarship. One may carry out research in anything from materials science to molecular biology with the hope that it may contribute to the well-being of others. Again, the fact that some atheists are also altruistic does not negate the Christian contribution to altruism.

(3)   Such motives may help shape a sub-field, specialty, or the questions a person asks about his or her research. For example, I readily confess that my scientific interest in interstellar molecules was initially inspired by the oft-repeated claims that this field will ultimately explain the origin of life. Ultimate questions tend to be of special interest to Christians.

(4)   When on occasion the scientist is asked to reflect on the wider implications of his or her scholarship, faith may have an important bearing on how that person sees the field, or its assumptions, fitting into a larger framework of meaning. This is, of course, precisely the purpose of the present book.

Concluding Remarks

My collection of scientists with Christian commitments is far from exhaustive. The publication of this essay will surely bring me correspondence from near and far with excellent new examples of the genre. Should a second edition be forthcoming, I will be happy to attempt to incorporate new material. Please do send cards and letters. But I should mention now a few others not included above. Among chemists, Professors Andrew Bocarsly (Princeton University) and James Tour (Rice University) have given Christian testimonies that have touched my heart and mind in a special way. Both Andy and Jim were born into Jewish families and gave their lives to Jesus Christ during their undergraduate years. Bocarsly is an inorganic photochemist and Tour a synthetic organic chemist turned materials scientist. Jim Tour's work on fullerenes, bucky tubes, and more generally nanochemistry is definitely on track for a trip to Stockholm some December, perhaps a decade from now.

The present discussion has focused on physics and chemistry for the obvious reason that I am a chemical physicist. This is my professional life. I suspect that it would be possible to make a similar case for the biological sciences. For example, Biochemistry Professor David Cole was the steadfast leader of the Christian faculty organization during my years on the Berkeley campus. Francis Collins is one of the most outstanding research biologists of our generation. While a professor at the University of Michigan, Collins discovered the cystic fibrosis gene. For the past decade, Francis Collins has been Director of the now successful National Institutes of Health (NIH) Human Genome Project, the largest scientific project ever undertaken.

Collin's paper "The Human Genome Project: Tool of Atheistic Reductionism or Embodiment of the Christian Mandate to Heal?" appeared in 1999 in the journal *Science and Christian Belief* (volume 11, number 2). Collins introduces his paper in this way: "Let me begin by saying a brief word about my own spiritual path. I did not come from a strongly Christian home. I was raised in a home where faith was not considered particularly relevant, sent to church to learn music, but instructed that it would be best to avoid the theology. I followed those instructions well and went off to college with only the dimmest idea of what saving faith in

Jesus Christ was all about. What little glimmers of faith I might have possessed were quickly destroyed by the penetrating questions of my freshman dorm colleagues who, as one will do at that phase in life, took great delight in destroying any remnants of superstition, which is what they considered faith to be. I became quite an obnoxious atheist with whom you would not have enjoyed having lunch. I too felt it was part of my mission to point out that all that really mattered could be discerned by science, and everything else was irrelevant . . . . Fortunately, through the guidance of some very patient people, who tolerated a lot of insolent questions, I was led to read C. S. Lewis and then the Bible, and so was led to understand many of the concepts that had completely eluded me before, and I gave my life to Christ 20 years ago."

> **"I became quite an obnoxious atheist with whom you would not have enjoyed having lunch."**
>
> **— Francis Collins**

I hope that this lecture has given you a flavor of the history of science. Those of you who have taken a freshman chemistry or physics course will surely recognize many of the names of the great scientists described here. In fact, the reason this first lecture in the series took its general shape was to present mini-sketches of the spiritual lives of scientists with whom my Berkeley freshman chemistry students would be familiar. There is a tremendous tradition, past and present, of distinguished scientist Christians. It gives me great joy to be a small part of that continuing tradition. And perhaps I have given you sufficient evidence that you will never again believe that it is difficult to be a scientist and a Christian. Finally, following the example of Oxford Professor Charles Coulson in his public lectures on science and the Christian faith, I encourage you to consider the advice of Psalm 34: "Taste and see that the Lord is good."

The Nondebate with Steven Weinberg

3

Steven Weinberg is considered by many to be the most distinguished physicist in the world. He shared the 1979 Nobel Prize in Physics with Abdus Salam and Sheldon Glashow for his work in unifying two of the fundamental forces of nature. Steven Weinberg is also unusual among physicists in that he is an outspoken, indeed sometimes angry, atheist. Among his more radical opinions Weinberg has stated: "Religion is an insult to human dignity." More to the subject of the present book, Weinberg dreams "I can hope that this long sad story, this progression of priests and ministers and rabbis and ulamas and imams and bonzes and bodhisattvas, will come to an end. I hope this is something to which science can contribute . . . . it may be the most important contribution that we can make." Steven Weinberg is obviously a much better scientist than historian. Just three atheists (Hitler, Stalin, and Mao) were responsible for more deaths in the 20th century alone than recorded in all military conflicts to date. During the year (1979-1980) I spent at the University of Texas, Austin, as Wilfred T. Doherty Professor of Chemistry and Director of the Institute of Theoretical Chemistry, Steven Weinberg was being courted by the Austin campus, a courtship that was highly successful. Following faculty appointments at Berkeley and Harvard, Weinberg moved to the University of Texas in 1982, reportedly in part because his wife Louise was offered a permanent faculty position in the UT Law School.

In September of 1999 I was approached by the organizers of a conference in Texas and asked if I would like to debate Professor Steven Weinberg on the question of God's existence. Having never debated anyone, I was less than enthusiastic. As things developed, Steve Weinberg was similarly inexperienced at debating and equally unenthusiastic about such an event. Eventually, a format was approved in which Weinberg would make prepared remarks for 40 minutes, I would do likewise for 40 minutes, Weinberg would comment for about 10 minutes, I would comment for a similar period, and the floor would be thrown open to questions from the audience. The great nondebate took place on April 13, 2000 as a part of a three-day conference at Baylor University titled "The Nature of Nature." In my mind the conference was a great success, mixing what appeared to be roughly equal numbers of Christians and others, from a broad range of disciplines, from philosophy to physics. Such a diverse group of distinguished academics had probably never gathered together under one roof for serious dialogue on this subject.

As I will explain later, Steven Weinberg has made some not entirely uncharitable remarks about biblical Judaism and Christianity in his published writings. But this was not the case on April 13, 2000. Weinberg equated Mohammed, Jesus, and Buddha with the nonexistent Zeus and called the three religious leaders "fairies." Being an equal abuser of all religions, Weinberg was every bit as dismissive of the faith of his forefathers, the religion of Abraham, Isaac, and Jacob. There was no levity in Weinberg's remarks. The flavor of his speech, albeit less sarcastically presented in print, may be found in Weinberg's 2001 book *Facing Up: Science and its Cultural Adversaries*, and in particular Chapter 20, "A Designer Universe?" Let me quickly note that there are some much better chapters in Weinberg's *Facing Up*, and I recommend in particular Chapters 12 and 13 on Alan Sokal's hoax. Weinberg's views therein overlap to a degree with some of my own comments in the chapter "Quantum Mechanics and Postmodernism" of the present book.

My lecture on April 13 quite literally began with a bang. The overhead projector exploded rather spectacularly when I turned it on. Although surprised, I was able to turn to Steve Weinberg and ask if he considered this to be an act of God. This did draw a big laugh from Weinberg, while the repair team swung into action. I was not embarrassed to tell the audience of about 300 (mostly professors) that Steven Weinberg was one of my scientific heroes. In addition to his scientific work, I have enjoyed his popular books *The First Three Minutes* and especially his 1992 book *Dreams of a Final Theory*. The latter book describes my own research favorably on pages 28 and 285, where Weinberg quotes at length from my 1986 *Science* paper entitled "Methylene: a Paradigm for Computational Quantum Chemistry." With as broad an audience as the Baylor gathering constituted, I thought it was fair to point out to the philosophers that Steve Weinberg is not "just another Nobel prize winning physicist." In the late 1960s Dr. Weinberg assumed from Richard Feynman the mantle of the most brilliant physicist in the world. In the minds of many, including myself, he has yet to relinquish the mantle, although Princeton string theorist Edward Witten seems to be nipping at his heels. I must add that to date string theory's ratio of scientific delivery to scientific promise seems rather low.

Since, as expected, Steve Weinberg spent most of his lecture claiming that science had disproved God, I felt that it was critical to review the development of modern physics and chemistry. Therefore I used about half of my lecture on the material contained in the chapter "Scientists and their Gods" of the present book. Although necessarily very selective, I noted that most of the pioneers of the physical sciences (Kepler, Pascal, Boyle, Faraday, Maxwell, Stokes, Kelvin, and Thomson, to name just a few) were committed Christians. If science has disproved God, how can it be that the pioneers of physics and chemistry were by their own testimonies motivated by their Christian faith? I also noted the Christian convictions of a good many (including four Nobelists) distinguished contemporary scientists.

The remainder of my lecture was intended to interact with Professor Weinberg through his own writings. For example, in *Dreams of a Final Theory*, Weinberg writes "Wolfgang Pauli was once asked whether he thought that a particularly ill-conceived physics paper was wrong. He replied that such a

> **"Scientists and others sometimes use the word 'God' to mean something so abstract and unengaged that He is hardly to be distinguished from the laws of nature."**
>
> **—Steven Weinberg**

description would be too kind—the paper was 'not even wrong.' I happen to think that the religious conservatives are wrong in what they believe, but at least they have not forgotten what it means to believe something. The religious liberals seem to me to be not even wrong." Despite his atheism, Steve Weinberg can express a clearer vision of who God is than many who would claim some nebulous sort of religious belief.

Weinberg continues in *Dreams of a Final Theory* with these words: "If the word 'God' is to be of any use, it should be taken to mean an interested God, a creator and lawgiver who has established not only the laws of nature and the universe but also standards of good and evil. Some personality that is concerned with our actions, something in short that it is appropriate for us to worship. . . . This is the God that has mattered to men and women throughout history. Scientists and others sometimes use the word 'God' to mean something so abstract and unengaged that He is hardly to be distinguished from the laws of nature." To which I can only add "Preach on, Steve!"

Unfortunately, Dr. Weinberg did not include this type of reasoning in his lecture on April 13, 2000. So I felt obligated, having brought the above Weinberg statements to the attention of the audience, to make a few reasonable extrapolations. Namely, that a vague impersonal belief in an organizing principle of the universe is definitely NOT what motivated:

(a)   William Wilberforce to devote the last 50 years of his life to the abolition of the slave trade in the British Empire;

(b)   Mother Teresa to commit her life to the relief of the suffering of the poorest individuals in Calcutta;

(c)   Or Jimmy Carter to spend several days each year pounding nails on behalf of Habitat for Humanity, a project to create affordable housing for the poor.

None other than Richard Feynman noted that the two pillars of Western civilization are the scientific enterprise and the Christian notion of love. Indeed, the lives of William Wilberforce, Mother Teresa, and Jimmy Carter were/are motivated by love for Jesus Christ and their fellow human beings. In his lecture at "The Nature of Nature" conference, Steve Weinberg took an uncompromising hard line against the design that human beings perceive in the universe. However, his words in *Dreams of a Final Theory* paint a less strident picture. He states "I have to admit that sometimes nature seems more beautiful than strictly necessary," and makes mention of blue jays, yellow-throated vireos, and a red cardinal. Weinberg continues "Although I understand pretty well how brightly colored feathers evolved out of competition for mates, it is almost irresistible to imagine that all this beauty was somehow laid out for our benefit."

> ...it is almost irresistible to imagine that all this beauty was somehow laid out for our benefit."
>
> —Steven Weinberg

Preach on, Steve! To see how Dr. Weinberg talks himself out of this painful predicament, you will have to read *Dreams of a Final Theory*, which I highly recommend. My point here is that all human beings experience the natural impulse that God exists and has created the universe for a purpose.

Equally revealing as the passage just quoted is the manner in which Weinberg concludes the chapter "What About God" in *Dreams of a Final Theory*. Remarkably, Weinberg quotes a substantial passage from the Venerable Bede's *Ecclesiastical History of the English* (ca. 700 A.D.). The Venerable Bede was one of the great Christians of English history before the Battle of Hastings. In this Bede passage a speech is given by one of the noblemen to King Edwin of Northumbria about the swift flight of a sparrow through the king's banqueting hall. The banqueting hall provides a picture of a person's fleeting life on planet earth, to be followed by an endless eternity. Weinberg is obviously touched by the juxtaposition of 70 years with eternity: "It is an almost irresistible temptation to believe with Bede and Edwin that there must be something for us outside the banqueting hall. The honor of resisting this temptation is only a thin substitute for the consolations of religion, but it is not entirely without satisfactions of its own." Thus Steve Weinberg again confirms that human beings are born with the intuition that God exists.

It is possible, albeit difficult and sometimes resulting in anger, to suppress this intuition. Concerning the question of "honor," I am not convinced that the categories honor and dishonor have meaning if God does not exist. In my lecture, it was necessary to note that contemporary atheism has led some scientists to dubious pseudo-scientific conclusions. Francis Crick's invention of the admittedly far-fetched notion of "directed panspermia" to explain the origin of life is discussed in the chapter "Climbing Mount Improbable" of this book. Martin Rees is so in awe of the anthropic constraints (the remarkable fine tuning of the universe for life) that he has concluded, in the total absence of evidence, that there must be a multitude of additional universes. And Frank Tipler, in his strange book *The Physics of Immortality*, has concluded that although God does not exist now, he/she/it will emerge in the future as a result of advances in computer technology. Atheistic presuppositions have led some very gifted scientific minds astray.

I concluded my formal remarks at "The Nature of Nature" conference in a highly dubious manner, namely by quoting myself. The cover story (page 62) of the December 23, 1991 *U.S. News and World Report*, was titled "The Creation: Religion's Search for a Common Ground with Science." Therein, I was quoted (correctly, to my amazement) as saying "The significance and joy in my science comes in those occasional moments of discovering something new and saying to myself, 'So that's how God did it!' My goal is to understand a little corner of God's plan."

One reporter at the conference noted that Professor Weinberg adopted a posture of indifference during my lecture. However, given his reputation, things could have been worse. Weinberg has been known at the University of Texas to take a wastebasket with him to a visiting professor's physics lecture and noisily open his copious mail during the seminar! Moreover, mine was the only lecture other than his own that Weinberg attended at the conference. The emotional crescendo of the conference was reached during Steve Weinberg's remarks in response to my lecture. He said he understood why so many famous chemists and physicists were Christians. At age 67, said Weinberg, he was beginning to appreciate the reality of death. One reporter quoted Weinberg as saying "It is horrifying to believe that we die and won't see our loved ones." I cannot confirm the exact words, but at about that point the great scientist paused for perhaps two or three seconds and seemed on the verge of breaking down. He did recover and admitted that it is hard to resist the consolations of the afterlife that religion may give.

In his response, Weinberg also said that the only point I had made that bothered him was my claim that the intelligibility of the universe using mathematical physics points to a sovereign creator God. I had quoted the revered physics Nobelist Eugene Wigner as noting "the unreasonable effectiveness of mathematics" and remarking that "the miracle of the appropriateness of the language of mathematics for the formulation of the laws of physics is a wonderful gift that we neither understand nor deserve." Of course the notion of a gift, raised by Wigner, requires a Giver. So perhaps I did make a small impression on Steve Weinberg that April afternoon.

Following the prepared remarks by Professor Weinberg and me and our responses to each other was a time of general questioning by the audience. One particularly dapper looking individual asked me a series of six or seven questions in machine gun rapid fire, allowing no possible response. Experience suggests that such persons are rarely looking for answers. One reporter described the questioner as "grandstanding to the cameras (smile included)." Participants sitting near this particular gentleman later noted that he had been muttering to himself throughout my lecture. I chose one of his many questions to explain that I had become a Christian following a careful examination of the historical evidence for the resurrection of Christ. Following the afternoon's session, it was pointed out that the dapper gentleman was Michael Shermer, previously unknown to me, but described by several at the conference as a swaggering gadabout.

Michael Shermer has two degrees in psychology and is a sometimes adjunct professor at Occidental College. He is also the editor of a magazine called *The Skeptic*. Shermer provided the most humorous description of the great nondebate in his "E-Skeptic" report dated April 20, 2000. Shermer begins his narrative with "The big showdown event of the conference, however, was Steven Weinberg versus Henry Schaefer." He continues with a charitable description of my scientific credentials, as well (obviously) as those of Steven Weinberg. In his essay, Shermer draws an analogy with the epic 1964 world heavyweight boxing championship fight between Sonny Liston (Weinberg) and Cassius Clay (yours truly). Shermer introduces my lecture in the following manner: "Schaefer is going to line up Weinberg's ducks, chamber load his 12-gage shotgun shells, and proceed to blow them apart like sparrows on a wire. Now we will surely hear the best of the new creationists, their would-be challenger.

Sonny "the big ugly bear" Liston is about to be knocked out by Cassius "ain't I pretty?" Clay. Schaefer comes out dancing, prancing, dodging, and weaving, tassels on his ankles and a smile on his face. Weinberg is his hero. Weinberg is The Man. You hate to destroy a god, but here goes. Ready?" As anticipated, this colorful introduction goes rapidly downhill, as Michael Shermer is downright furious about my bringing to his painful remembrance the fact that the pioneers of physics and chemistry were almost entirely committed Christians. But I can't help but give Shermer an "A" for his waggish writing skills.

Just before Dr. Weinberg was ferried back to Austin by his driver, we had a few moments of private conversation. I wanted him to be clear that my admiration for his scientific accomplishments was genuine and that there was absolutely no personal animosity on my behalf, despite our radically different views of the universe. Weinberg reciprocated and jokingly said he was happy to have me as a member of his fan club. I asked him to sign my personal copy of his book *Dreams of a Final Theory*. It reads, "Best wishes, Steve Weinberg, April 2000."

The Big Bang,
Stephen Hawking,
and God

4

The Big Bang

Cosmology is the study of the universe as a whole—its structure, origin, and development. The subjects cosmology addresses are profound, both scientifically and theologically. Perhaps the best way to define cosmology is in terms of the questions that it asks. Hugh Ross does an excellent job of stating these questions in his important book *The Fingerprint of God* (Second Edition, Whitaker House, 1989):

1) Is our universe finite or infinite in size and content?

2) Has this universe been here forever or did it have a beginning?

3) Was the universe created?

4) If the universe was not created, how did it get here?

5) If the universe was created, how was this creation accomplished, and what can we learn about the agent and events of creation?

6) Who or what governs the laws and constants of physics?

7) Are such laws the products of chance or have they been designed?

8) How do the laws and constants of physics relate to the support and development of life?

9) Is there any knowable existence beyond the apparently observed dimensions of our universe?

10) Do we expect our universe to expand forever, or is a period of contraction to be followed by a big crunch?

Let me begin by noting the relationship between my own research in molecular quantum mechanics and the field of cosmology. On November 5, 1973, my research group published its first paper on interstellar molecules, the molecules that exist in those relatively empty regions between the stars. Our paper appeared in the journal *Nature* and was titled "Theoretical Support for the Assignment of X-ogen to the HCO^+ Molecular Ion." The motivation for research on interstellar molecules has largely derived from the suggestion that these are the elementary materials from which life might have originated. My research group has continued its interest in molecules in space over the years, with many of our papers being published in the *Astrophysical Journal*, considered by some to be the premier journal in the field. Our most recent paper in this general area is titled "Reactions of Ethynyl Radicals as a Source of C_4 and C_5 Hydrocarbons in Titan's Atmosphere," and it appeared in the July 2002 issue of *Planetary and Space Science*. Two more recent astrophysical papers involving my research group are in different stages leading to publication.

The idea that the universe had a specific time of origin has been philosophically resisted by some very distinguished scientists. Hugh Ross has done an excellent job of summarizing this resistance. Ross begins with Arthur Eddington (1882-1944), who experimentally confirmed Einstein's (1879-1955) general theory of relativity in 1919. Eddington stated a dozen years later: "Philosophically, the notion of a beginning to the present order is repugnant to me. I should like to find a genuine loophole." Eddington later said, "We must allow evolution an infinite amount of time to get started."

Albert Einstein's response to the consequences of his own general theory of relativity may be reasonably interpreted to reflect a possible concern about the peril of a confrontation with the Creator. Through the equations of general relativity, we can trace the origin of the universe backward in time to some sort of a beginning. However, to evade this seemingly inevitable cosmological conclusion, Einstein introduced a cosmological constant, a "fudge factor," to yield a static model for the universe. He longed for a universe that was infinitely old. In fairness, Einstein later considered this to be one of the few serious mistakes of his scientific career. However, even this concession must have been painful, as Einstein had a strong conviction that all physical phenomena ultimately should be accounted for in terms of continuous fields everywhere (see Max Jammer's 1999 book *Einstein and Religion*).

Einstein ultimately gave at best reluctant assent to what he called "the necessity for a beginning" and eventually to "the presence of a superior reasoning power." But he never did embrace the concept of a personal Creator, a compassionate God who cares for men and women and children.

To understand the intensity of the objections to the idea that the universe had a beginning, an excursus may be helpful. Again following Hugh Ross, let us note the five traditional arguments for the existence of God. These arguments may be found in Augustine, and they were of course further elaborated by Thomas Aquinas. This may seem an unlikely starting point for our topic, but I think you will see as we proceed that these arguments keep coming up. I am not going to take a position on whether these arguments are valid, but I will state them, because throughout current discussions of cosmology these arguments are often cited:

1) The cosmological argument: the effect of the universe's existence must have a suitable cause.

2) The teleological argument: the design of the universe implies a purpose or direction behind it.

3) The rational argument: the operation of the universe according to order and natural law implies a mind behind it.

4) The ontological argument: man's ideas of God (his God-consciousness, if you like) implies a God who imprinted such a consciousness.

5) The moral argument: man's built-in sense of right and wrong can be accounted for only by an innate awareness of a code of law—an awareness implanted by a higher being.

So then, why has there been such resistance to the idea of a definite beginning of the universe? Much of it goes right back to that first argument, the cosmological argument. It may be useful to break down the cosmological argument into three parts:

(a) Everything that begins to exist must have a cause;

(b) If the universe began to exist, then

(c) The universe must have a cause.

You can see the direction in which this argument is flowing—a direction of discomfort to some physicists and others knowledgeable about these matters. Such a person was the Princeton physicist Robert Dicke (1916-1997), advocate of the infinitely oscillating theory of the universe, of which we will say more later. Dicke stated in 1965 that an infinitely old universe "would relieve us of the necessity of understanding the origin of matter at any finite time in the past." Walter Nernst (1864-1941), discoverer of the third law of thermodynamics, made a stronger statement: "To deny the infinite duration of time would betray the very foundations of science."

Dr. Stephen M. Barr, Professor of Physics at the University of Delaware has put his finger on the pulse of the problem (a problem, that is, to Einstein, Dicke, Nernst, and others of a non-theistic inclination): "The idea that the universe and time itself had a beginning really did enter Western thought from the Bible, and indeed from the opening words of the Bible. Virtually all the pagan philosophers of antiquity, including Aristotle, and, according to most scholars, Plato, held that time had no beginning. Modern materialists and atheists, for obvious reasons, have generally followed the ancient pagan view."

In 1946 George Gamow (1904-1968), a Russian-born American physicist, proposed that the primeval fireball, the "Big Bang," was an intense concentration of pure energy. It was the source of all the matter that now exists in the universe. The Big Bang Theory predicts that all the galaxies in the universe should be rushing away from each other at high speeds as a result of that initial event, which some have described as a singular explosion. A possible future dictionary definition of the hot Big Bang theory encompasses the idea that the entire physical universe, all the matter and energy and even the four dimensions of time and space, burst forth from a state of infinite or near infinite density, temperature, and pressure.

The 1965 observation of the microwave background radiation by Arno Penzias (1933-) and Robert Wilson (1936-) of the Bell

Telephone Laboratories (regrettably partially dismantled following the breakup of AT&T) convinced most scientists of the validity of the Big Bang Theory. Further observations reported in 1992 have moved the Big Bang Theory from a consensus view to the nearly unanimous view among cosmologists: there was an origin to the universe, perhaps 12-16 billion years ago. My former Berkeley colleague Joseph Silk and his coworkers gave a brief summary of the evidence for the Big Bang Theory in their February 17, 1995 review paper in *Science* magazine: "The hot Big Bang model is enormously successful. It provides the framework for understanding the expansion of the universe, the cosmic background radiation, and the primeval abundance of light elements, as well as a general picture of how the structure seen in the universe today was formed."

Many scientists have been willing to comment on the philosophical consequences of the Big Bang Theory. For example, Arno Penzias, co-discoverer of the microwave background radiation and 1978 Nobel Prize recipient in physics, stated to the *New York Times* on March 12, 1978: The best data we have (concerning the Big Bang) are exactly what I would have predicted, had I nothing to go on but the five books of Moses, the Psalms, the Bible as a whole."

When asked more recently (in Denis Brian's 1995 book *Genius Talk*) why some cosmologists were so affectionate in their embrace of the steady state theory (the idea that the universe is infinitely old) of the origin of the universe, Penzias responded: "Well, some people are uncomfortable with the purposefully created world. To come up with things that contradict purpose, they tend to speculate about things they haven't seen."

Perhaps the most amusing statement in this regard came from Cambridge University physicist Dennis Sciama, Stephen Hawking's thesis adviser and one of the most distinguished advocates of the steady state theory of the universe. Shortly after he gave up on the steady state hypothesis, Sciama stated: "The steady state theory has a sweep and beauty that for some unaccountable reason the architect of the universe appears to have overlooked." Of course we theoretical scientists have an abundance of excuses for why our cherished theories sometimes fail. But the notion of blaming our failures on the "architect of the universe" is very creative.

It is an unusual day when newspapers all over the world devote their front page headlines to a story about science. But that is exactly what happened on April 24, 1992. Announced on that date were the results of the so-called "Big Bang ripples" observations made by the cosmic background explorer (COBE) satellite of NASA. These ripples are the small variations in the temperature of the universe (about 2.7 degrees Celsius above absolute zero) far from heavenly bodies. These observations were remarkably consistent with the predictions of the Big Bang Theory. The particular item that the *London Times*, *New York Times*, etc. seemed to pick up on was a statement by George Smoot, the team leader from the Lawrence Berkeley Laboratory. He said, "It's like looking at God." For obvious reasons, this headline captured the attention of thinking people throughout the world. In the euphoria that followed, Stephen Hawking described the Big Bang ripples observations as "the scientific discovery of the century, if not all time."

A somewhat more sober assessment of the Big Bang ripples observations was given one week later in the *Los Angeles Times* by Frederick Burnham, a science-historian. He said, "These findings, now available, make the idea that God created the universe a more respectable hypothesis today than at any time in the last 100 years."

George Smoot, leader of the COBE team of scientists, and I were undergraduate classmates at M.I.T. We both arrived in September of 1962 and graduated in June of 1966. I do not remember meeting George Smoot, but his last name was famous within the M.I.T. community from the first day of our freshman year. However, the fame of the name Smoot was not such as to suggest that George would become one of the world's most famous scientists 26 years following his graduation from M.I.T. Social fraternities were very popular during our years at M.I.T. In fact, about one-third of the undergraduate student body lived in these fraternities, which were located across the Charles River from M.I.T. Students were encouraged to join a fraternity in the week before the beginning of their freshman year. One of the "better" fraternities was named Lambda Chi Alpha. I visited Lambda Chi Alpha, but chose instead the best fraternity at M.I.T., namely Sigma Alpha Epsilon. For those of you who believe that American social fraternities excel primarily in drunkenness and debauchery, let it be noted that it was a full ten years later that I became a Christian.

Returning to the story, in 1958 Oliver R. Smoot, Jr., a new member of Lambda Chi Alpha, is said to have consumed an excessive amount of a common chemical reagent, namely ethyl alcohol. In a semi-conscious state, as the story goes, this Smoot, 5'7" tall, was rolled across the Harvard Bridge by his fraternity mates numerous times. On the next day, the Harvard Bridge was smartly adorned with Smoot markers. At every ten Smoots (an interval of about 56 feet) brightly painted markers noted the achievement. The total length of the Harvard Bridge was boldly proclaimed at both ends to be 364.4 Smoots plus one ear. During the 1963-1964 academic year, my fraternity decided that Smoot was getting far more credit than he deserved. One of our members, Fred Souk, declared that he was fully the equal if not the better of Smoot in every respect. So we went out in the dark of night, painted out the Smoot marks, and replaced them with Souk marks. Fred was a bit taller than Smoot, so the total number of Souks did not quite match the old Smoots. As it turned out, this action enraged the members of the Lambda Chi Alpha fraternity. The Souk marks were obliterated the very next night, and replaced with the venerable Smoots, which continue to this date to be repainted regularly on the Harvard Bridge. I must confess to some surprise that when I read George Smoot's semi-autobiographical popular book about the Big Bang ripples, titled *Wrinkles in Time*, I found no mention of the most celebrated achievement associated with his name, the immortal Smoot marks. However, on his web site George Smoot acknowledges that Oliver R. Smoot, Jr. is "a distant relative." Apparently, the only Smoots ever to attend M.I.T. were Oliver R. Smoot, Jr., George Smoot, and Oliver's son Stephen Smoot.

Not everyone was ecstatic about the Smoot observations that revealed the so-called "Big Bang ripples." Certainly, those who had argued so strongly and passionately for a steady state model of the universe did not appreciate the interpretation of these results. The latter group included most prominently two senior scientists, Sir Fred Hoyle (1915-), the British astronomer, and Geoffrey Burbidge (1925-), a distinguished astrophysicist at the University of California at San Diego.

We may continue to probe the philosophical implications of

these Big Bang ripples observations by assessing a statement of Geoffrey Burbidge (made during a radio discussion with Hugh Ross) concerning these matters. Burbidge discounts the most obvious interpretation of the new experiments. He remains a strong advocate, in the face of seemingly overwhelming evidence, of the steady state theory. Remarkably, Burbidge stated that the COBE satellite experiments come from "the First Church of Christ of the Big Bang." Of course George Smoot took strong exception to this statement.

> **"There is no doubt that a parallel exists between the Big Bang as an event and the Christian notion of creation from nothing."**
>
> **—George Smoot**

In his popular 1993 book *Wrinkles in Time* Smoot does write cautiously "There is no doubt that a parallel exists between the Big Bang as an event and the Christian notion of creation from nothing." Burbidge did say something in the same interview that is indisputable, however. He predictably favored the steady state hypothesis and claimed that his view supports Hinduism and not Christianity. That is correct, because the steady state theory of the universe, were it to be true, would provide some support for the never ending cycles of existence taught by orthodox Hinduism.

Hugh Ross, an astrophysicist turned generalist, has written very persuasively on this topic. He again brings us to the philosophical implications. Ross states in his book *The Creator and the Cosmos* (Third Edition, Navpress, 2001) that: "By definition, time is that dimension in which cause and effect phenomena take place. If time's beginning is concurrent with the beginning of the universe, as the space-time theorem says, then the cause of the universe must be some entity operating in a time dimension completely independent of and pre-existent to the time dimension of the cosmos. This conclusion is powerfully important to our understanding of who God is and who or what God is not. It tells us that the creator is transcendent, operating beyond the dimensional limits of the universe. It tells us that God is not the universe itself, nor is God contained within the universe."

Perhaps some readers are inclined to say "So what?" If you fall into that category, may I remind you that well more than one billion people on this planet believe either that God is the universe itself or that God is contained within the universe. If the Big Bang Theory is true, it creates serious philosophical problems for these worldviews. Some scientific discoveries do have profound metaphysical implications. An entire book on this subject, titled *The Dancing Universe* (1997), has been written by Dartmouth College physics professor Marcello Gleiser. Without displaying any theistic sympathies, Gleiser confirms much of what Ross states above. His flow chart on page 303 labeled "A Classification of Cosmogonical Models" is of special interest. Gleiser asks the question "Is there a beginning?" to provide a primary sorting of worldviews. On the left side of Gleiser's diagram a positive answer to the above question leads via a particular path to creation by the sovereign God of the universe, as described in Genesis. On the right hand side, a "no" answer in regard to a beginning leads by another path to a rhythmic universe, as perhaps exemplified by the dance of Shiva in Hinduism. The resistance of several streams of Hinduism to the Big Bang Theory was recently highlighted at a symposium sponsored by the American Association for the Advancement of Science (AAAS) in Washington, D.C. (April 1999). In prepared remarks Hindu philosopher Anindita Baslev of Aarhus University in Denmark quoted from the ancient texts of her religion and summarily dismissed the discussions of Big Bang mechanics as "cosmological speculations."

Following the remarkable financial success of Stephen Hawking's 1988 book *A Brief History of Time*, a number of distinguished physicists have tried their hands at the same literary genre. In this context I would like to quote from a book that I do not necessarily recommend to the general reader. This particular book is by a brilliant physicist, Leon Lederman, a Nobel Prize winner and also a gifted and dedicated educator. Lederman's book is called *The God Particle* and although the title sounds very appealing, the best material is in the first few pages. The remainder of the book is largely a case for the building of the SSC, the Super Conducting Super Collider, a proposed massive particle accelerator south of Dallas, Texas, that was torpedoed by the U.S. Congress in late 1993. Therefore, reading the book today is a bit of a Rip Van Winkle experience. But the first section is wonderful; it is in fact a good summary of what I have attempted to say in this lecture thus far. Leon Lederman states:

"In the very beginning, there was a void—a curious form of vacuum—a nothingness containing no space, no time, no matter, no light, no sound. Yet the laws of nature were in place and this curious vacuum held potential. A story logically begins at the beginning. But this story is about the universe and unfortunately there are no data for the very beginning. None, zero! We don't know anything about the universe until it reaches the mature age of a billionth of a trillionth of a second—that is, some very short time after the creation in the Big Bang. When you read or hear anything about the birth of the universe, someone is making it up. We are in the realm of philosophy. Only God knows what happened at the very beginning."

In candid moments, outstanding cosmologists make statements rather similar to that quoted above. For example, Stephen Hawking states that "The actual point of creation lies outside the scope of the presently known laws of physics." M.I.T. professor Alan Guth, critical contributor to the "inflationary" understanding of the Big Bang Theory, is often considered to be the American counterpart of Hawking and has said analogously "The instant of creation remains unexplained."

Stephen Hawking

Stephen Hawking is probably the most famous living scientist. The tenth anniversary edition of his book, *A Brief History of Time*, is available in paperback and I strongly recommend it. The book has sold in excess of 20 million copies. For such a book to sell so many copies is essentially unheard of in the history of science writing. For the past five years I have used *A Brief History of Time* as the centerpiece of a course that I teach for a select group of 15-18 University of Georgia freshmen. For balance, the class also studies the novel *That Hideous Strength*, the third book in the C. S. Lewis space trilogy. My course falls in the "Get to know the professor" category that is becoming popular in large public universities to offset the sense of anonymity that many entering freshmen feel.

An excellent film (1991, director Errol Morris) has been made about *A Brief History of Time*, and we enjoy the film every year in my freshman seminar. There has even been another good book (*A Reader's Companion*, Bantam, 1992) made about the film. Hawking has a wonderful sense of humor. He displays it in the foreword of the *Reader's Companion*, stating "This is The Book of The Film of The Book. I don't know if they are planning a film of the book of the film of the book."

I want to begin our discussion of Stephen Hawking by saying something about his scientific research, without getting bogged down in details. Hawking has made his well-deserved scientific reputation by investigating in great detail one particular set of problems: the singularities and horizons around black holes and at the beginning of time. Now, every writer in this general area is convinced that if you encountered a black hole, it would be the last thing you ever encountered. A black hole is a massive system so centrally condensed that the force of gravity prevents everything within it, including light, from escaping. The reassuring thing is that, despite what our children see on the Saturday morning cartoons, no black hole appears to be in our neighborhood. That is, the closest black hole to planet earth is far more distant than could be traveled in the lifetime of a human being using conventional rockets.

Stephen Hawking's first major scientific work was published with Roger Penrose (a physicist very famous in his own right) and George Ellis (not as famous as Penrose and Hawking, but still very well known), during the period 1968-1970. They demonstrated that every solution to the equations of general relativity guarantees the existence of a singular boundary for space and time in the past. This landmark is now known as the "singularity theorem," and is a tremendously important finding, being about as close as we can get to a mathematical rationalization for the Big Bang Theory. Later, of course, Hawking began to carry out independent research, both by himself and with his own doctoral students and postdoctoral fellows. As early as 1973, he began to formulate ideas about the quantum evaporation of black holes, exploding black holes, "Hawking radiation," and so on. Some of Hawking's work is radical, exploratory, and even speculative in nature. However, by any reasonable standard Stephen Hawking is a great scientist. Even if time shows some of his more radical proposals to be incorrect, Hawking will have had a profound impact on the history of science.

The scientific centerpiece of *A Brief History of Time* would appear to fall in the speculative category of his research. In fact, I think it is fair to say that the scientific centerpiece of *A Brief History of Time* was not considered one of Hawking's most important papers prior to the publication of the book in 1987. I am referring to the "no boundary proposal" that Hawking published in 1984 in work with James Hartle, a physics professor at the University of California at Santa Barbara. Using a grossly simplified picture of the universe in conjunction with an elegant vacuum fluctuation model, Hartle and Hawking were able to provide a mathematical rationalization for the entire universe popping into existence at the beginning of time. This model has also been called the "universe as a wave function" and the "no beginning point." While such mathematical exercises are highly speculative, they may eventually lead us to a deeper understanding of the creation event. I postpone my analysis of the no boundary proposal for a few pages.

Hawking is certainly the most famous physicist in history who has not won the Nobel Prize. This has puzzled some people. Many people automatically assume that Professor Hawking has already won the Nobel Prize. Yet as of this writing (2003) he has not. This is probably because the Swedish Royal Academy demands that an award-winning discovery must be supported by verifiable experimental or observational evidence. Hawking's work to date remains largely unconfirmed. Although the mathematics and concepts of his theories are certainly beautiful and elegant, science waited until 1994 for rock solid evidence for even the existence of black holes. The verification of Hawking radiation or any of his more radical theoretical proposals still seems far off. In this context, we must recall that Albert Einstein was wrong about a number of important things scientific, especially quantum mechanics; yet we recognize him as one of the three great physicists of all time, along with Isaac Newton and James Clerk Maxwell. I should conclude this section by noting that a number of Nobel Prize Committees have shown themselves to be composed of rather savvy people, capable of compromise. So I would not be surprised to see the old gentlemen in Stockholm find a way to award the Nobel Prize in Physics to Stephen Hawking. Perhaps Hawking could share the prize with those responsible for the first definitive observations of black holes.

And God

Those who have not read *A Brief History of Time* may be surprised to find that the book has a main character. That main character is God. This was the feature of the book that the well known atheist Carl Sagan found a bit distressing. Sagan wrote the preface to the first edition of the book, but was less famous than Hawking by the time of arrival of the tenth anniversary edition, in which Sagan's preface does not appear. God is discussed in *A Brief History of Time* from near the beginning all the way to the crescendo of the final sentence. So let us try to put Hawking's opinions about God in some sort of a context. The context is that Stephen Hawking seems to have made up his mind about God long before he became a cosmologist.

Not surprisingly, the principal influence in Stephen's early life was his mother, Isobel. Isobel Hawking was a member of the Communist Party in England in the 1930's, and her son has carried some of that intellectual tradition right through his life. Incidentally, Hawking's fame is now such that he felt obligated to endorse one of the candidates in the 2000 United States presidential election. By the time he was 13, Hawking's hero was the brilliant agnostic philosopher and mathematician, Bertrand Russell. At the same age, two of Hawking's friends became Christians as a result of the 1955 Billy Graham London campaign. According to his 1992 biographers (Michael White and John Gribbin), Hawking stood apart from these encounters with "a certain amused detachment." There is little in *A Brief History of Time* that deviates in a significant way from what we know of the religious views of the 13-year-old Stephen Hawking. However, we must note that in public questioning Hawking insists that he is not an atheist. And I am told by eyewitness observers that in recent years Stephen Hawking has appeared "once or twice a month" in an Anglican church with his second wife.

Perhaps the most important event of Stephen Hawking's life occurred on December 31, 1962. He met his future wife of 25 years, Jane Wilde, at a New Year's Eve party. One month later, Hawking was diagnosed with a debilitating disease, ALS or amyotrophic lateral sclerosis, known in North America as Lou Gehrig's disease. He was given two years to live at the time. That was nearly 40 years ago. I have seen three chemistry professor friends die of this terrible disease. My three friends lasted two, three, and five years, respectively, the last surviving on an iron lung for his final tortuous year. By anyone's estimation, the preservation of Stephen Hawking's life is a medical miracle. And he is a man of great personal courage.

At this point in his life, 1962, Stephen was by all accounts an average-performing graduate student at Cambridge University. I hasten to add that even average doctoral students at Cambridge, still one of the five great universities in the world, can be very good. Let me quote from his biographers, White and Gribbin, on this point:

"However, there is little doubt that Jane Wilde's appearance on the scene was a major turning point in Stephen Hawking's life. The two of them began to see a lot more of one another and a strong relationship developed. It was finding Jane Wilde that enabled him to break out of his depression and regenerate some belief in his life and work. For Hawking, his engagement to Jane was probably the most important thing that ever happened to him. It changed his life, gave him something to live for and made him determined to live. Without the help that Jane gave him, he would almost certainly not have been able to carry on or had the will to do so."

They married in July of 1965, somewhat past the expected date of Stephen Hawking's death. The fact that three children followed is indisputable evidence that Stephen was not dead. Hawking himself said in an interview shortly following the publication of *A Brief History of Time* that "what really made a difference was that I got engaged to a woman named Jane Wilde. This gave me something to live for." Jane Wilde is an interesting person in her own right. I think she decided early on to pursue an academic discipline as far as possible from her husband. She received a doctorate for her research on the medieval lyric poetry of the Iberian Peninsula!

Jane Hawking is a Christian. She made the statement in 1986, "Without my faith in God, I wouldn't have been able to live in this situation (namely, the deteriorating health of her husband, with no obvious income but that of a Cambridge don to live on). I would not have been able to marry Stephen in the first place because I wouldn't have had the optimism to carry me through, and I wouldn't have been able to carry on with it."

The reason the book has sold more than 20 million copies, i.e., the reason for Hawking's success as a popularizer of science, is that he addresses the problems of meaning and purpose that concern all thinking people. The book overlaps with Christian belief and it does so deliberately, but graciously and without rancor. It is an important book that needs to be treated with respect and attention. There is no reason to agree with everything put forth in *A Brief History of Time* and you will see that I have a couple of areas of disagreement. It has been argued that this is the most widely unread book in the history of literature. I first began to prepare this material for a lecture in December 1992, because I was asked by a friend (John Mason) in Australia to come and speak on the subject. John wrote to me, "A great many people in Sydney have purchased this book. Some claim to have read it." So I encourage you to join the students in my University of Georgia class and become one of those who have actually read *A Brief History of Time*.

Stephen Hawking has made some eminently sensible statements on the relationship between science and Christianity. For example, "It is difficult to discuss the beginning of the universe without mentioning the concept of God. My work on the origin of the universe is on the borderline between science and religion, but I try to stay on the scientific side of the border. It is quite possible that God acts in ways that cannot be described by scientific laws." When asked by a reporter whether he believed that science and Christianity were competing worldviews, Hawking replied cleverly "Then Newton would not have discovered the law of gravity." Dr. Hawking is well aware that Newton had strong religious convictions.

A Brief History of Time makes wonderfully ambiguous statements such as, "Even if there is only one possible unified theory (here he is alluding to the envisioned unification of our understandings of quantum mechanics and gravity), it is just a set of rules and equations. What is it that breathes fire into the equations and makes a universe for them to describe?" In a similar vein Hawking asks "Why does the universe go to the bother of existing?" Although Hawking does not attempt to answer these two critical questions, they make wonderful discussion topics for university students, and I have enjoyed using them for this purpose.

Hawking pokes fun at Albert Einstein for not believing in quantum mechanics. When asked why he didn't believe in quantum mechanics, Einstein would sometimes say things like "God doesn't play dice with the universe." On one such occasion, Niels Bohr is said to have responded "Albert, stop telling God what He can do." Hawking's adroit response to Einstein is that "God not only plays dice. He sometimes throws them where they can't be seen." Of course, I like Hawking's response very much, having devoted my professional career to the study of molecular quantum mechanics.

For me (and for Hawking's now distinguished student Don Page; more on Professor Page later) the most precious jewel in *A Brief History of Time* reflects Hawking's interest in the writings of Augustine of Hippo (354-430 A.D.). Hawking states "The idea that God might want to change His mind is an example of the fallacy, pointed out St. Augustine, of imagining God as a being existing in time. Time is a property only of the universe that God created. Presumably, God knew what He intended when He set it up."

The first time I read *A Brief History of Time*, admittedly not critically, for the first 100 pages or so I thought, "This is a great book; Hawking is building a splendid case for creation by an intelligent being." But things then begin to change and this magnificent cosmological epic becomes adulterated by poor philosophy and theology. For example, Hawking writes on page 122 of the first edition, "These laws (of physics) may have originally been decreed by God, but it appears that He has since left the universe to evolve according to them and does not now intervene in it." The grounds on which Hawking claims "it appears" are unstated, and a straw God is set up that is certainly not the God who is revealed in time and space and history through Jesus Christ. What follows is a curious mixture of deism and the ubiquitous "god of the gaps." Stephen Hawking thus appears uncertain (agnostic) of his belief in a god of his own creation.

Now, lest any reader be uncertain, let me emphasize that Hawking strenuously denies charges that he is an atheist. When he is accused of atheism, he is affronted and says that such assertions are not true. For example, Hawking has stated "I thought I had left the question of the existence of a Supreme Being completely open . . . . . It would be perfectly consistent with all we know to say that there was a Being who was responsible for all the laws of physics." Stephen Hawking is probably an agnostic or a deist (a believer in an impersonal god) or something in between these two positions, his recent church attendance notwithstanding. He is certainly not an atheist and sometimes does not even appear very sympathetic to atheism.

One of the frequently quoted statements in *A Brief History of Time* is, "So long as the universe had a beginning, we would suppose it had a creator (the cosmological argument). But if the universe is really completely self-contained, having no boundary or edge, it would have neither beginning nor end: it would simply be. What place, then, for a creator?" Hawking's most famous statement is contained in the last paragraph of *A Brief History of Time*. Perhaps attempting to balance the quotation just cited, Hawking writes "However, if we do discover a complete theory. . . . . then we would know the mind of God." As a person who has dedicated his professional life to science, I am personally sympathetic to this statement. John Calvin was correct is stating that "All truth is God's truth." But I think Professor Hawking is claiming too much here. I would modify his statement to say that if we had a unified, complete theory of physics, we would know much more about the mind of God. To claim to know God comprehensively is beyond the capability of any human being.

The Anthropic Constraints

In 1955 G. J. Whithrow published a paper in the *British Journal of the Philosophy of Science* in which he argued that a "variety of astronomical conditions must be met if a universe is to be habitable." During the next 30 years, scientists continued to amass new evidence supporting this hypothesis. By 1986 British astronomer John Barrow and American mathematical physicist Frank Tipler were able to publish a 700-page book entitled *The Anthropic Cosmological Principle* with Oxford University Press. In their book Barrow and Tipler report that there are a surprising number of physical features of the universe that conspire to make life possible.

One statement of the anthropic principle would be that there are a number of fundamental constants (for example, the mass of the electron) or derived scientific parameters (for example, the dipole moment of the water molecule), any one of which changed just a little bit, would make the earth uninhabitable by human beings. In this regard a book that I strongly recommend is Hugh Ross's *The Creator and the Cosmos*. Ross has a substantial discussion of the anthropic principle and demonstrates why many physicists and astronomers have considered the possibility that the universe not only was divinely caused, but in fact divinely designed.

Such a person is Amherst College astronomy professor George Greenstein (a pantheist or something similar), who makes this statement: "As we survey all the evidence, the thought insistently arises that some supernatural agency, or rather Agency, must be involved. Is it possible that suddenly, without intending to, we have stumbled upon scientific proof of the existence of a Supreme Being? Was it God who stepped in and so providentially created the cosmos for our benefit?" Personally, I fear that Greenstein has gone, relative to Hawking, a little too far in the other direction. I do not think we have indisputable scientific proof of the existence of God. But I am convinced that we do have, in the Big Bang understanding, some very good evidence for the existence of the transcendent God of the universe.

Others have commented, sometimes inadvertently, on this evidence. A book I recommend is *Dreams of a Final Theory* by Steven Weinberg (1933- , Nobel Prize in Physics, 1979, and considered by many to be the greatest physicist of the last half of the twentieth century). Although Steven Weinberg is a staunch atheist, Chapter XI of his book is titled "What About God?" Therein Weinberg tells a story related by the Venerable Bede (672-735), English theologian and historian of the Pre-Middle Ages. In the story, a speech is made before King Edwin of Northumbria in favor of the adoption of Christianity. In this speech the term "banqueting hall" is used to describe the ordinary existence of human beings on planet earth. Weinberg's perceptive comment on the speech is, "It is an almost irresistible temptation to believe with Bede and Edwin that there must be something for us outside the banqueting hall." There must be something beyond strict reductionism or materialism. This view is echoed in the New Testament. For example, St. Paul wrote, "Ever since the creation of the world, God's eternal power and divine nature, invisible though they are, have been understood and seen through the things He has made" (Letter to the Romans 1:20). This is essentially what Steven Weinberg is attempting to describe—that almost "irresistible temptation" to believe in God.

It is relatively unusual that a physical scientist is truly an atheist. Why is this true? Some point to the anthropic constraints, the remarkable fine tuning of the universe. For example, Freeman Dyson, a Princeton faculty member, has said, "Nature has been kinder to us than we had any right to expect." Martin Rees, one of Hawking's colleagues at Cambridge, notes the same facts. Rees recently stated "The possibility of life as we know it depends on the values of a few basic, physical constants and is in some respects remarkably sensitive to their numerical values. Nature does exhibit remarkable coincidences." Science writer extraordinaire Paul Davies adds "There is for me powerful evidence that there is something going on behind it all . . . . . It seems as though somebody has fine tuned nature's numbers to make the Universe. The impression of design is overwhelming." Some scientists express surprise at what they view as so many "accidental occurrences." However, that astonishment quickly disappears when one sees purpose instead of arbitrariness in the laws of nature.

Against powerful logic, some atheists continue to claim, irrespective of the anthropic constraints, that the universe and human life were created by chance. The main argument seems to be "Since we human beings are here, it must have happened in a purely reductionist manner." This argument strikes me a bit like the apocryphal response of a person waking up in the morning to find an elephant in his or her bedroom. The individual in question concludes that this is no surprise, since the probability of the elephant being in the bedroom is a perfect 100%. Obviously this is a philosophical rather than scientific response to the situation.

A reply to this argument has been developed by the philosopher/historian William Lane Craig. The atheist's argument states that since we're here, we know every element of the creation must have happened by strictly material forces. Craig's philosophical counterargument, as reported by Hugh Ross, goes like this: Suppose a dozen sharpshooters are sent to execute a prisoner by firing squad. They all shoot a number of rounds in just the right direction, but the prisoner escapes unharmed. The prisoner could conclude, since he is alive, that all the sharpshooters missed by some extremely unlikely chance. He may wish to attribute his survival to some remarkable piece of good luck. But he would be far more rational to conclude that the guns were loaded with blanks or that the sharpshooters had all deliberately missed. Not only is life itself overwhelmingly improbable, but its appearance almost immediately (in geological terms), perhaps within as short a period as 10 million years following the solidification and cooling of our once-molten planet, defies explanation by conventional physical and chemical laws.

The No Boundary Proposal

Let us return to Hawking's no boundary proposal—the idea that the universe has neither beginning nor end. By treating the universe as a wave function, Hawking hopes to rationalize the universe's popping into existence 12-16 billion years ago. Critical to Hawking's research in this regard is the notion of imaginary time. The concept of imaginary time is a powerful mathematical device used on occasion by theoretical chemists and physicists. I remember clearly the day in October of 1965, during my Complex Variables class as a senior at M.I.T., when I learned that the result of contour integration was two pi i times the sum of the residues. For me, it was about as close to a revelation as I had received up to that time in my life. My closest colleague at Berkeley, Professor William H. Miller, in 1969 used imaginary time to understand the dynamics of chemical reactions, and it made him a household word in the world of science. The use of imaginary time is indeed a powerful tool.

Indulge me while I attempt to convey the essence of how imaginary time is exploited in theoretical physics and chemistry. One approaches a well defined problem, with all variables necessarily being real. This means, for example, real positions for all particles, real velocities, and so on. Real problems begin with all quantities real. Then one undertakes a carefully chosen excursion into the complex plane, making one or more variables complex. Subsequently we do some really cool things mathematically. Finally, all the variables revert to real values, and we find that something important has been mathematically derived that would have otherwise been impossible to prove.

Hawking and Hartle's no boundary proposal begins by adopting a grossly oversimplified model of the universe. Then the authors make time imaginary, and prove in their terribly restricted model that the universe has neither beginning nor end. The flaw in the exercise is that the authors never go back to real time. Thus the notion that the universe has neither beginning nor end is something that exists in mathematical terms only. In real time, to which we as human beings are necessarily attached, rather than in Hawking's use of imaginary time, there will always be a singularity, that is, a beginning of time.

In an obviously contradictory statement in *A Brief History of Time*, Hawking actually concedes this point. What we are seeing in this situation is Hawking versus Hawking. I view the following statement as Hawking speaking in his right mind: "When one goes back to the real time in which we live, however, there will still appear to be singularities. In real time, the universe has a beginning and an end at singularities that form a boundary to space-time and at which the laws of science break down" (first edition, page 144). Only if we lived in imaginary time (not coming soon to a neighborhood near you!) would we encounter no singularities. In real time the universe was created *ex nihilo* 12-16 billion years ago.

With some trepidation, I will venture further. A case can be made that the Hartle-Hawking "no boundary proposal" is only of marginal scientific interest. The reasons for this conclusion might include: (a) the theory is a mathematical construct that has no unique empirical support; (b) the theory makes no verifiable scientific predictions that were not achieved earlier with simpler models; (c) the theory generates no significant research agenda. The primary purpose of the theory seems to be an attempt to evade the cosmological argument for the existence of God, via the claim that nature is self-contained and effectively eternal.

Science is primarily concerned with facts, not motive, and thus a complete scientific description of the creation does not necessarily rule out a providential account at the same time. William Paley's famous design argument suggests that if you are taking a walk in the woods and find a watch on the path, you should not conclude that the watch just assembled itself—despite the fact that we can take the watch apart, look at every single part and completely understand how it works. We look at the watch on the path and prudently conclude that it was designed by some higher intelligence.

In *A Brief History of Time*, Hawking states, "If the no boundary proposal is correct, He [God] had no freedom at all to choose initial conditions." This statement strikes me as a leap into irrationality. Why does Hawking find, within the functioning of the universe, aspects that appear to him to be limitations of God's power? This stems not from any attitude of an infinite God, but rather from the attributes of finite man. Namely, we as human beings are able to scientifically discern characteristics of the Creator only as they are related to that which is created, that which we can observe. This limitation of ours immediately reduces what might be infinite to the finiteness of our existence. Of course, Biblically, there is no problem in accepting divine constraints to divine options, if the Creator chooses to run the universe according to His stated and established laws. Divine tenacity to His own laws is, of course, the very essence of the Biblical God.

Another of Hawking's controversial statements needs to be addressed. Although it is not original with him, Hawking states: "We are such insignificant creatures on a minor planet of a very average star in the outer suburbs of one of a hundred billion galaxies. So it is difficult to believe in a God that would care about us or even notice our existence." I take a different position. In their recent writings, Hugh Ross and Guillermo Gonzalez (a professor of astronomy at Iowa State University) have demonstrated that our solar system, and in particular the sun and planet earth, are in fact quite extraordinary in many respects. The work of Ross and Gonzalez follows the excellent book *Rare Earth*, published in 2000 by Peter Ward and Donald Brownlee. There is no compelling evidence to date that life exists elsewhere in the universe. Human beings, thus far, appear to be the most advanced species in the universe. Maybe God does care about us! Stephen Hawking surveys the cosmos and concludes that the principal characteristic of humankind is obscurity. I consider the same evidence and conclude that human beings are special. I must be quick to add that a Christian worldview does not exclude the possibility of life, even sentient life, elsewhere in the universe. Precisely this possibility is addressed by C.S. Lewis in his two science fiction novels *Out of the Silent Planet* and *Perelandra*.

Before moving on, two related issues need to be addressed. The first concerns the infinitely oscillating model of the universe, which posits a ceaseless sequence of Big Bang/big crunch pairs. This model, popularized by Robert Dicke, makes the universe effectively eternal. The infinitely oscillating universe model, as noted above, comports nicely with Hinduism's dance of Shiva. Since the hypothesized period between the present Big Bang and its imagined big crunch would be just one of an infinite number of such periods, any problems relating to the time scale that might be needed for evolution are resolved by the conclusion that our interval must be "just right." On many occasions when I have presented this lecture, the Q&A time includes a question concerning this cosmological model. Actually, this issue was resolved for most cosmologists in 1983 in a critical paper by Alan Guth (best known for his pioneering work on the inflationary features of the Big Bang Theory) appearing in the influential journal *Nature*, volume 302, beginning on page 505. The title of Guth's paper tells the story: "The Impossibility of a Bouncing Universe." Therein Guth showed that even if the universe contained sufficient mass to halt the current expansion, any collapse would end in a thud, not a bounce. Incidentally, the weight of opinion among cosmologists has shifted over the past five years to the position that, short of direct intervention by God, the universe will continue to expand forever. The critical research in this regard was Saul Perlmutter and Brian Schmidt's apparently simultaneous discovery that the expansion of the universe is actually speeding up. *Science* magazine named their finding the "Breakthrough Discovery of the Year" in 1998.

The second and perhaps most recent attempt to evade the (theistic) logical consequences of the fine tuning of the universe (anthropic constraints) is the proposal that there are an infinite number of universes. This proposal has been given wide attention through the popular 2000 book by Martin Rees entitled *Just Six Numbers*. Rees's logic flows something like this: (a) he concedes that a universe like ours is overwhelmingly improbable; but (b) we know that God doesn't exist, or if He does He had nothing to do with the design of the universe; (c) thus there must be a near infinite number of universes; (d) ours just happens to be the universe that is just right for human life. Since no evidence for other universes is provided, Rees's argument is less than convincing, particularly for those who are prepared to consider the possibility of the existence of a personal God.

The Rees proposal might be broadened a bit by adding that other universes might have their own forms of intelligent conscious life, very different from what is observed on planet earth. One could go further and state that there is no need for life in the proposed other universes to be based on carbon. John Polkinghorne has responded to these ideas as follows: "Those who make such a claim are drawing a very large intellectual blank check on a totally unknown bank account. Consciousness seems to demand very great physical complexity to sustain it (the human brain is the most complicated physical system we have encountered). It is far from persuasive that there are many alternative routes to the generation of such complexity."

In his paper in the April 2001 issue of the journal *Science & Christian Belief* Rodney Holder critiques the proposal for the existence of many universes as an alternative to design. Holder states some of the problems associated with the postulate of an infinite number of universes:

(a)   the existence of infinitely many universes depends critically on parameter choices;

(b)   the probability that any universe in an ensemble is fine-tuned for life is zero;

(c)   the physical realization of any ensemble will exclude an infinity of possibilities;

(d)   the hypothesis is untestable and unscientific;

(e)   the hypothesis is not consistent with the amount of order found in our universe, nor with the persistence of order.

In completing this discussion, I note that a Christian worldview does not exclude the possibility of other universes. One of the great hymns of the Christian faith in fact begins with the words "O Lord my God, when I in awesome wonder, consider all the worlds Thy hands have made." However, a plausible scientific case for an infinite or near infinite number of universes has yet to be made.

A Broader View

Does everyone agree with Stephen Hawking concerning the metaphysical consequences of recent cosmological discoveries? Certainly not. Alan Lightman, a MIT professor with no obvious theistic inclinations, states in his book *Origins: The Lives and Worlds of Modern Cosmologists* (Harvard University Press, 1990), "Contrary to popular myths, scientists appear to have the same range of attitudes about religious matters as does the general public." This fact can be established either from anecdotes or from statistical data. Sigma Xi, the scientific honorary society, conducted a systematic poll a few years ago which showed that, on any given Sunday, around 41 percent of all Ph.D. scientists are in church; for the general population the figure is perhaps 42 percent. So, whatever influences people in their beliefs about God, it does not appear to have much to do with having a Ph.D. in science. It is true in science, as well as in essentially all other professions, that after income levels reach perhaps $75,000. per year (in North America), further increases in salary may be correlated with higher percentages of agnosticism. In his 1998 paper in *Nature* Edward Larson showed that for incomes above $150,000. per year, belief in God falls off significantly. The same trend holds, for example, for lawyers at these income levels. This finding, of course, is consistent with the words of Jesus on the difficulty of a rich person entering the kingdom of heaven.

There are many prominent scientific counterexamples to Stephen Hawking. One is my former colleague at Berkeley for 18 years, Charles Townes (1915-). Townes won the Nobel Prize in Physics in 1964 for discovering the maser, which led quickly to the laser, surely one of the most important scientific advances of the twentieth century. In a statement from his recent book *Making Waves* (American Physical Society, 1995) Professor Townes appears to take dead aim on Hawking. Charles Townes states "In my view, the question of origin seems to be left unanswered if we explore from a scientific view alone. Thus, I believe there is a need for some religious or metaphysical explanation. I believe in the concept of God and in His existence."

Arthur Schawlow (1921-1999) was another Physics Nobel Prize winner (1981), honored for his work in laser spectroscopy.

Schawlow was a professor at Stanford until his recent death and did not hesitate to identify himself as a protestant Christian. He stated, "We are fortunate to have the Bible and especially the New Testament, which tells us so much about God in widely accessible human terms." I view this statement as uniquely scientific, knowing that Professor Schawlow was convinced that his discoveries in laser spectroscopy were telling him something about God's handiwork. However, unlike the New Testament, Schawlow's research was difficult to express in "widely accessible human terms."

The other chaired Professor of Theoretical Physics at Cambridge (Cambridge is still very stingy about handing out Professor titles; most tenured faculty members retire at the rank of Senior Lecturer) for much of Hawking's career was John Polkinghorne, a nuclear physicist. He left the chair of mathematical physics at Cambridge in 1979 in order to train for the ordained ministry of the Church of England. Upon ordination, Polkinghorne became a parish priest for five years. He returned to Cambridge in 1986 as Dean of Trinity Hall and subsequently President of Queens' College. I am very familiar with the grounds of Queens' College, as it is immediately adjacent to St. Catherine's College, where I stay in Cambridge courtesy of my longtime collaborator, Professor Nicholas Handy. John Polkinghorne's statement of belief is straightforward: "I am a Christian believer and believe that God exists and has made Himself known in human terms in Jesus Christ."

Probably the world's greatest living observational cosmologist is Allan Sandage. Sandage works in Pasadena, California at the Carnegie Observatories. In 1991 he received the Crafoord Prize, given by the Royal Swedish Academy every six years for cosmology and worth nearly the same amount of money as the Nobel Prize (there is no Nobel Prize given for cosmology). Sandage has been called "the grand old man of cosmology" by the *New York Times* and is viewed as the successor to his mentor, Edwin Hubble (1889-1953), who is considered the father of modern cosmology.

At the age of about 50, Sandage became a Christian. Sandage has stated "The nature of God is not to be found within any part of the findings of science. For that, one must turn to the Scriptures." When asked the famous question regarding whether it is possible to be a scientist and a Christian, Sandage replied, "Yes. The world is too complicated in all its parts and interconnections to be due to chance alone. I am convinced that the existence of life with all its order in each of its organisms is simply too well put together."

Of Hawking's two earliest collaborators (1970, the singularity theorem), Roger Penrose seems to be some sort of an unconventional theist, while George Ellis is a Christian. Ellis is Professor of Applied Mathematics at the University of Cape Town, South Africa. In the book *Quantum Cosmology and the Laws of Nature*, Ellis states his position with respect to ultimate questions:

(1) God is the creator and sustainer of the universe and of humankind, transcending the universe but immanent in it;

(2) God's nature embodies justice and holiness, but is also a personal and loving God who cares for each creature (so the name "father" is indeed appropriate);

(3) God's nature is revealed most perfectly in the life and teachings of Jesus of Nazareth, as recorded in the New Testament of the Bible, who was sent by God to reveal the divine nature, summarized in "God is Love;"

(4) God has an active presence in the world that still touches the lives of the faithful today.

One of the scientists closest to Stephen Hawking and prominent in the movie about *A Brief History of Time* is Donald Page. Page is Professor of Physics at the University of Alberta, where he hosted my lecture on this topic in July 1997. Our discussions following my lecture lasted for four hours spread over three days. Don Page has had an excellent physics career in quantum cosmology in his own right, but he began to achieve fame as a postdoctoral fellow with Stephen Hawking. The Hawkings were not financially well off in the years prior to publication of his best selling book and needed some help to keep going. So Don Page went to live with the Hawkings for the period 1976-1979.

Page describes these years in the book (the book about the film about the book!). He said, "I would usually get up around 7:15 or 7:30 AM, take a shower, read in my Bible and pray. Then I would go down at 8:15 and get Stephen up. At breakfast, I would often tell him what I'd been reading in the Bible, hoping that maybe this would eventually have some influence. I remember telling Stephen one story about how Jesus had seen the deranged man, and how this man had these demons, and the demons asked that they be sent into a herd of swine. The swine then plunged over the edge of the cliff and into the sea. Stephen piped up and said, 'Well, the Society for the Prevention of Cruelty to Animals would not like that story, would they!'"

Page has stated, "I am a conservative Christian in the sense of pretty much taking the Bible seriously for what it says. Of course I know that certain parts are not intended to be read literally, so I am not precisely a literalist. But I try to believe in the meaning I think it is intended to have." Expressing the universal goal of theoretical physicists for simplicity in their methods, Page makes an interesting connection to the spiritual world: "If the universe basically is very simple, the theological implications of this would need to be worked out. Perhaps the mathematical simplicity of the universe is a reflection of the personal simplicity of the Gospel message, that God sent His Son Jesus Christ to bridge the gap between Himself and each of us, who have rejected God or rejected what He wants for us by rebelling against His will and disobeying Him. This is a message simple enough even to be understood by children."

My final example is Chris Isham, Professor of Theoretical Physics at Imperial College of Science and Technology, University of London. The superb popular writer and former research physicist Paul Davies has described Isham as "Britain's greatest quantum gravity expert." This is high praise indeed when one considers that Stephen Hawking's research area is quantum gravity. I had the pleasure of chatting with Professor Isham for a while when I gave this lecture at Imperial College in May 2000. Alluding to the philosopher Paul Tillich, Chris Isham states "The God of Christianity is not only 'the ground of being.' He is also Incarnate." Essential therein "is the vision of the Resurrection (of Jesus Christ) as 'the new creation out of the old order' and . . . the profound notion of the 'redemption of time' through the life and death of Jesus Christ. I think it will be rather a long time before theoretical physics has anything useful to add to that." Let me be quick to extinguish one possible interpretation of Professor Isham's last sentence. By no means is Chris Isham belittling the importance of theoretical physics. Isham has committed his entire professional life to the pursuit of theoretical physics. Isham is passionate about theoretical physics. Isham is rather saying that what he has found in Jesus Christ surpasses anything that physics could hope to provide in terms of ultimate meaning.

The Limits of Science

A statement that I think gives some balance to this discussion was made by one of my scientific heroes, Erwin Schrödinger, after whom the most important equation in science is named: the Schrödinger Equation. I have spent a good bit of my professional life trying to solve this equation for atoms and molecules. Toward the end of Schrödinger's career he began to write more expansively. His 1942 book *What is Life?* is thought to have inspired an entire generation of molecular biologists. The statement I would like to quote comes from Schrödinger's 1954 book *Nature and the Greeks*. In it he takes a dim view of what we might call scientific imperialism. The Schrödinger statement in question is:

"I am very astonished that the scientific picture of the real world around me is very deficient. It gives us a lot of factual information, puts all of our experience in a magnificently consistent order, but it is ghastly silent about all and sundry that is really near to our heart, that really matters to us. It cannot tell us a word about red and blue, bitter and sweet, physical pain and physical delight; it knows nothing of beautiful and ugly, good or bad, God and eternity. Science sometimes pretends to answer questions in these domains but the answers are very often so silly that we are not inclined to take them seriously."

Although science is an inspiring pursuit in its proper domain, and a genuine delight to me and others, it is not the whole story. Jane Hawking commented on this aspect of her husband's work following the publication of *A Brief History of Time*. She said "Stephen has the feelings that because everything is reduced to a rational, mathematical formula, that must be the truth. He is delving into realms that really do matter to thinking people and in a way that can have a very disturbing effect on people—and he's not competent. "

In a similar vein my longtime friend and Berkeley faculty colleague Phillip Johnson states "The irony of the situation is that Hawking's professional life currently is devoted to telling a story about the cosmos in which the elements that make his life interesting—love, faith, courage, and even creative imagination— disappear from view. Aspiring to know the mind of God, he can imagine nothing more interesting than a set of equations governing the movement of particles. A unified field theory would be a major scientific accomplishment, of course. But to Hawking it is just a step toward a distant but attainable goal of what he calls 'a complete understanding of the events around us, and of our own existence.' The way to this goal does not seem to require reading the Bible or Shakespeare, living in a variety of cultures, experiencing art, climbing mountains, or falling in love and having children. All it involves is 'the intellectually challenging task of developing better approximation methods.'" Although Phil does not seem to appreciate the great affection with which persons such as Hawking and I hold equations, there is much that is worthy of consideration in Professor Johnson's analysis.

Richard Feynman states in his 1990 book, *The Character of Physical Law*, that "Everything in physical science is a lot of protons, neutrons and electrons (parenthetical remark by HFS— and don't we love them, especially electrons!), while in daily life, we talk about men and history, or beauty and hope. Which is nearer to God—beauty and hope or the fundamental laws? To stand at either end, and to walk off that end of the pier only, hoping that out in that direction is a complete understanding, is a mistake." I would have to say that, at least in the final sentence of *A Brief History of Time*, Stephen Hawking has walked off one end of Feynman's pier.

Where Do We Go from Here?

In his book *The Fingerprint of God*, Hugh Ross seeks to construct a bridge between cosmology and matters of ultimate importance. With minor modifications, I wholeheartedly concur. Having presented the opinions of many others in this lecture, the following represents my own position:

1. The Big Bang represents an immensely powerful yet carefully controlled release of matter, energy, space, and time within the strict confines of very carefully fine-tuned physical constants and laws which govern their behavior and interactions. The power and care this explosion reveals exceed human potential for design by multiple orders of magnitude.

2. A Creator must exist. The Big Bang ripples (April 1992) and subsequent scientific findings are clearly pointing to an *ex nihilo* creation consistent with the first few verses of the book of Genesis.

3. The Creator must have awesome power and wisdom. The quantity of material and the power resources within our universe are truly immense. The information, or intricacy, manifest in any part of the universe, and (as Allan Sandage has well stated) especially in a living organism, is beyond our ability to comprehend. And what we do see is only what God has shown us within our four dimensions of space and time!

4. The Creator is loving. The simplicity, balance, order, elegance, and beauty seen throughout the creation demonstrate that God is loving rather than capricious. Further, the capacity and desire to nurture and to protect, seen in so many creatures, makes sense if their Creator possesses these same attributes. It is apparent that God cares for His creatures, for He has provided for their needs.

5. The Creator is just and requires justice. Inward reflection and outward investigation affirm that human beings have a conscience. The conscience reflects the reality of right and wrong and the necessity of obedience.

6. Each of us falls hopelessly short of the Creator's standard. We incur His displeasure when we violate any part of God's moral law in our actions, our words, and our thoughts. Who can keep his or her thoughts and attitudes pure for even an hour? Certainly not me. If each person falls short of his or her own standards, how much more so of God's perfect standards? For many years I sought to get a "passing grade" with God by comparing myself with other sinners.

7. Because the Creator is loving, wise and powerful, He made a way to rescue us. When we come to a point of concern about our personal failings, we can begin to understand from the creation around us that God's love, wisdom, and power are sufficient to deliver us from our otherwise hopeless situation.

8. If we trust our lives totally to the Rescuer, Jesus Christ, we will be saved. The one and only path is to give up all human attempts to satisfy God's requirements and put our trust solely in Jesus Christ and in His chosen means of redemption, namely, His death on the cross.

The above outline is, of course, just an outline. To fill in the outline of this bridge over the troubled waters of human experience, the reader may turn to Chapter 8, my essay entitled "The Ten Questions that Intellectuals Ask about Christianity." Several of these questions arise persistently during Q&A times following the Big Bang lecture on cosmology.

Climbing Mount Improbable: Evolutionary Science or Wishful Thinking? 5

Introduction

Of all the lectures in this series, this is the one I most assiduously try to avoid having to present. I have manufactured all sorts of entirely valid reasons to convince different universities that my "Big Bang" lecture was far more suitable to their environments than would be this evolution talk. Of all the topics treated in this book, evolution is the most inflammatory. The ratio of heat to light produced reaches a maximum for this lecture, irrespective of how the material is treated. On the other hand, for many prospective readers, this is the chapter to which they will turn first. Regrettably, for many I will probably fail a litmus test that prevents them from considering the other chapters, which may be more helpful.

This is a topic that can potentially alienate even good friends. Trite though it may seem, it is true that several of the people in this world I most appreciate are agnostics or atheists. My Berkeley chemistry faculty colleagues, Professors Robert Harris and Richard Saykally, are two such friends. They are going to be offended by this chapter, because I am convinced that, ultimately, nothing in the universe makes sense apart from a belief in the sovereign God of the Bible. My Theistic Evolutionist friends Professors David Cole (Berkeley) and Don Page (Alberta) will be disappointed because I find the current evidence for the standard evolutionary model to be unconvincing. Finally, my Recent Creationist friends, for example Professor William Pelletier, distinguished natural products chemist and former Provost of the University of Georgia (the single person most responsible for the remarkable transformation of the University of Georgia into a modern research university), will be similarly dismayed. Their unhappiness will arise from my conclusion that the original intent of Moses in writing (3400 years ago) of the six "days" in chapter one of Genesis was to denote indefinite periods of time, rather than literal 24 hour periods. Since my wife Karen also holds to the Recent Creation position, one will look in vain in this book to find criticisms of that view of origins.

The nature of the evolution debate has changed radically over the past decade. Prior to that time the anti-evolution case was primarily put forth by those with connections to Biblical literalism. The persons doing the heavy lifting were usually Henry Morris (formerly a respected engineering professor at Virginia Tech) and Duane Gish, a Berkeley Ph.D. in biochemistry. Although Drs. Morris and Gish had solid academic credentials, they were pejoratively referred to by many in academia as "fundamentalists." Although Morris and Gish disagreed with the standard evolutionary model at many points, perhaps most central was their insistence that the earth is not more than 10,000 years old.

An initially unheralded but very significant event occurred in 1985 with the publication of the book *Evolution: A Theory in Crisis*, by the Australian biologist Michael Denton. Dr. Denton was an agnostic, so his work was not in the least religiously motivated. In 1986 my Berkeley faculty colleague Professor Phillip Johnson began to ask me a few questions about evolution. Johnson is a mainline Presbyterian with absolutely no history of Biblical literalism. The next year he read Denton's monograph and asked if I could find a few reviews of the book. I found one, in the *Journal of the American Scientific Affiliation*, as I remember. The rest is history. Phil Johnson's 1991 book *Darwin on Trial* became the manifesto for a new generation of younger people skeptical of the claim that all of life can be understood in terms of mutations and natural selection. Johnson has a brilliant analytical mind, and I consider him one of the two most intellectually gifted faculty members I came across during my 18 years as a Berkeley professor. The precision of Johnson's logic reduced some of his opponents to appeals to specialized scientific knowledge, purportedly inaccessible to a legal scholar. To some unbiased observers this seemed a bit disingenuous, since the same defenders of the standard evolutionary model had used oceans of ink explaining how very simple were all the concepts required to understand evolution.

The next trumpet blast in the battle was a full length article in the respected Jewish intellectual magazine *Commentary* by the distinguished mathematician and popular writer (*A Tour of the Calculus*) David Berlinski. Berlinski's June 1996 review, entitled *The Deniable Darwin* was sufficiently incisive to fill up a large fraction of the September 1996 issue of *Commentary* with letters to the editor, pro and con. Dr. Berlinski identified himself as an agnostic Jew, putting a great deal of room between his view of the universe and biblical literalism. Berlinski was followed by Michael Behe's book *Darwin's Black Box*. Behe is a Professor of Biochemistry at Lehigh University and a Roman Catholic. Next came William Dembski, with Ph.D.s in both mathematics and philosophy, publishing *The Design Inference* with Cambridge University Press, one of the most distinguished academic publishers. Dembski's religious history includes a period with Eastern Orthodoxy, hardly a stronghold of "fundamentalism." The most recent of the popular anti-evolution books is *Icons of Evolution*, by the Berkeley molecular biology Ph.D. Jonathan Wells. Wells is a follower of the religious charlatan Sun Myung Moon.

What do Phillip Johnson and the above-described authors (and several others with scholarly books in the works) have in common? First, these people are not Biblical literalists. Second, none of them wishes to make an issue of the age of the earth. Thus the debate necessarily takes on a very different character than that observed before 1991. One might think that this would remove much of the old animosity associated with the origins debates. This is not necessarily so. Although the likes of Richard Dawkins may have earlier railed against the young earth chronology of the dreaded "fundamentalists," with these folks no longer in the limelight, the wrath of Dawkins et al., if anything, seems to have redoubled. Perhaps the age of the earth was not as big a problem as advertised.

Before concluding this introduction, I should say a few words about my own cultural heritage. In the loving family in which I was so very privileged to be raised, evolution was a fundamental belief. This became evident to me on an evening in 1960 after I returned from seeing the classic Spencer Tracy film *Inherit the Wind*. The film is a caricature of the 1925 Scopes evolution trial in Dayton, Tennessee. A historical account of the Scopes trial is given in the Pulitzer Prize winning 1997 book *Summer for the Gods*, by Edward Larson. While waiting to purchase my ticket to the movie, to my amazement, I observed a protest outside the theater, with individuals waving placards saying "Fight Godless Evolution" and similar things. Protests were unheard of in Midwestern America in 1960, four years before the trouble began in Berkeley. My dad was awake when I returned from the theater, so I naturally asked if he could explain this unique situation to me. Without batting an eyelash, my father replied, "Son, those people are religious fanatics. They don't even believe in evolution." So there it is, evolution—a sacred belief in the household in which I grew up.

I believed everything in evolution when I received Christ into my life in 1973. Perhaps this is the reason I still fail to see evolution as a major hindrance to a person becoming a Christian (of course there are exceptions), and prefer to focus on the other chapters of the present book. I continued to embrace the standard evolutionary model for at least five years after I became a Christian. By this time a number of people in the church I attended were expecting me to be able to explain to them how the whole evolution business fit in, or did not fit in, with an orthodox understanding of the Christian faith. Honesty compels me to admit that between 1973 and 1978 I was not very interested in the relationship between science and the Christian faith. I was coming to know Jesus in a personal way, and that was the passion of my life, as it remains. However, eventually I became weary of telling inquirers "I haven't thought seriously about it yet" and decided it would be easier to research the topic than to continue to be viewed as an unbalanced scientist. I had been interested in origin of life issues for some time, due to my research on interstellar molecules. Gradually, I began to study general interest articles on evolution in the highly respected professional journals *Science* and *Nature*. In hindsight, it is most curious that becoming a Christian would cause me to become a much broader scientist than would have otherwise been the case! But now I'm getting ahead of my story.

Climbing Mount Improbable

Richard Dawkins is the author of the 1996 book *Climbing Mount Improbable*. After Stephen Hawking, Richard Dawkins is perhaps the best known living popularizer of science. His books

The Selfish Gene (1976) and *The Blind Watchmaker* (1986) were bestsellers among science books for a general audience. Unlike Stephen Hawking, however, Richard Dawkins is an angry atheist. In fact, the Atheist Alliance International Convention presents an annual Richard Dawkins Award to the most effective atheist on the planet. Dawkins' fulminations against those of differing opinions include the statement recorded in the April 9, 1989 *New York Times*: "It is absolutely safe to say that, if you meet somebody who claims not to believe in evolution, that person is ignorant, stupid, or insane (or wicked, but I'd rather not consider that)." Richard Dawkins was a member of the Berkeley faculty (Assistant Professor of Zoology) during 1967-1969, leaving as I began my 18 years as a professor of chemistry at Berkeley. Dawkins achieved tenure (a permanent faculty position) at Oxford University, but was never promoted to the coveted position of Professor of Zoology. He abandoned his career as an original scientist about 20 years ago and immersed himself in the publication of popular books. Eventually, Microsoft multimillionaire Charles Simonyi made a large gift to Oxford University, with the stipulation that Richard Dawkins be named the Professor of the Public Understanding of Science.

Richard Dawkins has occasional spells of candor, which cause some to question the validity of his argumentation. For example, the back cover of *Climbing Mount Improbable* states: "The metaphor of 'Mount Improbable' represents the combination of perfection and improbability that we find in the seemingly 'designed' complexity of living things." Ten years earlier, in *The Blind Watchmaker*, Dawkins made a related concession: "Biology is the study of complicated things that give the appearance of having been designed for a purpose." The dispassionate observer may wonder, given Dawkins' confessions of the appearance of design, why it is "ignorant, stupid, insane, or wicked" to assume that there might just be a Designer.

Not entirely surprisingly, the indignant atheist has his detractors. Had Dawkins been active three-quarters of a century ago, the ever-quotable G. K. Chesterton would surely have included him among those who "fail to believe in the sovereign God of the universe, but are willing to believe almost anything." David Berlinski, author of the highly influential *Commentary* essay *The Deniable Darwin*, states: "The theory of evolution is the great white elephant of contemporary thought. It is large, almost entirely useless, and the object of superstitious awe." And Dawkins' *bête noire*, Berkeley Professor Phillip Johnson takes dead aim on Dawkins in stating (November, 1996) "The first step for a 21st century science of origins is to separate materialist philosophy from empirical science."

Richard Dawkins, author of *Climbing Mount Improbable*, is the very model of a modern materialist reductionist. For example, Dawkins describes love as "a product of highly complicated, nervous equipment or computing equipment of some sort." This does not immediately strike me as the sort of language that is likely to be found attractive by most members of the opposite sex. Although he is now reported to be married once again, one individual at Oxford opined that Dawkins was, at least for a while, testing as much of this "computing equipment" as he could discretely get his hands on. When asked if such a worldview is depressing, Dawkins responds "I don't feel depressed about it. But if somebody does, that's their problem. Maybe the logic is deeply pessimistic, the universe is bleak, cold and empty. But so what?" To complete this set of inspiring quotations, Dawkins has stated that the universe "has precisely the properties we should expect if there is, at bottom, no design, no purpose, no evil and no good, nothing but pointless indifference."

It would be unfair to Richard Dawkins to pretend that he alone holds such depressing views. In his 1965 book *The Identity of Man*, Jacob Bronowski states "Man is a part of nature, in the same sense that a stone is, or a cactus, or a camel." Again G.K. Chesterton responds, once more far ahead of his time, in *The Everlasting Man* (1925): "It is not natural to see man as a natural product. It is not common sense to call man a common object of the country or the seashore. It is not seeing him straight to see him as an animal. It is not sane. It sins against the light; against that broad daylight of proportion which is the principle of all reality."

The skeptical ideas outlined above are not restricted to Dawkins, Bronowski, and a few others to be discussed later. Such philosophizing occasionally enters even the relatively sober world of molecular quantum mechanics that I inhabit. In 1977, the *International Journal of Quantum Chemistry* reported this example of naturalistic evolutionary thinking by Cambridge scientist

Andrew McLachlan: "Living systems are wonderfully well-suited to their purpose, but the design is shaped by blind evolution instead of imaginative intelligence." Since a theistic evolutionist would consider evolution to be the grandest example of God's imaginative intelligence expressed in the natural world, McLachlan's statement leaves room for none but atheists.

What This Chapter is Not About

This discussion does not concern the age of the earth. I am happy to accept the view that the age of the earth is roughly 4.6 billion years (*Science*, June 6, 2003) and that the age of the universe is something like 14 billion years. Current estimates of the reliability of the latter estimate are in the range of two billion years. Following the university lecture on this topic I usually do answer a question or two on this topic, but it is not a burning issue for me. Those who want to argue about the age of the earth have my approval, as long as both sides remain civilized. I am comfortable with what might be called "The Standard Timetable of Creation," which goes approximately as follows:

14,000 Million Years Ago	The Big Bang
4,600 Million Years Ago	Earth is Formed
3,860 Million Years Ago	Life Begins
3,500 Million Years Ago	Recognizable Fossil Cells
550 Million Years Ago	Cambrian Explosion
~0.1 Million Years Ago	Human Beings Appear

What else is the current origins debate *not* about? It does not concern the fact that micro-evolution is responsible for observed variations at or below the species level. Of course the most popular of such examples is the peppered moth story, or the case of industrial melanism. Although the peppered moth scenario is now considered factually dubious (see Wells, *Icons of Evolution*), there is no reason in principle why related examples of microevolution might not be demonstrated. Microevolution is not a generally disputed matter, although the scientific research related to specific cases (e.g., industrial melanism) may be shoddy.

What appears to be an exceptionally well-documented case for micro-evolution has been made by Peter and Rosemary Grant, two Princeton academics who have spent a significant part of their lives studying finches in the Galapagos Islands. The May 8, 1994 issue of the *New York Times Sunday Magazine* cites their work as an example of "Evolution in Action." The Grants reported that the Galapagos experienced a terrible La Nina-related drought in 1977 on Daphne Island. The generation of finches following the drought had beaks roughly 4% bigger than usual, better adapted for opening the last tough seeds that remained on the island. However, in 1983 Daphne Island experienced spectacular floods, and many finches died as the island quickly turned from desert to jungle. Subsequently, the first postflood generation of finches again had smaller beaks, to enjoy the multitude of tiny seeds that became available.

Is it possible to give precise definitions to evolution of the micro and macro varieties? In fact, this has been done most capably by Professor Ernst Mayr, one of the most distinguished defenders of the standard evolutionary model. In his book *One Long Argument* (Harvard University Press, 1991), Mayr defines "microevolution" as evolution at or below the species level, and states that it generally refers to relatively minor variations that occur in populations over time. Mayr in the same text defines "macroevolution" as evolution above the species level. Mayr gives as examples the evolution of higher taxa and the production of evolutionary novelties such as new structures. Macroevolution generally refers to major innovations such as new organs, structures, or body plans. The contemporary evolution debate is focused on macroevolution, not the non-controversial micro variety.

Finally, the origins discussion is not centered on a statement purportedly made by the Pope a few years ago. Pope John Paul II was quoted as saying that "New knowledge has led to the recognition that evolution is more than a theory." In fact, this juicy morsel appeared prominently on the front page of the New York Times in November of 1996. When this quotation created an uproar, the Vatican appeared to be genuinely confused. It turned out that the above English rendition was a translation from the French. The situation was sufficiently embarrassing that in January of the next year the Vatican released an official English version of the Pope's statement: "Some new findings lead us toward the recognition of more than one hypothesis within the theory of evolution." The latter statement, of course, refers to the sort of battles we observe between the proponents of variations of the standard evolutionary model.

Before leaving the last point, let me provide one example of the turf wars of the general type mentioned by the Pope, within the family of those totally committed to the standard evolutionary model. Richard Lewontin is a Professor of Genetics at Harvard, a Marxist, an atheist, and a much better scientist than Richard Dawkins. A recent blast by Professor Lewontin goes like this: "Dawkins' vulgarizations of Darwinism speak of nothing in evolution but an inexorable ascendancy of genes that are selectively superior, while the entire body of technical advance in experimental and theoretical evolutionary genetics of the last fifty years has moved in the direction of emphasizing non-selective forces in evolution." There is indeed more than one hypothesis within the theory of evolution.

So, What is the Contemporary Origins Debate About?

A major feature of the ongoing controversy is the mechanism by which one attempts to explain the macro-evolutionary changes (distinctly abrupt, on the geological time scale) observed as a function of time in the fossil record. A critical question in this context is "Where did the phyla come from?" The vast majority of the known phyla (over 95%) appear within a geologically brief period (perhaps 5-40 million years, figures that are necessarily upper bounds). This period, a bit more than half a billion years ago, is known as the Cambrian Explosion, the latter word chosen for obvious reasons. Following the Cambrian Explosion no new phyla are added throughout the geological record. The phyla are the major groups of life forms, based upon large differences in morphology, especially basic body plans. Currently there are about 38 phyla; shortly after the Cambrian explosion there were about 50 phyla.

With respect to this fossil explosion of 545 million years ago, Richard Dawkins uncharacteristically admitted in *The Blind Watchmaker* that "It is as though (the Cambrian phyla) were just planted there, without any evolutionary history." Thus a major challenge for advocates of the standard evolutionary model is to demonstrate that the Cambrian Explosion was preceded by a multitude of essentially invisible evolutionary developments. For a discussion of current controversies along these lines, the reader may examine the review by Richard Fortey (Oxford University faculty member) in the July 20, 2001 issue of *Science* magazine.

The other major bone of contention in our great debate is the absolute origin of life. More correctly, how did the simplest self-replicating biochemical system, the simplest thing that might be called "living," come into being? When most people with a general education imagine simple life forms, the amoebae they observed through microscopes in high school quickly come to mind. In fact, small though it may have seemed, an amoeba is a very complicated molecular machine. The simplest self-replicating biochemical system is much simpler than an amoeba. However, that said, the molecular information content in the simplest living thing is still staggering, requiring a technical description more than a thousand pages long if an attempt was made to discuss stereochemical features. Thus the second critical question in the debate is "How did all this information come together?"

Dr. Howard C. Berg is the Herschel Smith Professor of Physics and also Professor of Molecular and Cellular Biology at Harvard University. His August 2000 letter to *Physics Today* gives a clear picture of what is meant in the previous paragraph by the simplest living thing. Berg writes: "No free-living (independently replicating) organism has been synthesized from scratch. The possibility of doing so is still remote. The simplest case, a wall-less bacterium called 'Mycoplasma,' requires DNA encoding of about 300 genes for growth under laboratory conditions. The functions of about 100 of these (genes) are unknown." For those not into biochemistry, I should note that even a single gene is a very complicated molecular system. If the synthesis of life has eluded the tremendous design capacities of modern science, is there any good reason to be confident that these incredibly intricate molecular systems just assembled themselves by chance?

The Oparin-Haldane Hypothesis

In 1924 the Russian biochemist Alexander Oparin made a proposal for the origin of life on planet earth. However, it was apparently 1938 before Oparin's ideas appeared in English. In the meantime (1929), the eccentric Cambridge biochemist J.B.S. Haldane (more about him in the C.S. Lewis chapter of the present book) expressed similar ideas in the more readily accessible English language. Since 1940 their ideas have often been grouped together as the Oparin-Haldane hypothesis. Oparin and Haldane contended that the earth's early atmosphere contained very little oxygen and that life arose in the ancient oceans, using sunlight as an external energy source. The Oparin-Haldane scenario became very popular following a famous experiment in 1952 by Stanley Miller and Harold Urey at the University of Chicago. Miller passed a mixture of water vapor, methane, ammonia, and molecular hydrogen through an electric spark discharge for several days and observed a number of reaction products, including traces of amino acids. The results appeared to Miller and Urey to be broadly supportive of the early stages of the Oparin-Haldane mechanism for the origin of life.

In the two decades following the Miller-Urey experiment, the public imagination ran wild with their praises. The hype included favorable comparisons with what is usually considered the most important discovery in biology of the entire 20th century, namely James Watson and Francis Crick's identification of the double helix structure of DNA. Miller's experimental results received widespread coverage in popular publications such as *Time* magazine and gave the Oparin-Haldane model the status of textbook orthodoxy almost overnight. As one writer put it: "James Watson and Francis Crick unraveled the chemical basis of life . . . . . Stanley Miller discovered how matter and energy could create the building blocks of life without a preexisting cell. Unleashed from paralysis and spurred by the Space Age, research on the origin of life was launched by these . . . momentous achievements into an era of discovery and achievement."

The Miller-Urey experiments encouraged the creation of the field of interstellar molecules, a subject very dear to my own scientific heart. Since the molecules (water, methane, ammonia, and hydrogen) used as reactants in the Miller-Urey apparatus were so simple, perhaps a good bit of the origin of life chemistry might take place in the most sparsely settled regions of the universe, the vast expanses between the stars. The discovery of interstellar water and ammonia by Nobel Laureate Charles Townes (see the chapter "Scientists and their Gods" for a discussion of his outspoken belief in the God of the universe) in the early 1960s added to this stream of thought. In 1973, when I published my first paper on interstellar molecules in the journal *Nature*, the excitement of the field was certainly the challenge of contributing to an eventual understanding of the origin of life. My research group has continued for the past thirty years to carry out studies of molecules in space, publishing regularly on this topic in the *Astrophysical Journal* and elsewhere.

As the 1970s arrived, resistance to the Oparin-Haldane hypothesis began to emerge. In November 1972, the respected monthly *Physics Today* reported the following words from Ilya Prigogine (winner of the chemistry Nobel Prize five years later): "The probability that at ordinary temperatures a macroscopic number of molecules is assembled to give rise to the highly ordered structures and to the coordinated functions characterizing living organisms is vanishingly small. The idea of spontaneous genesis of life in its present form is therefore highly improbable, even on the scale of billions of years during which prebiotic evolution occurred."

The most scholarly and consistent source of the early (1970s) resistance to the Miller-Urey conclusions was Professor Dean Kenyon of San Francisco State University. Kenyon, a Stanford University Ph.D. in biophysics, was a highly unlikely source of opposition to the prevailing view. His 1969 monograph entitled *Biochemical Predestination* was the first major book on the origin of life and laid down the party line in great detail in favor of Miller and Urey's interpretation of their experiments. However, in 1976, just seven years later, Kenyon published a paper in the *Journal of Molecular Evolution* in which he raised grave questions concerning the plausibility of the Oparin-Haldane hypothesis. Subsequently, Kenyon has abandoned his 1969 views entirely. Another blow to the Oparin-Haldane hypothesis was dealt by the 1980 monograph *The Mystery of Life: Reassessing Current Theories*, by Charles Thaxton, Walter Bradley, and Roger Olsen. Bradley, a respected professor at Texas A&M University, has remained one of the important contributors to this research area in the succeeding 23 years. In 1986 New York University chemistry professor Robert Shapiro continued the academic discussion with his book Origins: *A Skeptic's Guide to the Creation of Life on Earth*. Shapiro's skepticism was directed at the Miller-Urey deductions, and his book is unrelenting in its criticism of the Oparin-Haldane hypothesis.

Those who claim that the Miller-Urey experiments are telling us something fundamental about the origin of life make extensive use of circular reasoning. This is obvious in their treatment of the earth's physical properties 3.86 billion years ago, the date of the oldest signs of life discovered thus far. Dean Kenyon states this criticism clearly: "If one wishes to know whether a chemical evolutionary origin of life could have taken place, one cannot simply assume that it did take place and then argue that conditions on the prebiotic Earth must have been such as to allow it to occur."

Stanley Miller and other chemical evolutionists begin by assuming that some naturalistic process brought about the first life. Then, arguing from the properties of organic molecules and the results of simulation experiments (the thousands of descendants of the original Miller-Urey experiments) they draw dubious conclusions about conditions on the primitive surface of the Earth. For example, organic compounds are well known to decompose in the presence of O_2; therefore, O_2 must have been virtually absent from the primitive atmosphere. Other reasons for believing that the Earth's early atmosphere contained very little O_2 are mentioned, but none appear to be as compelling. If one considers the possibility that life originated non-naturalistically, it may be appropriate to reason differently about the question of O_2 in the primitive atmosphere: The primitive atmosphere may or may not have contained substantial amounts of O_2. The issue, however, must be decided on the basis of independent evidence, not on the results of simulation experiments or the requirements of the Oparin-Haldane hypothesis. A fairly dispassionate assessment of the earth's early oxygen may be found in two articles in the August 3, 2001 issue of *Science* magazine.

Dean Kenyon continues that this circular reasoning has also been applied to the analysis of the temperature of the Earth 3.86

billion years ago. In discussing the temperature of the primitive Earth, Stanley Miller states: "The temperature of the primitive ocean is not known, but it can be said that the instability of various organic compounds and polymers makes a compelling argument that life could not have arisen in the ocean unless the temperature was below 25 C." Here again the requirements of a chemical evolutionary origin of life are used to constrain the primitive surface conditions. Is it not more reasonable, however, to try to construct an argument about the temperature of the primitive oceans that is independent of these requirements? If the information to answer the question is not yet at hand one should suspend judgment. When one doesn't know the answer to a scientific question, the good scientist simply states that he or she does not know.

Concerning other details of the primitive atmosphere's composition Stanley Miller is cautious, but the same kind of argumentation is discernible: "Some of the organic chemistry (i.e., of the simulation experiments) makes explicit predictions about atmospheric constituents. Such considerations cannot prove that the earth had a certain primitive atmosphere, but the prebiotic synthesis constraints should be a major consideration." Here Miller is referring to the experimental fact that the more reducing the experimental atmosphere (e.g., rich in CH_4, NH_3, and H_2, as opposed to O_2, CO_2 and N_2) the greater is the production of such organic compounds as amino acids, the building blocks of proteins. The results of simulation experiments are taken to lend powerful support to the view that the Earth's primitive atmosphere was reducing. But again, such reasoning is persuasive only if one assumes that chemical evolution must have taken place.

Is There a Crisis in Origin of Life Studies?

Perhaps the single most painful blow to the Oparin-Haldane hypothesis came in July 1973 with the publication of a paper by Francis Crick and Leslie Orgel. Crick is a self-proclaimed atheist who was known to tell fellow students in the tea room at Cambridge in the 1940s that his purpose in studying biochemistry was to disprove the existence of God. Thus Francis Crick was philosophically very sympathetic to the conventional interpretation of the 1952 Miller-Urey experiments. Nevertheless, Crick realized the bankruptcy of the Oparin-Haldane hypothesis in the early 1970s. The result of this enlightenment was his publication of the paper titled "Directed Panspermia" in the journal *Icarus*. Since the Miller-Urey interpretation was no longer plausible, Crick and Orgel in "Directed Panspermia" proposed that the first living molecular assemblies were imported from a much earlier civilization in another solar system. Fred Hoyle and N. C. Wickramasinghe took this fanciful idea and ran with it, publishing in 1981 the monograph *Evolution from Space*. Hoyle argued therein that biomolecules are so enormously complex that "Quite explicit instructions" were necessary for their assembly. From the scientific perspective of interstellar molecule studies, I always viewed "Directed Panspermia" as little more than a highly improbable avenue for escaping the evidence for the God of the universe. The real issue was science's unexpected inability to understand why even the simplest self-replicating biochemical system has a staggeringly high information content.

The *Icarus* article with Orgel was only the beginning of Francis Crick's ruminations on the origin of life. Eight years later, in his book *Life Itself*, Crick stated: "An honest man, armed with all the knowledge available to us now, could only state that in some sense, the origin of life appears at the moment to be almost a miracle, so many are the conditions which would have had to have been satisfied to get it going."

Francis Crick spoke out once again on the Origin of Life twelve years later in his preface to the 1993 book *The RNA World*. Crick writes: "The real fossil record suggests that our present form of protein-based life was already in existence 3.6 billion years ago and evolved rather slowly for a billion or so years after that. This leaves an astonishingly short time to get life started. The rather far-fetched hypothesis of Directed Panspermia would predict that life was sent here in the form of "bacteria" suitable for growth in anaerobic conditions, and several somewhat different forms would probably have been sent at the same time, in the hope that at least one would survive. All are likely to have evolved originally from a common ancestor (on another planet) that existed some billions of years before the formation of our solar system. Therefore, the final question about the RNA world and the pre-RNA world (if it existed) is: Where did it occur? Are we totally confident that our form of life started here, or did it perhaps originate elsewhere in the universe? It might have been easier to start elsewhere because, for example, the atmosphere there was more reducing than the Earth's early atmosphere appears to have been."

Francis Crick's coworker on the Directed Panspermia hypothesis, Leslie Orgel, made an equally striking statement in his own article in *The RNA World*. Orgel writes: "We conclude that the direct synthesis of the nucleosides or nucleotides from the prebiotic precursors in reasonable yield and unaccompanied by larger amounts of related molecules could not be achieved by presently known chemical reactions. The *de novo* appearance of oligonucleotides on the primitive earth would have been a near miracle."

When the second edition of *The RNA World* was published in 1999, Francis Crick felt no obligation to revise the preface. Indeed, the 1990s were not kind to the Oparin-Haldane hypothesis. One of the brightest contributors to this area is Professor Steven Benner, who began his faculty career as an assistant professor at Harvard. Benner then moved to the finest chemistry department in continental Europe, the Swiss Federal Institute of Technology in Zürich, as Professor. After a decade in Zürich, Benner moved back to the USA for personal reasons. In the March 26, 1999 issue of *Science* magazine, Benner writes: "The classical approaches to the origins of life . . . . . have characterized the second half of the 20th century . . . . . These classical approaches did not solve the problem surrounding life's origin. Prebiotic chemistry could produce a wealth of biomolecules from nonliving precursors. But the wealth soon became overwhelming, with the "prebiotic soups" having the chemical complexity of asphalt (useful, perhaps, for paving roads but not particularly promising as a wellspring for life). Classical prebiotic chemistry not only failed to constrain the contents of the prebiotic soup, but also raised a new paradox: How would life (or any organized chemical process) emerge from such a mess? Searches of quadrillions of randomly generated RNA sequences have failed to yield a spontaneous RNA replicator."

Some critics have been less humorous but more harsh than Benner in their assessments of 50 disappointing years of Oparin-Haldane research. For example, M.I.T. biologist Hymann

Hartman wrote in the March 29, 1999 issue of *The Scientist* the following: "The Urey-Miller experiment is wrong, completely wrong as a historical document." Even the recent report (*Science*, May 2, 2003) most friendly to Miller and Urey states: "Contemporary geoscientists tend to doubt that the primitive atmosphere had the highly reducing atmosphere used by Miller."

The February 2001 issue of *Physics Today*, published by the American Physical Society, contains several retrospective articles on the life of Wolfgang Pauli (1900-1958, Nobel Prize in Physics 1945). Several knowledgeable scientists (for example Max Born) considered Pauli to be the greatest physicist of the 20th century. His genius was a towering and ruthlessly penetrating intellect. In one of the retrospective articles in *Physics Today*, Engelbert Schucking describes a meeting he had with Pauli in 1958. The following interesting paragraph appears midway in the story: "Pauli asked me whether I thought the evolution of life could be explained by random mutations. I said yes, citing the resistance of bacteria to penicillin and mosquitoes to DDT. If this can happen in just a few years, why shouldn't a trilobite, in 500 million years, evolve into a Pauli? He had heard these arguments before and wasn't convinced by them. Pauli wanted to see calculated probabilities for large-scale evolution."

When all the scientific evidence currently at our disposal is examined, and all the problems given honest consideration, I conclude that Dean Kenyon is correct. Namely, we should seriously consider the possibility that life owes its inception to a source outside of nature. Some of the main lines of evidence and reasoning supporting this view are as follows (Kenyon, 1985):

(1) The statistical challenges associated with a spontaneous origin of genetic information, even in a period as long as 10 billion years, that elapsed between the Big Bang and the earliest fossils discovered thus far.

(2) The fact that the dominant trend in the Miller-Urey experiments and their successors is toward the production of non-biological, intractable macromolecular material, described as asphalt by Steven Benner. Biopolymers are not found in these experiments. Interfering cross-reactions predominate in the most realistic simulation experiments.

(3) Simulation experiments routinely produce racemic mixtures (equal numbers of dextro and levo isomers) of organic compounds. To date, all experimental attempts to find a plausible naturalistic basis for the preferential primeval accumulation of L amino acids have been inconclusive.

(4) Geochemical evidence seems to be consistent with the conclusion that some oxygen was present in the Earth's early atmosphere. This O2 might have quenched any presumed chemical evolution at its earliest stages.

Another indication of the apparent failure of the Oparin-Haldane hypothesis is the range of alternative explanations that have been proposed for the origin of life. Let me mention just the three most prominent such ideas. Dr. A. Graham Cairns-Smith is a faculty member in chemistry at the University of Glasgow in Scotland. In his 1982 Cambridge University Press book *Genetic Takeover and the Mineral Origins of Life*, Cairns-Smith argues that life began in clays. More recent is the idea that it all began in hot (near the boiling point of water) ocean vents. The 1998 book by Juergen Wiegel and Michael Adams, *Thermophiles: the Keys to Molecular Evolution and the Origin of Life?* captures the flow of recent developments in this direction. Third is the notion of German patent lawyer Guenter Wachtershauser that simple compounds necessary for life formed on lumps of pyrite. Wachtershauser's ideas were the subject of a feature article in the March 15, 2002 issue of *Science*. It seems unlikely that one of these three newer hypotheses will ever achieve the near hysteria that once surrounded the Miller-Urey experiments.

More General Concerns

The Modern Synthesis, which is an exaggeration of what I have been calling the standard evolutionary model, dates from the 1940s, with Julian Huxley being one of the prime movers. This standard model postulates that all species originate by slow processes contingent upon gradual genetic changes. Natural selection, or the survival of variants best adapted to their environments, is asserted to determine the direction of such changes. While embracing the Modern Synthesis, Richard Dawkins goes farther and claims that all such changes are the result of a vast number of very small changes. That is, a nearly infinite number of nearly infinitesimal changes. And Dawkins is not loath to make up stories of why such processes could benefit the life forms in question at every step along the way. Dawkins' critics, including some as staunchly atheistic as he, like to describe these Dawkinsisms as "Just So Stories," more representative of Rudyard Kipling tales than contemporary science. As Norman Platnick stated in his 1977 *Systematic Zoology* article: "Evolutionary biologists are . . . . . spinners of tales, bedtime storytellers, instead of empirical investigators." In the same vein but referring specifically to human evolution, Yale anthropologist David Pilbeam in the *American Scientist* stated in May 1979: "The theories are more statements about us and ideology than about the past. Paleoanthropology reveals more about how humans view themselves than it does about how humans came about."

Dawkins' nemesis in the evolution wars was for many years Steven Jay Gould. Gould, professor at Harvard since 1967, died of cancer in 2002. An unwavering atheist to the end, Gould enjoyed saying that he learned his Marxism at his father's knee. Although fiercely defending the standard evolutionary model, Gould's view of species changes was very different from that of Dawkins, or even Julian Huxley. Gould accepted the fact that the fossil record speaks of relatively sudden rather than purely continuous changes. In one of his more feisty moments Gould declared that the modern synthesis was "effectively dead." He insisted that the "jerkiness" of the fossil record "is not the result of gaps, it is the consequence of the jerky mode of evolutionary change."

Gould also liked to say: "We are not likely to detect the event of speciation itself. It happens too fast, in too small a group, isolated too far from the ancestral range." Ironically and quite unintentionally, Gould has presented scientific boundary conditions that correlate very well with the Biblical account of the creation of the first man and the first woman. The *Genesis* account of human speciation does indeed take place very "fast." The creation of the first man and of the first woman were both accomplished instantaneously. The group was indeed "small," as there were just the two human beings at the start. Finally, the first man and woman were very "isolated from the ancestral range," as there were no ancestors.

As early as 1968, in his book *Language and Mind*, Noam Chomsky, no friend of religion, was able to state: "It is perfectly safe to attribute this development (human language) to natural selection so long as we realize that there is no substance to this assertion, that it amounts to nothing more than a belief that there is some naturalistic explanation for these phenomena." This overall picture does not appear to have changed very much in the succeeding 35 years. Dr. Michael Covington, a highly respected artificial intelligence scholar at the University of Georgia, recently (2003) stated: "The emergence of human language and consciousness happened quickly and required major changes in the architecture of the brain. There is no plausible mechanism for how it happened as quickly as it did." A related but more general conclusion in the April 2002 issue of *Scientific American* was drawn by Ian Tattersall: "In light of what we know about evolution, it seems most likely that our extraordinary cognitive capacity was somehow acquired as a unit, rather than in a gradual process of modular accretion, for it is plainly wrong to regard natural selection as a long-term fine-tuning of specific characteristics, however much we like the resulting stories."

What should one make of these evolutionary controversies among atheists? The individuals engaging in the controversies would tell us that these are simply family fights about details. Just be patient, they explain, and all the controversies will be resolved in favor of a universe in which God is irrelevant. My view is that several of the disputes appear to be about basics, not details. And I think there is some probability that the entire paradigm may come crashing down at some time in the future. How might this happen? In November 1992 *Time* magazine published an entire issue dedicated to futurism. *Time* asked a number of prominent authors to speculate on what the year 2092 would reveal. The article about science and religion was noteworthy and, in my opinion, very insightful: "It seems amazing now that there was a time when science was supposedly the enemy of faith, and religion was deemed hostile to technological investigation. The end of atheism and agnosticism became inevitable as soon as computer calculations made improbable the odds that random natural selection could be the sole explanation for the ever increasing intricacies found in biology." As a computational chemist, I do suspect that future computers, more powerful than we can currently imagine, may have bad news in store for atheism.

Evolution and Christian Theism

For many observers the first question to be raised in this context is the age of the universe. I would attempt to deal with that controversy with as little rancor as possible. In this spirit, perhaps a good place to begin is with the statement of St. Augustine from more than 1500 years ago: "It is a laborious and difficult task for the powers of our human understanding to see clearly the meaning of the sacred writer (Moses) in the matter of the six days (Genesis 1)." Augustine of Hippo, 415 A.D., *The Literal Meaning of Genesis*. In my opinion, Augustine was right—the task continues to be difficult.

The distinguished theologian Dr. Carl F. H. Henry has noted that four main views of the origin of man fix the perimeters of debate in the current controversy over human beginnings. With a few modifications, these are:

1. Naturalistic Evolution: Impersonal processes, e.g., natural selection, mutations, chance, or some combination of these, account for all forms and species of life; so that man, whether emerging gradually or appearing suddenly, is the product of unthinking, nonpurposive forces. The age of the universe is about 14 billion years and the age of the Earth 4.6 billion years. This is the only position available for most atheists.

2. Theistic Evolution: God as immanent agent sustains and directs the natural processes that shape the evolution of life from the simplest self-replicating biochemical system to man. This position is scientifically identical to the first, but presupposes the sovereign activity of God in planning and executing the evolutionary process.

3. Progressive Creation: God immanently supports and directs an extensive development of species. He acts transcendently at special stages of this process to create the main biological orders of being. Man is not dependent physically on any intermediate species. And in further distinction from the primates he is specially made in God's image. The age of the universe is about 14 billion years and the age of the Earth is 4.6 billion years.

4. Recent Creation: All life-forms are created *de novo* by supernatural agency. No late orders of creation are dependent on earlier kinds of being. The age of the Earth is not more than 10,000 years.

By this point in the book, the conscientious reader will have observed that my own position is the third given above, namely progressive creation or old earth creation. Specifically, my opinion is that it was Moses' intention in composing the book of Genesis 3400 years ago that the Hebrew word "yom," or "day" in English, be understood as an indefinite period of time. What I consider to be an excellent and temperate discussion of this controversial subject may be found in Volume 6 of Carl Henry's epic work *God, Revelation, and Authority.*

With this introduction, the question remains, how are the scientific details of the six days to be understood? I think that my friend James Montgomery Boice, now with the Lord, did a fine job of describing the six days in his excellent commentary on the first eleven chapters of Genesis:

Day 1. Genesis 1:1-5. Formation of the sun and other heavenly bodies.

Day 2. Genesis 1:6-8. Formation of the atmosphere.

Day 3. Genesis 1:9-13. Emergence of land masses.
Plants and trees.

Day 4. Genesis 1:14-19. God parts the cloud cover sufficiently for direct sunlight to fall on the earth and for accurate observations of the movements of sun, moon, and stars to take place.

Day 5. Genesis 1:20-23. Marine life, freshwater life, and flying creatures.

Day 6. Genesis 1:24-31. All the land animals, culminating in the creation of the first man and the first woman.

Now, and perhaps most important, how critical is this ever-continuing controversy to the future of orthodox Christian belief? My conviction is that the age of the Earth is not a matter of Christian orthodoxy. In contrast, let me note two statements that are essentials (non-negotiables) of the historic Christian faith.

A. Jesus' affirmation that He was and is Almighty God, the One through Whom the universe was created.

B. Jesus' insistence that eternal life (heaven) is accessible only to those who place their exclusive trust in His death on the cross as an all-sufficient payment for their many failings.

Although other points critical to Christian orthodoxy might be chosen, I emphasize the above two, because they were completely foreign to me before I became a Christian. You may be a wonderful person as the world counts people wonderful. But if you cannot affirm the factuality of the above two points, your position falls short of saving faith in Christ. Now, having taken a hard line on points A and B above, are there other points on which Christians can agree to disagree? Of course. I am happy to make the Christian big tent as large as is consistent with the words of Jesus recorded in the New Testament. Although others are certainly possible, let me here note five points of respectful diversity among Christians:

1. Modes of Christian worship.
2. Expected chronology and details of the return of Jesus Christ.
3. Precise interpretation of the six days of creation of *Genesis*.
4. Models of church government
5. The method of and appropriate age for baptism.

It will be seen that I place the understanding of the days of Genesis 1 right in the middle of a group of issues about which Christians should be free to disagree, without abusing each other. This is not an issue that appears to be heading for a resolution, so Rodney King's advice to "just get along," although sometimes dubious in other contexts, is pretty good here.

The Standard Evolutionary Model: Science or Dogma?

Phillip Johnson has forcefully made the argument that Richard Dawkins' perspective is not science at all, but philosophical materialism. I personally find very little with which to disagree with Dawkins concerning the observable scientific facts. Of course a skeptic of Dawkins such as I will be less prone to fall for the next fossil hoax, but this is a relatively minor point. The disagreement, and a monumental disagreement it is, concerns the interpretation of the facts. For Dawkins, Gould, and Carl Sagan, the commitment to atheism appears stronger than their commitment to follow the scientific evidence wherever it leads. Perhaps nowhere is this philosophical opposition to God seen more clearly than in the *New York Review of Books* essay by Harvard's Richard Lewontin that appeared on January 9, 1997:

"We take the side of science in spite of the patent absurdity of some of its constructs, in spite of its failure to fulfill many of its extravagant promises of health and life, in spite of the tolerance of the scientific community for unsubstantiated just-so stories, because we have a prior commitment, a commitment to materialism. It is not that the methods and institutions of science somehow compel us to accept a material explanation of the phenomenal world, but, on the contrary, that we are forced by our *a priori* adherence to material causes to create an apparatus of investigation and a set of concepts that produce material explanations, no matter how counterintuitive, no matter how mystifying to the uninitiated. Moreover, that materialism is absolute, for we cannot allow a Divine Foot in the door."

One cannot help admire Lewontin for his candor and his disdain for Dawkins' just-so stories. However, the bottom line is the same, an uncompromising atheism. And there are many others who share the views of Dawkins, Gould, Sagan, and

Lewontin. Harvard biologist Edward O. Wilson is a gentler, kinder Alabama-bred version of Dawkins. As early as 1978, however, Wilson stated: "The final decisive edge enjoyed by scientific naturalism will come from its capacity to explain traditional religion, its chief competition, as a wholly material phenomenon. Theology is not likely to survive as an independent intellectual discipline." The last sentence is reminiscent of the prediction by Voltaire (1694-1778) that Christianity would disappear in Europe within a few decades.

The radical views of Lewontin, Wilson, and the others have even troubled a few self-proclaimed agnostics and atheists. The March 7, 2003 issue of *Science* magazine includes the article "Is Evolution a Secular Religion?" by Florida State University Professor Michael Ruse. Writing an essay like the above is a tricky business, even for a tooth and claw evolutionist like Ruse, because there is a significant danger of being "thrown out of the club". Individuals like E.O. Wilson are extremely influential movers and shakers in the world of scientific politics. Ruse's closing remarks dance on the edge of his expulsion from the club: "We who cherish science should be careful to distinguish when we are doing science and when we are extrapolating from it, particularly when we are teaching our students. If it is science that is to be taught, then teach science and nothing more. Leave the other discussions for a more appropriate time."

Having shared my own views, I must give Phillip Johnson the opportunity to present his case. In his 1998 book *Objections Sustained*, Johnson wrote: "The a priori commitment (to the standard evolutionary model) explains why evolutionary scientists are not disturbed when they learn that the fossil record does not provide examples of gradual macroevolutionary transformation, despite decades of determined effort by paleontologists to confirm neo-Darwinian presuppositions. That is also why origin-of-life chemists like Stanley Miller continue in confidence even when geochemists tell them that the early earth did not have a reducing (oxygen-free) atmosphere, essential for producing the chemicals required by the prebiotic soup scenario. They reason that there had to be some source (comets?) capable of providing the needed molecules, because otherwise life would not have evolved. When evidence showed that the period available on the early earth for the evolution of life was extremely brief in comparison to the time previously posited for chemical evolution scenarios, Carl Sagan calmly concluded that the chemical evolution of life must be easier than we had supposed, because it happened so rapidly on the early Earth.

That is also why neo-Darwinists like Richard Dawkins are not troubled by the Cambrian Explosion, where all the invertebrate animal groups appear suddenly and without identifiable ancestors. Whatever the fossil record may suggest, those Cambrian animals had to evolve by accepted neo-Darwinian means, which is to say by material processes requiring no intelligent guidance or supernatural input. Materialist philosophy demands no less. That is also why Niles Eldredge, surveying the absence of evidence for macroevolutionary transformations in the rich marine invertebrate fossil record, can observe that 'evolution always seems to happen somewhere else,' and then describe himself on the very next page as a 'knee-jerk neo-Darwinist.' Finally, that is why Darwinists do not take critics of materialist evolution seriously, but speculate instead about 'hidden agendas' and resort immediately to ridicule. In their minds, to question materialism is to question reality."

In the contest between Phillip Johnson and Richard Dawkins, I find no difficulty in throwing my support to Johnson. Of course, there are still other positions. The discoverer of the laser, Nobelist Charles Townes, is no admirer of Johnson, but he is equally unsatisfied with Dawkins' view of reality. Townes has stated: "In my view the question of origin seems always left unanswered if we explore from a scientific view alone. Thus, I believe there is a need for some religious or metaphysical explanation. I believe in the concept of God and in His existence." Townes and those in the theistic evolution camp (David Cole, Francis Collins, Don Page, and others) want to hold positions somewhere intermediate between the advocates of intelligent design and the likes of Richard Dawkins. In fact, one of my two most faithful proofreaders for this book is such a theistic evolutionist, Dr. Paul Hartman, a radiation oncologist and former faculty member in the medical school at Yale University.

I should give the reader just a bit of the flavor of Lehigh University biochemistry professor Michael Behe's work. Behe's best-selling 1996 book *Darwin's Black Box* caused a furor among some theistic evolutionists, as well as the followers of Dawkins. I have selected two statements from Behe not found in his book.

The first is from an interview in October 1997. At that time Behe stated: "The interactive complexity of the bacterial flagellum, the intra-cellular-transport system, and many other cellular machines is strikingly similar to that of designed objects we encounter in our daily lives. Therefore, the inference that those biological systems were in fact intentionally designed comes straight from the physical data. In addition to biochemical findings, a hypothesis of intelligent design fits well with data from other areas of modern science, such as the discovery that the universe had a beginning; the many 'anthropic coincidences;' and the intractability of the origin-of-life problem. These empirical results all point in the same direction: The universe and life were somehow planned. Dismissing the plain implication is not good science; rather, it is a failure of nerve, which is very bad for science."

My second selection from Behe is perhaps even more to the point: "Darwinian assumptions are not needed for the day-to-day work of science. If you look at the biochemical literature for scientific papers that try to explain how biochemical systems developed step-by-step in Darwinian fashion, there aren't any. It's startling. Most biologists completely ignore evolution in their work, and the ones that think about it simply look for relationships and don't bother with Darwinism." My University of Georgia colleague in biochemistry, Professor Russell Carlson, has expressed the same sentiment to me privately.

What's a Chemical Physicist to Do?

Perhaps arrogantly, I think that physical scientists have something to contribute to the evolution discussion. I quoted physics Nobelist Wolfgang Pauli's skeptical view of origin of life dogma for this reason. My own research and that of others is beginning to extend the tentacles of quantum mechanics into molecular biology (our latest research concerns the radical anions of DNA base pairs). It has occurred to me that the standards of truth for the physical sciences are sometimes higher than those of many biologists. Physical scientists should occasionally challenge the claims some biologists make that go beyond what is genuine science. They can tell us what they know as biologists, and we want to absorb and honor that specialized knowledge. But when, as biologists, they tell us that they are believers of materialism as philosophy, we will reply with Michael Behe: Is this relevant? You don't know that as biologists, and intellectual integrity requires us to challenge you on your claims of expertise over philosophical issues.

In October 2001, I agreed to have my name appear first on a list of 100 research scientists who made the following modest statement: "We are skeptical of claims for the ability of random mutations and natural selection to account for the complexity of life. Careful examination of the evidence for Darwinian theory should be encouraged." Given that skepticism is the hallmark of good science, I was a bit surprised by the response this statement received. In its November 1 issue (page 22) the *London Review of Books* puzzled over our statement. The expected rebuke from the U.S. National Academy of Sciences followed quickly. Given the widely proclaimed open-endedness of science, the uncontested benefits of "skepticism" to science, and everyone's expressed desire for "careful examination" of everything in science, one could not help but feel that all the fuss over our statement was a bit much.

Is Evolution a Good Theory?

My most recent contribution to the public discussion of the evolution issue was instigated by an urgent invitation from the *Atlanta Journal and Constitution*, the largest newspaper in the South. This request came at the time of a controversy in the Cobb County (suburban Atlanta, Georgia) schools. My solicited discourse was published on September 28, 2002, the title I chose being "Is Evolution a Good Theory?" This invited essay (slightly modified) is a suitable note on which to conclude the present chapter: As a theorist who uses quantum mechanics to solve problems ranging from biochemistry to astrophysics, the subject of this essay is of great interest to me. It is a question that is discussed in depth in my University of Georgia freshman seminar entitled *Science and Christianity: Conflict or Coherence?* This semester eighteen gifted UGA students and I are spending six weeks examining Stephen Hawking's best-selling book, *A Brief History of Time*. Therein Hawking states: "A theory is a good theory if it satisfies two requirements. It must accurately describe a large class of observations on the basis of a model that contains only a few arbitrary elements. And it must make definite predictions about the results of future observations." I consider Hawking's statement to be an excellent definition of a good theory. How does evolution stack up to the two demands of a good theory? By the term evolution I mean the claim that random mutations and natural selection can fully account for the complexity of life, and particularly macroscopic living things.

I think that the standard evolutionary model does a good job of categorizing and systematizing the fossil record. It serves as an effective umbrella or big tent under which to collect a large number of observations. If evolution has a weakness in this regard, it is that the tent is too big. Thus 20th century paleontology witnessed a series of hoaxes, beginning in 1908 with Piltdown Man and continuing to recently fabricated fossil "discoveries" in China, that have been embraced as missing links by distinguished scientists. Nevertheless, I give evolution a B grade with respect to Hawking's first category. The second requirement for a good theory is far more problematical for the standard evolutionary model, sometimes called the modern synthesis. Over the past 150 years evolutionary theorists have made countless predictions about fossil specimens to be observed in the future. Unfortunately for these seers, many new fossils have been discovered, and the interesting ones almost always seem to be contrary to the "best" predictions. This is sometimes true even when the predictions are rather vague, as seen by the continuing controversies associated with the relationships between dinosaurs and birds.

Is the expectation that a good theory be predictive unrealistic? Let us consider two theories to which evolution is often favorably compared. The theory of gravity precisely predicted the appearances of Halley's comet in 1910 and 1986. On the latter occasion I was on sabbatical from Berkeley at the University of Canterbury in Christchurch, New Zealand. The newspaper (informed by classical mechanics and the law of gravity) told me exactly when I had to wake up in the middle of the night to enjoy the wonder of Halley's Comet. And in fact, the theory of gravity never fails for the macroscopic objects to which it is applicable. A second successful theory, the atomic theory, is grounded in Schrödinger's Equation and the Dirac Equation. Atomic theory is able to make many predictions of the spectra of the hydrogen molecule and the helium atom to more significant figures than may be currently measured in the laboratory. We are utterly confident that these predictions will be confirmed by future experiments. By any reasonable standard the theory of gravity and the atomic theory are good theories, well deserving of A grades. In comparison with these quantitative theories of the physical sciences, when it comes to Hawking's second requirement for a good theory, the standard evolutionary model fails, and should probably be given a D grade.

Might I be more detailed in stating my reservations concerning the standard evolutionary model? Sure. Let me preface these closing remarks by reiterating that the scientific evidence for God's creation of the universe 12-16 billion years ago is good. My first evolution concern is that, with the collapse of the Miller-Urey model, there is no plausible scientific mechanism for the origin of life, i.e., the appearance of the first self-replicating biochemical system. The staggeringly high information content of even the simplest living thing is not readily explained by evolutionists. Second, the time frame for speciation events seems all wrong to me. The major feature of the fossil record is stasis, long periods in which new species do not appear. When new developments occur, they come rapidly, not gradually. My third area of reservation is that I find no satisfactory mechanism for macro-evolutionary changes. Analogies between a tiny change in the beak size of a Galapagos finch species and the transition from dinosaur to bird appear to me inappropriate at present.

Quantum Mechanics and Postmodernism

6

This essay had its origin with a series of four lectures that I gave at the Ohio State University in April 1996. The four lectures comprised a Veritas Forum, sponsored by a number of student and faculty organizations at Ohio State. One of the faculty sponsors, Professor Jeffrey Chalmers of the Department of Chemical Engineering, insisted that one of the lectures be on this topic. I objected that no more than a handful of persons would be interested in such a discussion. But Jeff (a former student of mine at Berkeley) eventually prevailed, and the lecture was given in the physics department to an audience of perhaps 200.

Postmodernism is one of the more influential forces in universities in North America and Western Europe in the early days of the twenty-first century. Driven by the quest for novelty, essentially all major universities have made appointments to their faculties of persons holding to this particular worldview. Postmodernism holds that there is no genuine knowledge. There are merely stories (or narratives) devised to satisfy the human need to make sense of the world. All purported knowledge is local or situated, the product of interactions of a social class, rigidly circumscribed by its interests and prejudices (Paul Gross and Norman Levitt, *The Academic Left and its Quarrels with Science*).

Without the time to discuss its historic and cultural origins (e.g., Jacques Derrida), suffice it to say that postmodernism holds to an epistemology of radical skepticism. Postmodernism believes that humans are hopelessly subjective and unable to say anything meaningful about reality. Interestingly, this inability to communicate does not prohibit postmodernists from writing many papers and books. Postmodernists maintain that our senses cannot be trusted to accurately represent reality; and reason is a Western cultural construct that gives no insight into the actual nature of things. Given these presuppositions, such scholars hold that insistence upon any version of reality is an effort to subjugate and marginalize others. All assertions of so-called truth are thinly veiled efforts to dominate others.

Jerram Barrs (Autumn 1996 newsletter, Francis Schaeffer Institute, St. Louis) has done a fine job in summarizing four key ingredients of postmodernism:

1. Postmodernism says that nothing can be known by reason. Reason is inadequate. There is no objective truth. This concept, of course, dovetails with a popular opinion, held long before the introduction of the term "postmodernism," namely "You have your truth and I have my truth, and that is all that matters."

2. One logical consequence of postmodernism is the rejection of authority. Postmodernism believes that there is no book, no idea, and no social structure that could command or deserve respect. If there is no authority which engenders respect, then all styles are equally valid. No art is better than any other art; there is no high culture. Andy Warhol's depictions of tomato soup cans (my friend Professor Carl Moser in Paris has a superb collection) are just as great as Rembrandt's *Night Watch*. This follows from the conviction that there is no measure against which we can evaluate such things.

3. For the postmodernist there can be no transcendent or binding commandments. No one has the right to tell another person what to do. The individual becomes the moral authority. Again, this resonates with the popular idea that long preceded postmodernism, namely "Who are you to give me instructions for my life?"

4. A fourth consequence of postmodernism may be practical idolatry. Though persons no longer have truth to provide meaning, they sometimes hunger for what might be called "idols of the mind." Certain individuals may thus be inclined to believe almost anything, no matter how irrational it might appear. In fact, some may not even ask the question "Is it reasonable?" If people have no objective values to direct their lives, they often demand idols for their wills. People usually live for something, whether it is achieving respect, making money, or being successful; and it may completely control their lives.

The essence of postmodernism has been captured by philosopher/sociologist Richard Rorty, who retired from the University of Virginia in 1998 to accept a five-year term appointment at my doctoral alma mater, Stanford University. In the July 31, 1995 issue of *The New Republic*, Professor Rorty states that philosophers "try to explain how social democrats can be better than Nazis, modern medicine better than voodoo, and Galileo better than the Spanish Inquisition, even though there are no neutral, transcultural, ahistorical criteria that dictate these rankings."

Another visible postmodernist is Stanley Fish, formerly professor at Duke University, now a dean at the University of Illinois, Chicago. In his October 15, 2001 essay in the *New York Times*, Fish responds to the concerns of some that the destruction of the World Trade Center one month earlier may have dealt a blow to postmodernism. Nonsense, says Fish. He denounces the use of the word "terrorist" to describe those who carried out the 9/11 action. Fish also dismisses notions such as "We have seen the face of evil" as "inaccurate and unhelpful . . . . false universals." According to Fish, good and evil are meaningless concepts, devised to brutalize those with whom we disagree.

Prior to five years ago, most scientists would have dismissed the above discussion with a comment like "So what does all this have to do with science?" At this stage in the lecture I turn to what is perhaps the most obvious laboratory manifestation of quantum mechanics, the spectra of molecules. I first show a fifty-year-old, but obviously patterned, spectrum of the lowest vibrational transition of the hydrogen bromide molecule. I point out that each of the thirty peaks in this old spectrum splits into a number of marvelously ordered peaks when observed under contemporary high resolution spectroscopy. Then I show an even more beautiful spectrum of a carbon cluster at the highest resolution currently possible. Both spectra immediately impress the human mind as examples of design. And, as is the case with many observations in science, both spectra seem to be pointing to some sort of intelligible truth, not just a social context.

In fact, postmodernist writers for some time have been using examples from science to justify their postmodern beliefs. For the most part these activities flew under the radar of practicing scientists. However, in 1996 an event occurred that finally brought postmodernism out of the closet, as far as scientists were concerned. This was the publication by New York University physics professor Alan Sokal of a paper entitled "Transgressing the Boundaries: Toward a Transformative Hermeneutics of Quantum Gravity." Sokal's paper was carefully reviewed and published by the (previously) highly respected American cultural studies journal *Social Text*. Unfortunately for the journal, Sokal's paper found its way to the attention of scientists, who immediately recognized the paper as a humorous parody. To add insult to injury, in 1998 Sokal published with Jean Bricmont the book (St. Martin's Press) *Fashionable Nonsense: Postmodern Intellectuals' Abuse of Science*. As the title indicates, the Sokal-Bricmont book is an open assault on postmodernism.

A concise review of the Sokal paper in *Social Text* was given by David Miller in June 1999 in *Science* magazine, one of the two most influential science journals in the world. Miller states "In 1996 Alan Sokal enraged cultural theorists by planting in a leading periodical a spoof article that ridiculed the way in which some prominent French intellectuals of recent years have ornamented their writing with uncomprehending, and certainly incomprehensible, passages of bewitching scientific jargon, borrowed mainly from theoretical physics (quantum theory, chaos) and from pure mathematics (topology, mathematical logic)."

A related review by Cornell University physics professor David Mermin appeared in the April 1999 issue of *Physics Today*. Mermin starts out in a similar vein to David Miller: "These passages (written by postmodern humanities scholars) do indeed sound like irredeemable rubbish to one who has learned to use in the original contexts the technical terms they employ. Not only is it impossible to extract from the excerpts any meaningful use of those terms, but it is clear that, if they are being used in anything like their conventional senses, then the authors of these excerpts have utterly failed to grasp their original meaning." However, Mermin then turns on his heel and criticizes Alan Sokal for being too harsh on the postmodernists and for failing to interact with them in a constructive manner.

With this background, let us take a look at the origin of our understandings of quantum mechanics, with an eye to appreciating what the postmodernists are attempting to say. I acquired a modest notoriety in my freshman chemistry classes at Berkeley and more recently at the University of Georgia by attempting to convince the students that quantum mechanics may turn out to be the greatest intellectual achievement of the twentieth century. This is despite the fact that quantum mechanics from one perspective had an entirely pragmatic birth. Quantum mechanics came to be understood due to the existence of three important problems that could not be solved by the methods of what we now call classical physics (a discipline largely due to the genius of Isaac Newton and James Clerk Maxwell).

The first of the problems insoluble to classical physics was the problem of black body radiation. This historic descriptor refers to ideal radiation from a perfect absorber and emitter of radiation. In 1900 Max Planck provided the first satisfactory explanation of this phenomena, devising a formula $E=h\nu$, which relates the energy (E) and the frequency of radiation (ν) through what is now known as Planck's constant (h). Planck thus established that electromagnetic radiation comes in discrete packets or quanta. The second critical problem for physics as the twentieth century began was the photoelectric effect. This was explained in 1905 by Albert Einstein using Planck's formula $E=h\nu$ and the principle of conservation of energy.

The third mysterious problem for classical physics illustrates most clearly the trial-and-error beginnings of quantum mechanics. The formula for the positions of the spectral lines of the hydrogen atom had been discovered in 1885 by the Swiss mathematics teacher Johann Jakob Balmer. But the origin of the Balmer formula was perplexing. The first acceptable explanation was provided by the Danish physicist Niels Bohr. Bohr (and every other theoretical physicist in the world) knew what had to be derived—it was just a matter of how to get there. In 1913 Bohr got there first, by brilliantly juggling a critical sequence of postulates to yield, following some straightforward mathematical physics, the known Rydberg formula. Although one of Bohr's postulates (that electrons move in fixed circular orbits) turned out to be wrong, his insight was nevertheless marvelous.

In hindsight, the justification for quantum mechanics is that quantum mechanics works. That is, it provides predictions consistent with laboratory observations. Given the trial-and-error beginnings of quantum mechanics [above examples plus Louis de Broglie's particle waves – 1924, Erwin Schrödinger's equation governing the motions of electrons and protons – 1926, Paul Dirac's incorporation of relativity into quantum mechanics – 1927, and Werner Heisenberg's uncertainty principle – 1927 (note, however, as discussed below, we have reservations about placing the uncertainty principle in such an exalted position)], would one have expected this zigzag path to give rise to profound philosophical insights, as some postmodernists have suggested? Certainly not.

Let me note here several excellent books on quantum mechanics that I have read, enjoyed, and recommend to others. The first is Max Jammer's classic *The Conceptual Development of Quantum Mechanics*, first published by McGraw-Hill in 1966. The other books are all by Jagdish Mehra and Helmut Rechenberg and form their series *The Historical Development of Quantum Theory*. I have been through Volumes 1 (Parts 1 and 2), 2, 3, 4, and 5 (Parts 1 and 2), published by Springer-Verlag between 1982 and 1987. I have just acquired Parts 1 (2000) and 2 (2001) of Volume 6, stated to be the final volume of the series. Since Volume 6 is 1612 pages long, its enjoyment awaits an extended vacation at the beach.

There is little of postmodernism in the books just described. So whence comes the much discussed relationship with quantum mechanics? We can point squarely to the Heisenberg Uncertainty Principle. Stated in perhaps its simplest form, the Heisenberg Uncertainty Principle says that the position and velocity of a particle cannot be simultaneously measured to an unlimited precision. Taken to the extreme, one can construct a problem for undergraduates in which the position of an electron is so tightly constrained that nothing at all is known about its velocity (literally, the uncertainty in the electron's velocity exceeds the speed of light, and thus the entire range of possible velocities).

For the benefit of those who are neither physicists nor chemists, let me quickly point out that the effects of the uncertainty principle are so small for macroscopic objects (such as a human body) as to be invisible. Another example from my days of teaching physical chemistry at Berkeley will suffice. Suppose we take a Honda Civic automobile (weight about one ton) and specify its velocity to within one-billionth of a mile per hour (i.e., 0.000000001 mph), obviously much greater precision than currently measurable. Given this uncertainty in the velocity, what is the uncertainty in the position of the vehicle? The Heisenberg principle tells us that the position of the Honda Civic is uncertain by about one-billionth of one-billionth of one-billionth of a meter (i.e., 0.000000000000000000000000001 meter). This was my way of proving to the students that the Heisenberg uncertainty principle would never provide an excuse for their getting lost on the freeway on the way to class after a long weekend at home.

The point of contention is not the formula describing the uncertainty principle but rather the proper interpretation of the Heisenberg Uncertainty Principle. Of course, scientists and philosophers have been discussing the meaning of the uncertainty principle for more than seven decades, often in serious academic circles. However, these 70 years have also seen an abundance of silly statements like "The uncertainty principle allows a way for God to exist." But the notion that quantum mechanics supports postmodernism is relatively recent, at least in its popular appeal. In their excellent 1994 book *The Soul of Science*, Nancy Pearcey and Charles Thaxton describe several current interpretations of the Heisenberg Uncertainty Principle. With minor modifications by the present author, these are:

1. Albert Einstein, Max Planck, and Louis de Broglie considered the uncertainty in quantum mechanics to be merely a statement of human ignorance. Their followers on this particular point continue to insist that events in the quantum world, like those in the world of classical physics, are fully causal and deterministic. Einstein spent a good part of the last thirty years of his life (without success) in search of such a precise theory. Einstein expressed his resistance to the probabilistic interpretation of quantum mechanics with his famous statement "God does not play dice with the universe."

2. Niels Bohr was of the opinion that uncertainty is not a result of temporary ignorance, solvable by further research. Uncertainty is a fundamental and unavoidable limitation on human knowledge. Bohr thought that we must remain agnostic about the ontology of the atomic

world and talk only about the results obtained under certain experimental conditions. Note, however, that when I gave this lecture at the Swiss Federal Institute of Science and Technology (ETH Zürich) in July 2000, Professor Hans Primas did not like Pearcey and Thaxton's description of Bohr's view. Primas has been studying the historical views of Bohr and Heisenberg for the past 30 years and insisted that Bohr had a different view of the uncertainty principle every year of his life after 1930 (Bohr died in 1962). So perhaps we should take the present description as the time-averaged Bohr interpretation of the uncertainty principle.

3. Werner Heisenberg ascribed uncertainty to nature. According to Heisenberg, nature is not deterministic, as classical physics assumed; it is indeterminate. When a scientist intrudes his/her measuring device into an atomic system, he/she forces a particular outcome to be actualized from what was before a fuzzy realm of potentialities.

4. I will refer to this fourth view as the subjective interpretation. Its proponents claim that when we choose which property will be measured via an experiment, this is essentially equivalent to saying that we "create" a particular property. This is the view of many of the postmodernists who have attempted to relate their ideas to quantum mechanics. The subjective view also resonates with Hinduism and with the popular Eastern/New Age books *The Tao of Physics* and *The Dancing Wu-Li Masters.*

Although I was vaguely aware of some aspects of the fourth view above, the spread of these ideas first hit me squarely in 1985. I was returning to Berkeley via the Newark airport following a day of consulting for a solar energy company (Energy Conversion Devices). The ride from Morristown, New Jersey to the Newark airport was of considerable duration, and the taxi driver was very interested that I was a theoretical chemist. When he found out that my specialty was quantum mechanics, his exhilaration was sufficient for me to question his driving ability. With great emotion, the taxi driver related to me his recent experience of reading of *The Dancing Wu-Li Masters*. It is indisputable that such books have had a significant impact on nonscientists in the general public. As you will see, I am afraid that I was not able to encourage my taxi driver that day in the direction he had chosen for what was essentially a spiritual journey.

We now turn to a discussion of the subjective interpretation of the Heisenberg Uncertainty Principle. Let us begin with some questionable statements from this direction. Science writer John Gribbin has stated "What quantum mechanics says is that nothing is real." Fritjof Capra, author of *The Tao of Physics* claims "The electron does not have properties independent of my mind." Michael Talbot, author of the 1993 book *Mysticism and the New Physics*, has written "It is the consciousness of the observer that intervenes and triggers which of the possible outcomes is observed." And distinguished physicist John Wheeler has given some dubious support to this group with his statement "No elementary phenomenon is a real phenomenon until it is an observed phenomenon."

Perhaps the first comment to be made concerning the above is that Fritjof Capra's best-selling book *The Tao of Physics* has been harshly criticized by physicists with no theistic inclinations whatsoever. And these criticisms ring true with my own studies in theoretical chemistry. For example, in my group's research, we have developed (subsequent to the pioneering work of Josef Paldus and Isaiah Shavitt) and applied the unitary group approach to the problem of electron correlation in molecules. Capra concludes that the frequent use of the word "unitary" in theoretical physics in some way amounts to support for the idea ubiquitous to Eastern religions that "all is one." As Capra's critics have documented, and I can confirm, these are nothing more or less that accidental coincidences in language.

John Polkinghorne, Professor of Mathematical Physics at Cambridge University and later President of Queens' College at Cambridge, has addressed some of these questions in his fine little book *The Quantum World*. In response to statements like those of Capra, Polkinghorne states "I submit that it might be wise to look for an interpretation of quantum mechanics which comes as near as possible to being in accord with the attitude so widespread among its users." Having been a developer and user of molecular quantum mechanics for more than 30 years, I like this statement very much. Polkinghorne adds soberly that "Your average quantum mechanic is about as philosophically minded as your average garage mechanic." The latter quote reminds me of comments heard (behind closed doors) at the Berkeley faculty club in informal discussions among some physicists: "If Bohr had been able to do anything else in physics after reaching the age of 50, he wouldn't have wasted his time on all that philosophy garbage. It's another case of the Nobel Disease." The "Nobel Disease" is a crude allusion to the inability of a few prize winners to press on with original scientific research after making the trip to Stockholm to receive science's highest accolade.

As hinted above, many physicists and chemists, myself included, are uncomfortable with placing the uncertainty principle in such a prominent position within quantum mechanics. First, this philosophical fixation on the uncertainty principle detracts from Werner Heisenberg's earlier (1925) more innovative and foundational work (with Pascual Jordan and Max Born) on matrix mechanics. Second, the uncertainty principle is not really one of the fundamental tenets of quantum mechanics. Berkeley professor William H. Miller, a brilliant expositor of the relationships between classical and quantum mechanics, has expressed this most forcefully: "The uncertainty principle is an elementary consequence of the Schrödinger equation, derivable from it as one does in a standard graduate quantum mechanics course, and resulting from the Fourier transform relation between position and velocity (or between time and energy). The revolutionary thing is that the particles are to be described by a wave equation. Once this is accepted, i.e., the de Broglie relation and the Schrödinger equation that quantifies it, all else is arithmetic, including the uncertainty principle. The uncertainty principle existed for classical waves long before quantum mechanics; again, the intellectual breakthrough is that particles need to be represented by a wave equation."

Whatever philosophers of science may propound, most working scientists remain realists—not only in regard to the ontological status of the quantum world, but also in regard to scientific knowledge. The realist believes that theories aim to describe the world and therefore may be true or false, not just useful; and that science consists largely of discovery, not just construction. Even in particle physics, scientists speak of the discovery—not the invention—of a new particle.

Hugh Ross (*The Creator and The Cosmos*, 2000) has put his finger on the critical question surrounding the purported relationship between quantum mechanics and postmodernism. Namely, does quantum mechanics show that the observer creates reality? Ross notes that Niels Bohr seemed to think that in the invisible atomic world of quantum phenomena, reality in the absence of an observer does not exist. Bohr implied that there is a sense in which the act of observing creates the reality. This has led certain individuals so far as to conclude that quantum events do not take place without an observer. Some postmodernists have extrapolated Bohr's conclusions about the invisible atomic world to the entire universe. If an observer can give reality to a microscopic event, why not to the whole of the cosmos itself?

My view is that this stream of logic is flawed from beginning to end. Molecules emit and absorb photons whether anyone observes them or not. Atmospheric chemistry took place long before the techniques of modern chemical kinetics were developed. Molecules existed in interstellar space billions of years before the appearance of humankind. Etc., etc., etc.

In *The Creator and the Cosmos* Hugh Ross has done an excellent job of summarizing the evidence against an observer created reality. With modest additions, deletions, and nuancing by the present author:

1. There is no movement from imprecision to precision in quantum phenomena. All that happens is that the observer can choose where to put the imprecision. If the observer chooses to measure the position of the quantum particle sufficiently precisely, he or she loses the potential for some degree of precision in measuring the particle's velocity. Conversely, if the experimenter decides to measure the velocity of the quantum particle sufficiently accurately, the potential for unlimited precision on the position of the particle will be irretrievably lost.

2. Experiments are obviously designed and directed by human beings. But this does not mean that the observer gives reality to the quantum event. One can always

imagine a set of natural circumstances (involving no human being) that could give rise to the same quantum event. The observer can choose some aspect of reality he/she wants to discern in a particular experiment. Though in quantum entities, indefinite properties (see discussion below following point 5.) become definite to the observer through measurements, the observer cannot determine how and when the indefinite property becomes definite.

3. Rather than affirming the postmodernist view that human beings are more powerful than we might have imagined, quantum mechanics tells us that we are weaker. In classical physics (Newton and Maxwell, pre-1900) no apparent limit exists on our ability to make accurate measurements. In quantum mechanics, a fundamental and easily determinable limit exists. In classical physics, we can see all aspects of causality. But in quantum mechanics some aspect of causality always remains hidden from human investigation.

4. The time duration between a quantum event and its observed result is always very brief, briefer by many orders of magnitude than the time period separating the beginning of the universe from the recent appearance of human beings. Speculations to the contrary, for both the universe and people, time is not reversible. Thus, no amount of human activity can ever affect events that occurred billions of years ago. The idea that one can create his or her own universe receives no support from quantum mechanics.

5. An experiment designed with insufficient foresight or performed with insufficient care may be unintentionally disrupted. And there are observations that cannot be understood without taking the uncertainty principle into consideration. Nevertheless, experiments consistently reveal that nature is described correctly by the condition that the human consciousness is irrelevant. A properly described experiment carried out in Berkeley, California can be reproduced by a different group of scientists in Cambridge, England one year later. Furthermore, there is

nothing particularly special about human observers. Inanimate objects, such as microwave, infrared, and ultraviolet spectrometers, are far more capable than humans of detecting quantum mechanical events.

Somewhat more should be said to complete this discussion. I acknowledge helpful comments in this regard by Professor Tucker Carrington of the University of Montreal. According to quantum mechanics, an observation will, to some degree (an imperceptible degree for macroscopic objects visible to the human eye) disrupt the system. But this does not imply that an observer can obtain whatever result he or she wishes. According to quantum mechanics we cannot predict the results of a particular experiment with absolute certainty. But this does not imply that all results are equally probable. Quantum mechanics tells us precisely how to compute the probability of obtaining a specific result. It is not true that according to quantum mechanics one can obtain any result whatsoever, and quantum mechanics is

For the reasons outlined here, very few scientists are sympathetic to the subjective (or postmodern) interpretation of the Heisenberg Uncertainty Principle. Scientists believe that there is knowledge, not merely a collection of stories; there is a reality not contrived by human beings; and there is truth. These are not merely human constructions.

therefore not consistent with the idea that the experimenter may manipulate the experiment to obtain any desired result. Using the equations of quantum mechanics one may precisely compute the possible values of an observable. Only those values predicted by quantum mechanics are observed. It is not possible using quantum mechanics to argue that observables can take on values dictated by the experimenter. Thus quantum mechanics does not suggest that reality is determined by the experimenter.

We must conclude that the purported symbiotic relationship between quantum mechanics and postmodernism is a nonrelationship. For the reasons outlined here, very few scientists are sympathetic to the subjective (or postmodern) interpretation of the Heisenberg Uncertainty Principle. Scientists believe that there is knowledge, not merely a collection of stories; there is a reality not contrived by human beings; and there is truth. These are not merely human constructions. These realist convictions were an important motivation for the pioneers of modern science, beginning perhaps around 1500 with Copernicus. And it is not an accident that virtually all of these pioneers were persons of Christian belief. By their own testimony these individuals were driven in their scientific investigations by the conviction that, through Jesus Christ, God the Father had created a perfectly ordered universe. The resulting intelligibility of the universe is absolutely critical to the scientific endeavor.

C. S. Lewis: Science and Scientism

7

Introduction

The origin of this lecture, first given at the University of Tennessee, was with my friend Dr. Terry Morrison. Terry has a Ph.D. in chemistry and was a faculty member at Butler University in Indianapolis, Indiana, reaching the rank of full professor in 1972. However, in 1974 Dr. Morrison left Butler University to (eventually) become Director of Faculty Ministries for InterVarsity Christian Fellowship. One of Terry's many activities in recent years has been to organize an annual C. S. Lewis Lecture at the University of Tennessee. Terry asked me to give the Fifteenth Annual C. S. Lewis Lecture, and the event took place on April 7, 1997.

Furthermore, Dr. Morrison had the temerity to assign a particular title for my C. S. Lewis Lecture, namely the title given here. I protested that this was a subject matter with which I was not terribly familiar. Terry responded glibly "Not to worry. I can give you a couple of unpublished dissertations that will get you started. I'm sure you can take it from there." One of these dissertations, the 1971 Texas A&M Master's Thesis of Faye Ann Crowell, turned out to be extremely helpful to me, and I will shamelessly use material from her work. To my knowledge, Faye Ann Crowell's thesis has not been published, and I hope that my lecture has given, and this essay will give, due attention to what I consider an excellent scholarly work. The title of Faye Ann Crowell's thesis is "The Theme of the Harmful Effects of Science in the Works of C. S. Lewis."

A short book with title somewhat similar to the present is Michael D. Aeschliman's *The Restitution of Man: C. S. Lewis and the Case against Scientism*. Although the titles are related, the concerns of my essay are different from those of Aeschliman. As an active scientist with a vigorous research group of 30 people, it is probably inevitable that I would not take as ambiguous an attitude toward science as Aeschliman. I have a strong love—

121

indeed, passion—for science, and have devoted my entire professional career to its pursuit. Perhaps it should be added that the present essay has changed a bit since its original presentation as a lecture in April 1997. This is largely because in August of the same year I began to teach a freshman seminar at the University of Georgia in which Lewis's two books *Out of the Silent Planet* and *That Hideous Strength* are required reading. Although I had read the entire Lewis space trilogy (of which these are the first and last books, respectively), I am now much more familiar with the two books, having made up examinations on them for each of the past five years.

This is not the place for an introduction to the writings of C. S. Lewis. For those desiring such an introduction, I will note that I have thoroughly enjoyed Walter Hooper's 940 page *C. S. Lewis Companion & Guide*, published in 1996 by HarperCollins. Lewis spent most of his life as a student and faculty member at Oxford University. For the last eight years of his career, he was Professor of Medieval and Renaissance English at Cambridge University. Lewis is considered the most widely read and influential serious Christian writer of the 20th century. Although I would disagree with him on many smaller points, I find Lewis's writing to be largely (OK, I really zone out on the last 30 pages of *Till We Have Faces*) very insightful and am happy to be a member of his fan club. I also consider C. S. Lewis to be the best example we have for constructive engagement by a Christian scholar with the secular world of the university.

What are the questions we hope to address in this essay? First and foremost, what did C. S. Lewis think about science and scientism? Second, is scientism alive and well in the twenty-first century? When this material is presented as a stand-alone lecture, a third question is addressed, namely, do nearly all scientists believe in scientism? In the present book, however, that third question is treated in the introductory chapter, entitled "Scientists and their Gods."

What Was the Attitude of C. S. Lewis Toward Science and Scientism?

Let us begin with Webster's standard dictionary definition of the word "scientism." C. S. Lewis liked to use this word, but it is unfortunately less frequently employed today than was the case 50 years ago. Webster's first definition of scientism is "the methods, mental attitude, doctrines, or modes of expression characteristic or held to be characteristic of scientists." This is not the sense in which C. S. Lewis uses the word. Webster's second definition fits Lewis's usage well: "a thesis that the methods of the natural sciences should be used in all areas of investigation including philosophy, the humanities, and the social sciences: a belief that only such methods can fruitfully be used in the pursuit of knowledge."

It is well to note that at least two other terms carry meanings related to the one Lewis intended by the word scientism. The first is "logical positivism," a system of thought that became popular in the 1920s. The second is "reductionism," a more recently accepted word that is becoming rather common, particularly among philosophers of science. Taken to the limit, reductionism claims that human behavior is simply a matter of neurons firing in the brain, and the latter can be further reduced to atomic physics. In such a purely reductionist worldview, human responsibility does not exist. Although popular in three different eras, the three terms scientism, logical positivism, and reductionism are sufficiently closely related that distinctions may be subtle. They represent a belief system toward which C. S. Lewis was not receptive. As a more specific example of scientism, consider my relationship with my wife, to whom I have been happily married for more than 30 years. Scientism tells us that if one could make enough accurate scientific measurements on myself and on my wife, the resulting analysis would fully explain my strong attraction to her in preference to all others.

Although C. S. Lewis had no training in the sciences, he conceded that his atheism, up to the age of 30, was due to his false perception of the sciences. This is stated perhaps most clearly in Lewis's autobiography of his early life, entitled *Surprised by Joy*. Therein, Lewis writes "You will understand that my (atheism) was inevitably based on what I believed to be the findings of the sciences; and those findings, not being a scientist, I had to take on trust—in fact, on authority." In other words, some authority figure had told him that science had disproved God, and Lewis unquestioningly believed that person.

In my opinion, Lewis's views on science and scientism are expressed most effectively in his space trilogy: *Out of the Silent Planet*, published in 1938; *Perelandra*, appearing in 1943; and the concluding *That Hideous Strength*, produced in 1945. Although some would disagree, I consider *That Hideous Strength* to be Lewis's masterpiece of fiction. I concede that the juxtaposition of the scientism theme with Lewis's take on the 1500-year-old King Arthur/Merlin legend can be a bit confusing on first read. However, the second time through (Lewis was convinced every good book was more enjoyable upon a second reading, and I concur), the two threads fall perfectly into place. In his May 21, 1946 review in the *New York Times*, Orville Prescott hits the nail on the head in stating: "*That Hideous Strength* is a parable (concerning) the degeneration of man which inevitably follows a gross and slavish scientific materialism which excludes all idealistic, ethical and religious values."

Faye Ann Crowell's summary statement (Texas A&M Master's Thesis, 1971) is equally perceptive: "C. S. Lewis feared what might be done to all nature and especially to mankind if scientific knowledge were to be applied by the power of government without the restraints of traditional values. These fears are presented dramatically in the space novels. To Lewis the possibility was great that men would not survive as men."

Lewis's writings have been quite incorrectly viewed by some as trenchantly anti-science. For example, Philip Deasy wrote in 1958 ("God, Space, and C. S. Lewis," *Commonweal*, page 422, July 25) that the "total and unrelenting attack on science was for many readers . . . . . an insuperable stumbling block." It is difficult for me to believe that Deasy read *That Hideous Strength* carefully. The hero of the early part of the novel is William Hingest, affectionately called "Bill the Blizzard" in admiration of his formidable intellect. Dr. Hingest is a physical chemist (a noble profession!) and the only fellow of Bracton College with an international scholarly reputation. Although Hingest is most regrettably murdered about a fifth of the way through *That Hideous Strength*, he is the only character at that stage of the book to resist the scientism that C. S. Lewis so opposes.

Faye Ann Crowell clearly recognized the truth of the matter in stating "Many writers have referred to elements in the (space) trilogy which they think show that Lewis was completely opposed to science, but those who knew him personally and/or who have made the most detailed studies of his works—Chad Walsh, Clyde Kilby, Richard Cunningham, and William Luther White—have insisted that it was not science which Lewis was attacking but certain ideas held by people usually not scientists."

Chad Walsh, author of the first book-length study of Lewis's works and ideas, published *C. S. Lewis: Apostle to the Skeptics* in 1949. From his personal conversations with Lewis, Chad Walsh concluded quite correctly that Lewis "had noticed that the 'pure sciences' seem to have no dehumanizing effect on those who study them, but that the closer a science approaches to human affairs the more it tends to strip its specialists of their humanity; sociologists and psychologists are in greater peril than chemists and mathematicians."

The main character of the science fiction trilogy (1938, 1943, 1945), the hero Elwin Ransom, is a theist who embraces the values of pity, kindness, honesty, and respect for individuals. In striking contrast, the villain Professor Weston in the first two novels (he is killed by Ransom in *Perelandra* after a Herculean struggle) is a brilliant physicist who believes there are no absolute truths. Weston is willing to sacrifice anyone or anything to his goal of propagating human life into other parts of the universe. In the third novel, *That Hideous Strength*, the leaders of the National Institute of Coordinated Experiments (NICE) exhibit the ruthless disregard for people that Lewis feared would begin to appear in those who rejected Christian values.

The fictitious Elwin Ransom is a Cambridge University faculty member, and most particularly a philologist. Philology is commonly defined as the study of literature that includes or may include grammar, criticism, literary history, language history, systems of writing, and anything else that is relevant to literature or to language as used in literature. However, as pointed out by Thomas Lessl, philology is much more influenced by science than is literature. Some historical implications seem inevitable, as Lewis's close friend J. R. R. Tolkien was a philologist. In Lewis's own academic specialization, literary studies, philology was disdained by many.

Faye Ann Crowell's analysis picks up on Ransom's activities beginning in the second chapter of *Out of the Silent Planet*, the first book of the space trilogy. She notes that the partially drugged Elwin Ransom hears a conversation which reflects both Dick Devine's selfishness and his lack of concern for life, and Professor Weston's lack of compassion as well as his zeal for wrong goals. Weston is perfectly willing to sacrifice a mentally retarded boy because he was "incapable of serving humanity and only too likely to propagate idiocy. He was the sort of boy who in a civilized community would be automatically handed over to a state laboratory for experimental purposes." The physicist does not like the idea of kidnapping Ransom (for the journey to Mars) because he is "human." Conceding the latter, Weston argues with himself that Ransom is "only an individual, and probably a quite useless one." Weston had in Chapter I dismissed Ransom's work in philology as "unscientific tomfoolery" which was "wasting money that ought to go to (scientific) research."

In defending his view of planetary colonization, the physicist villain Weston tells Ransom "You cannot be so small-minded as to think that the right or the life of an individual or of a million individuals are of the slightest importance in comparison with this." Lewis's hero the philologist Ransom in turn expresses his contempt for "the off chance that some creatures or other descended from man as we know him may crawl about a few centuries longer in some part of the universe." Weston is unimpressed, countering "It would be easier if your philosophy of life were not so insufferably narrow and individualistic . . . . . even a worm, if it could understand, would rise to the sacrifice . . . . . all educated opinion—for I do not call classics and history and such trash education—is entirely on my side."

The narrator of *Perelandra*, the second book of the space trilogy, makes a statement that undoubtedly reflects Lewis's own view of the above debate. *Perelandra* notes that Professor Weston "was a man obsessed with the idea which is at this moment circulating all over our planet in obscure works of 'scientifiction,' in little Interplanetary Societies and Rocketry Clubs, and between the covers of monstrous magazines, ignored or mocked by intellectuals, but ready, if the power is ever put into its hands, to open a new chapter of misery for the universe. It is the idea that humanity, having now sufficiently corrupted the planet where it arose, must at all costs contrive to seed itself over a larger area: that the vast astronomical distances which are God's quarantine regulations, must somehow be overcome."

In the concluding book of the space trilogy, *That Hideous Strength*, Lewis's horror of the forcibly planned society appears as the National Institute of Coordinated Experiments (NICE) is introduced. The NICE is glowingly described by its advocates as "the first fruits of that constructive fusion between the state and the laboratory on which so many people base their hopes of a better world." The bursar James Busby, a member of the Progressive Element which controls Bracton College, expresses the popular notion of the purpose of the NICE: "It's the first attempt to take applied science seriously from the national point of view."

The aims of the NICE, according to Lord Feverstone (who was Weston's co-conspirator Dick Devine in the first book of the space trilogy) include "sterilization of the unfit, liquidation of backward races (we don't want any dead weights), selective breeding. Then real education, including prenatal education. By real education I mean one that has no 'take-it-or-leave-it' nonsense. A real education makes the patient what it wants infallibly: whatever he or his parents try to do about it. Of course, it'll have to be mainly psychological at first. But we'll get on to biochemical conditioning in the end and direct manipulation of the brain." In contrast, Lewis was certain that a union of applied science and social planning with the power of government would result in the loss of freedom and individuality.

Lord Feverstone continues in *That Hideous Strength* as follows: "It does really look as if we now had the power to dig ourselves in as a species for a pretty staggering period, to take control of our own destiny. If Science is really given a free hand it can now take over the human race and re-condition it: make man a really efficient animal . . . . . Man has got to take charge of Man. That means, remember, that some men have got to take charge of the rest." Note again that Feverstone is the same Dick Devine, who helped Professor Weston to kidnap Ransom in *Out of the Silent Planet*.

The evil forces in *That Hideous Strength* mostly reside at Belbury, a florid Edwardian mansion built for a millionaire who admired Versailles. Belbury is set in the English countryside, perhaps 15 miles from the fictitious University of Edgestowe, home of Bracton College. Belbury is the site of the NICE, a government-supported organization supposedly scientific, with a physiologist (Professor Filostrato) and a psychologist (Augustus Frost) as important but evil characters.

Some critics have incorrectly regarded *That Hideous Strength* as an attack on science. In this regard Faye Ann Crowell correctly draws attention to Lewis's unpublished (in his own lifetime) reply to Professor J.B.S. Haldane's highly critical review. Lewis answered Haldane's criticism by explaining just what he was attacking: "Firstly, a certain view about values: the attack will be found, undisguised, in *The Abolition of Man*," Lewis's 100 page work of nonfiction on the same subject. The latter essay addresses the dangers Lewis saw in the twentieth century abandonment of traditional, objective values. Lewis's second aim in *That Hideous Strength* was to illustrate the folly of devoting one's life to gaining the power and prestige of belonging to a ruling clique or inner circle. Finally, Lewis continued, he was attacking not scientific planning, as Professor Haldane had thought, but the kind of planned society which first Adolf Hitler and then European Marxists had instituted: "the disciplined cruelty of some ideological oligarchy."

Some attention in the above context should be drawn to J. B. S. Haldane (1892 - 1964). There can be no question that Haldane was gifted with a brilliant intellect, studying physiology and genetics at Oxford University. At the tender age of 31 Haldane became a Reader (at the time a highly distinguished faculty appointment) in Biochemistry at Cambridge in 1923. Haldane became Professor of Genetics at University College London in 1933. Haldane was well known as an atheist; during the 1930s he was an outspoken Marxist and served for a time as chairman of the editorial board of the London *Daily Worker*. Haldane eventually left the Communist Party, disillusioned by the fame that Russia accorded to the bogus biologist Trofim Lysenko. Haldane emigrated to India to join the Biometry Research Group in Orissa in 1957. He became an Indian citizen in 1961 and died of cancer there at the age of 72. Today Haldane is best known generally as the co-author of the largely discredited Haldane-Oparin mechanism for the origin of life. This subject is discussed at length in my essay "Climbing Mount Improbable." Along with a British contemporary, the crystallographer J. D. Bernal, Haldane continues to be something of an icon to some Marxists and atheists in the sciences.

C. S. Lewis almost certainly reflected some of what he perceived as the qualities of Haldane in the space trilogy character of Professor Weston. Particularly relevant to Lewis's space trilogy is the last chapter of J. B. S. Haldane's 1927 collection of essays entitled *Possible Worlds*. There Haldane states that if the human race were to continue to survive and progress, mankind would have to colonize the planets. On November 15, 1948, Haldane spoke in Lewis's presence at the Oxford Socratic Club on the topic "Atheism". He departed abruptly without answering questions.

The most negative statement about science in the space trilogy is that of the narrator of *That Hideous Strength*, toward the end of Chapter 9, entitled "The Saracen's Head." The passage reads as follows: "The physical sciences, good and innocent in themselves, had already, even in Ransom's own time, begun to be warped, had been subtly maneuvered in a certain direction. Despair of objective truth had been increasingly insinuated into the scientists; indifference to it, and a concentration upon mere power, had been the result." Lewis is addressing his concern that some scientists had abandoned the historic Christian view of a rational universe. Although the above narrator's language may be a bit overblown, I would agree with Lewis that science is endangered when it fails to understand why the universe is intelligible.

In the above-cited unpublished response to J. B. S. Haldane's criticism of the novel *That Hideous Strength*, Lewis wrote: "If any of my romances would be plausibly accused of being a libel on scientists it would be *Out of the Silent Planet*. It certainly is an attack, if not on scientists, yet on something which might be called 'scientism' — a certain outlook on the world which is usually connected with the popularization of the sciences, though it is much less common among real scientists than among their readers. It is, in a word, the belief that the supreme moral end is the perpetuation of our own species, and this is to be pursued even if, in the process of being fitted for survival, our species has to be stripped of all those things for which we value it—of pity, of happiness, and of freedom." Source: *Of Other Worlds*, Editor Walter Hooper; indirect source, Faye Ann Crowell.

One of the most revealing characters in *That Hideous Strength* is the highly regarded physiologist, Professor Filostrato. Filostrato would prefer artificial trees made of aluminum, with artificial birds which would sing at the touch of a switch, thus eliminating feathers, eggs, dirt, and decay. Filostrato tells the wimpy sociologist Mark Studdock (husband to the book's heroine, Jane Studdock) what he sees as the true purpose of the NICE. "It is for the conquest of death: or for the conquest of organic life if you prefer. They are the same thing. It is to bring out of that cocoon of organic life, which sheltered the babyhood of mind, the New Man, the man who will not die, the artificial man, free from Nature. Nature is the ladder we have climbed up by, now we kick her away."

The fact that Lewis is not negative about science per se is seen in his treatment of sociology and psychology in *That Hideous Strength*. When Mark Studdock uses the phrase "sciences like sociology" in a conversation with Bracton College's most outstanding scientist, William Hingest, the physical chemist interrupts him with, "There are no sciences like sociology." Mark goes on to speak of studying "the reality" of the ordinary man, and Hingest interrupts even more abruptly, analyzing what happens when sociologists study men: "I should want to pull it to bits and put something else in its place. Of course. That's what happens when you study men: you find mare's nests. I happen to believe you can't study men; you can only get to know them, which is quite a different thing."

In a posthumously published (Cambridge University Press, 1964) essay contained in the collection *The Discarded Image*, Lewis continues his argument that the problem is not with "the pure sciences." He states "In our age . . . the ease with which a scientific theory assumes the dignity and rigidity of fact varies inversely with the individual's scientific education . . . . The mass media which have in our time created a popular scientism, a caricature of the true sciences." This statement seems to reflect Lewis's embarrassment that he was an atheist for many years, in part because someone who knew little about science told him authoritatively that the latter had disproved God.

Faye Ann Crowell notes that although the space trilogy was completed in 1945, C. S. Lewis did not alter the concerns expressed therein. In 1963, the year of his death (on the same day

President John F. Kennedy was assassinated), Lewis wrote: "If we encounter in the depths of space a race, however innocent and amiable, which is technologically weaker than ourselves . . . we shall enslave, deceive, exploit, or exterminate; at the very least we shall corrupt it with our vices and infect it with our diseases. We are not fit yet to visit other worlds . . . . Must we go to infect other realms?" ("The Seeing Eye," in *Christian Reflections*, Eerdmans, 1967).

Lewis directly addresses those who accuse him of being an enemy of science in *The Abolition of Man*. He writes therein "Nothing I can say will prevent some people as describing this lecture as an attack on science. I deny the charge, of course: and real Natural Philosophers (there are some now alive) will perceive that in defending value I defend *inter alia* the value of knowledge." Let the reader note that the term "natural philosophy" was used in the 19th century to describe science. Referring in *That Hideous Strength* to the excesses of some contemporary scientists, Lewis's narrator states "You could not have done it with nineteenth century scientists. Their firm objective materialism would have excluded it from their minds; and even if they could have been made to believe, their inherited morality would have kept them from touching dirt." Lewis of course is referring indirectly to the Christian convictions of Michael Faraday, James Clerk Maxwell, J. J. Thomson, Lord Kelvin, and so many other great pioneers of the physical sciences.

Lewis also touches on these matters in *The Screwtape Letters* (1942), probably his most widely read book after *Mere Christianity*. Screwtape, an experienced demon, advises his nephew Wormwood, at work on a "patient" in England, "Do not attempt to use science (I mean, the real sciences) as a defense against Christianity. They will positively encourage him to think about realities he can't touch and see. There have been sad cases among the modern physicists. If he must dabble in science, keep him on economics and sociology . . . . But the best of all is to let him read no science but to give him a grand general idea that he knows it all and that everything he happens to have picked up in casual talk and reading is 'the results of modern investigation.'" Once again we see an allusion to Lewis's personal experience, his unsuspecting absorption of the false premise that science had disproved the existence of the God of the universe.

Lewis was concerned that the modern rejection of absolute standards and objective values would leave mankind with no defense against what some persons might do with the powers of science. His love of individual freedom and his appreciation for people as creatures made in the image of God caused him to fear what might be done to humanity if science, without Christian standards to restrain it, were to be given the power of government to enforce what a few persons might plan for all the rest.

Lewis reminded his readers that naturalism, determinism, and rigid empiricism all view man as a biological accident with no meaning and no unmeasureable qualities like soul or spirit. These philosophies presuppose that there is neither a God nor absolute truth of values. The study of humankind by sociologists, psychologists, and anthropologists has reduced persons to things having minimal dignity or worth, having little or no individual responsibility for their choices and actions. In explaining nature and man, scientists have "explained away" his value and meaning.

Is Scientism Alive and Well in the Twenty-First Century?

The answer to this question is certainly "yes." C. S. Lewis's concerns in this regard remain valid. The most famous statement of belief in scientism of the last century is still fresh in the minds of most educated adults in the USA: "The cosmos is all there is or ever was or ever will be." This statement is the opening salvo in Carl Sagan's famous television series "The Cosmos." How curious for a program supposedly concerned with science to begin with a statement of atheistic faith! But so it was with Sagan to the end. On his deathbed, Sagan instructed his wife to give a full account of his final moments, that no one might conclude he had stopped shaking his fist at God. Not to worry. C.S. Lewis liked to say that deathbed conversion experiences were rare, and that he did not feel like thinking about spiritual things when he had a toothache.

Daniel Dennett is a philosopher/sociologist at Tufts University in Massachusetts. His book *Darwin's Dangerous Idea* is a model reductionist work and represents precisely the sort of scientism that so concerned C. S. Lewis. Dennett writes therein "My own spirit recoils from a (personal) God in the same way my heart sinks when I see a lion pacing neurotically back and forth in a small zoo cage. I know, I know the lion is beautiful but dangerous; if you let the lion roam free, it would kill me. Safety demands that it be put in a cage. Safety demands that religions be put in cages, too . . . . . We just can't have the second-class status of women in Roman Catholicism." Although C. S. Lewis did not live to read Dennett's book, Dennett is precisely the sort of person that Lewis would not want to influence society—namely, a philosopher who writes about science from a reservoir of ignorance on the subject. A less successful expositor of the same scientism as Dennett is Michael Shermer, a sometime adjunct professor at Occidental College with two psychology degrees. A bit more will be said about Shermer in my short essay "The Nondebate with Steven Weinberg."

Even my own research area of molecular quantum mechanics has not entirely escaped the phenomenon of scientism. C. S. Lewis never sought to pick a fight with evolutionists, and that is not the purpose of this essay either. However, sometimes evolutionists cannot seem to avoid putting their foot into scientism. For example, in the 1977 Symposium Issue of the *International Journal of Quantum Chemistry*, Andrew McLachlan provides an example of the consequences of indiscriminate naturalistic evolutionary thinking. McLachlan states "Living systems are wonderfully well-suited to their purpose, but the design is shaped by blind evolution instead of imaginative intelligence." The notion that God does not exercise "imaginative intelligence" is clearly offensive to anyone who believes in a higher power.

Richard Dawkins, author of *The Blind Watchmaker*, is the very ideal of a modern materialist reductionist. It has been noted above that the word "reductionism" serves the purpose today that "scientism" played in the 1940s. Let me attempt to give just a flavor of Dawkins' worldview. For example, he describes love as "a product of highly complicated... nervous equipment or computing equipment of some sort." Free advice to young people: this is not likely to be an effective way to win the heart of that person with whom you are infatuated. If you do feel that way about your sweetheart, it may be better to keep the conviction to yourself. When asked if such a worldview is depressing, Dawkins responds "I don't feel depressed about it. But if somebody does, that's their problem. Maybe the logic is deeply pessimistic, the universe is bleak, cold and empty. But so what?" Dawkins is without question the most influential apostle of scientism on the planet. My essay "Climbing Mount Improbable" deals with Dawkins' views in more detail.

Is there resistance within the academic world to the scientism of Sagan, Dawkins, and Dennett? Of course. Among more than a thousand Berkeley faculty colleagues, one of the two most brilliant for the 18 years I served as a professor there was Professor Phillip Johnson of the Boalt School of Law. For more than a decade, Phillip Johnson has been challenging the philosophical underpinnings of scientism. One of his best essays on this subject was invited by the *Wall Street Journal* and appeared there on May 10, 1993. Professor Johnson writes "But how tolerant do the triumphant scientists plan to be toward those who don't think that reductionist naturalism is a rational philosophy? Many well-educated people think that there is an intelligence behind the cosmos, and that life and consciousness cannot be explained in terms of physics and chemistry alone. Such people may want to dispute undemonstrated reductionist claims about such subjects as the origin of life and the reducibility of mental life to chemical reactions in the brain. May these persons obtain a fair hearing?"

Johnson concludes his essay in this manner: "Naturalistic metaphysics relegates questions like how we should live or what we should value to the realm of subjective opinion. It provides no sacred common ground, other than a supposedly value-free science, to unite differing human groups and give them a foundation to reason from. Is it any wonder that the great universities that are permeated by this philosophy are themselves being torn apart by groups that demand separate academic departments to promote their ideologies?"

Reductionists who purport to be consistent are obligated to try to explain away all nonscientific aspects of human experience. From the consistent reductionist perspective, Beethoven's music really is just meaningless vibrations in the air; the *Mona Lisa* really is just an improbable collection of specks of paint of readily determinable chemical composition. It is hard to exaggerate the implausibility of this limited view of reality. All that is most profound, and all that makes human life worth living, is devalued and discarded, sacrificed to an unjustified scientific imperialism. One needs to go a bit further in this reduction of scientism to the absurd. The consistent reductionist must argue that torturing children is neither right nor wrong. Our society's decision not to torture children is just a conventional agreement to see things this way. The reductionist similarly has no definitive basis for his or her decision to greet or to eat a stranger. Such a worldview should be resisted, as Lewis did so well. I know, as surely as I accept Coulomb's Law (like charges repel; opposite charges attract), that love is better than hate, and that the truth is better than a lie.

Do Nearly All Scientists Believe in Scientism?

The clear answer to this question is certainly no. The first chapter of the present book deals decisively and at length with this question. The average Ph.D. scientist is not likely to be more attracted to scientism than your average truck driver. Perhaps the simplest way to display this fact is by listing just a few of the great scientist Christians of the past and present.

Past	Present
Francis Bacon	Richard Bube
Robert Boyle	David Cole
Charles Coulson	Francis Collins
Michael Faraday	Robert Griffiths
Lord Kelvin	Chris Isham
Johannes Kepler	Norman March
James Clerk Maxwell	Donald Page
Isaac Newton	William Phillips
Blaise Pascal	John Polkinghorne
William Henry Perkin	John Pople
Michael Polanyi	Allan Sandage
Arthur Schawlow	Marlan Scully
George Stokes	John Suppe
J. J. Thomson	James Tour

Conclusions

First, we should ask, is C.S. Lewis's critique of scientism valid today? In the broad sense, yes. There may be somewhat less enthusiasm among intellectuals today for proliferating human sinfulness to other planets than was the case in 1938. However, one would not come to that conclusion based on Roger Highfield's November 16, 2001 story in *The Telegraph*. In that article Stephen Hawking, the most famous scientist in the world, is quoted as saying "I don't think the human race will survive the next thousand years, unless we spread into space. There are too many accidents that can befall life on a single planet. But I'm an optimist. We will reach out to the stars." The apparent lack of introspection in Hawking's words is a concern. He seems to naively assume that the readers of *The Telegraph* will unanimously view the achievement of space colonization as something about which to feel good. My opinion is that it would serve Professor Hawking well to study C.S. Lewis's space trilogy. Also sobering in light of the space trilogy are the continuing popularity of Star Wars and Star Trek, not to mention the tragic suicidal demise of the "Heaven's Gate" cult.

Second, scientism is indeed alive and well in the 21st century. There can be little doubt that C. S. Lewis would have been as skeptical of the modern reductionist Richard Dawkins today as he was of J. B. S. Haldane in 1938. Further, Lewis almost certainly would have some reservation about state-supported research on frozen human embryos. Lewis would not likely have been supportive of the use of human genome research to terminate the lives of fetuses that were less than genetically perfect. His opinion on human cloning is equally predictable.

Do most scientists believe in scientism today? Not according to a poll of 3332 members of the scientific honorary society Sigma Xi. The November 7, 1988 issue of *Chemical & Engineering News* reports "Scientists are anchored to the U. S. mainstream. Half participate in religious activities regularly." Moreover, as I have documented, many distinguished contemporary scientists have found the truth claims of Jesus Christ to be intellectually compelling. My challenge to those of you who are not familiar with C. S. Lewis's writings is to read his classic *Mere Christianity* and consider the claims of Jesus.

The Ten Questions
Intellectuals Ask About
Christianity

8

It may strike some readers as peculiar to find a chapter with this title included in a volume on science and Christianity. Twenty years ago, as I began giving this series of lectures as a Professor of Chemistry at the University of California at Berkeley, I would have shared this opinion. However, my hosts always try to schedule a "Question and Answer" time of perhaps 30 minutes to one hour following each lecture. And gradually it dawned on me that many of the same questions were being asked at one university after the next. Moreover, many of these recurring questions had little or nothing to do with science. About ten years ago, someone came to the front of the auditorium after the post-lecture questions were exhausted, perhaps at Stanford University, and had the temerity to say "Professor, you did better on the questions than you did on the lecture. Why don't you make up a lecture from your answers to these nonscientific questions?" So here we are. I am indebted to many sources for the answers to these questions, but I regret that many of these sources have been lost. My comments in the preface are especially applicable here. I do recommend in this context Paul Little's book *Know Why You Believe* and acknowledge several helpful answers from my friend Steve Brown of Reformed Theological Seminary, Orlando.

1. Is it reasonable to be a scientist and a Christian?

This is actually the first question that many intellectuals ask about Christianity. Since the majority of the present book is devoted to answering this question, my answer here will be exceedingly brief. Namely, that the answer must be "Yes," because so many of the pioneers in the physical sciences were committed

Christians. Further, many of today's most distinguished physicists and chemists are Christians.

2. What about Adolf Hitler? Wasn't he a Christian?

I have found that in a university audience of 200 students and faculty, there is invariably at least one person for whom this question absolutely dominates. I answer this question by quoting Hitler himself: "The heaviest blow that ever struck humanity was the coming of Christianity. Bolshevism is Christianity's illegitimate child. Both are inventions of the Jew." Christianity is, of course, Jewish in its origin, but the rest of the above statement is pure human depravity. Shortly after assuming power in Germany in 1933, Adolf Hitler stated that he intended "to stamp out Christianity root and branch," for "One is either a Christian or a German—you cannot be both." Christianity should be destroyed by force or "left to rot like a gangrenous limb," Hitler argued, so that most Germans will be Christian "never again. That tale is finished . . . . . but we can hasten matters. The parsons will be made to dig their own graves. They will betray their God to us." Source of last quote: Marvin Olasky.

3. Who made God?

This is a universal question, in the sense that it is asked in all cultures by persons of all ages above perhaps three years old. God never needed to be made, because He was always there. Prior to the creation of our universe God existed in one or more time dimensions that human beings have not experienced. God exists in a different way from human beings. We exist in a derived, finite, and fragile way, but the Creator exists as eternal, self-sustaining, and necessary, in the sense that there is no possibility of Him ceasing to exist. In philosophy, many errors result from supposing that the conditions and limits of our own finite existence apply to God.

4. Can God make a rock so big that he can't lift it?

I had thought this question was a joke until I was asked to answer it on October 13, 1995 before an audience of 1300 people at the University of Michigan. It is indeed true that God is omnipotent. But omnipotence does not mean that God can do literally everything. As the *Westminster Shorter Catechism* says "God can do all His holy will." God cannot sin. God cannot lie. God cannot change His nature. God cannot deny the demands of His holy character. God cannot make a square circle, for the notion of a square circle is self-contradictory. God cannot cease to be God. But all that God wills and promises, He can and will do.

5. Doesn't the inherent subjectivity of morality prove that God does not exist?

The pervasiveness of this question in contemporary society requires a substantive answer:

People commonly say that "morality is subjective" or that it is "relative." But when they speak in a moral vein—which is to say, when they pass judgment on human behavior—they do so as moral realists. Most atheists are just as convinced as Christians that Adolf Hitler was an evil person.

A. People resist moral realism because they think it leads to intolerance. In doing so they make two fundamental mistakes. First, they fail to realize that tolerance itself is a value and that they are simply making this particular goal rule over all others. This is itself a form of moral realism. Second, they fail to understand that tolerance and moral realism can coincide, and indeed do in healthy societies.

B. People disagree about how to achieve objectives, but in the abstract they do not usually clash over the truth of any specific value.

i. One rarely hears it said that "justice" or "fairness" or "kindness" or "bravery" or "charity" are not sound principles —in the abstract.

ii. Moral disagreements typically involve the implementation of values, the challenge of trying to integrate them into our behavior. This involves taking into account issues of knowledge as well as concerns about right and wrong.

D. There are essentially no new or revolutionary ideals. People sometimes assume there are new values, simply because the language through which ideas are expressed changes. For instance, an important concept today is "diversity." While you may not find this precise word in the traditional language of morality, such as that used in the New Testament, you will find the concept (e.g., I Corinthians 12:14-31). There Paul talks about the different roles played by different (i.e., diverse) parts of the body of Christ.

E. People are attracted to moral subjectivism or relativism because it exonerates them of guilt. But the very fact that they so strongly desire to perceive themselves as righteous reveals an unacknowledged commitment to moral realism.

Allow me to acknowledge explicitly the fact that the thrust of points A–E came from a source that is now lost to me.

6. Is the New Testament picture of Jesus reliable?

Given the unprecedented claims of Jesus, this is an important question. Shortly after becoming a Christian, I came upon a remarkable book by the British classics scholar Professor F. F. Bruce of the University of Manchester. Dr. Bruce made his academic reputation as a scholar of ancient Greek and Latin manuscripts. Bruce's book is titled *The New Testament Documents:*

Are They Reliable? Therein Professor Bruce argues that "The grounds for accepting the New Testament as trustworthy compare very favorably with the grounds on which classical (Greek, Roman) scholars accept the authenticity and credibility of 'reliable' ancient documents." As just one example, Bruce notes Julius Caesar's *Gallic Wars*, of which there are nine or ten existing manuscripts, the oldest of which dates from 850 A.D.

My immediate response to this bit of information from Professor Bruce was "I wish I had known that when I began second-year Latin at East Grand Rapids High School on the first day of school in September of 1959." We spent the entire academic year trying to translate Caesar's *Gallic Wars*. I need to confess here that my behavior in Miss Hill's Latin class was less than exemplary. Miss Hill was an elderly unmarried lady, and some of the names we attached to her person cannot be repeated here. If she's in heaven, I've got some apologizing ahead of me. We received marks for both academic performance and behavior at East Grand Rapids High School, and my marks for behavior in Miss Hill's class placed me right on the edge of expulsion from the school. But I would have cheerfully risked it all on that first day of second-year Latin to say in front of the class "Miss Hill, I am regrettably going to have to request a different translation assignment for the year. It has come to my attention that the oldest existing copy of Caesar's *Gallic Wars* is a copy, probably fraudulent, made nearly 900 years after the book was purported to have been composed. I respectfully refuse to be involved in translating a book that is not reliable."

In the above context, the comparison of Caesar's *Gallic Wars* to the New Testament could hardly be more stark. Specifically, there are some 4,000 extant Greek manuscripts of the New Testament, in whole or in part. The best complete documents go back to 350 A.D. Parts of John's Gospel are authoritatively dated at 130 A.D., perhaps only 50 years after its composition.

John Warwick Montgomery has well summarized this situation: "To express skepticism concerning the resultant text of the New Testament books . . . is to allow all of classical antiquity to slip into obscurity, for no documents of the ancient period are as well attested bibliographically as is the New Testament."

7. How could an intelligent 20th century person believe that Jesus rose physically from the dead?

For me this was the most important question, as I have discussed in the chapter "From Berkeley Professor to Christian." Recognizing the truth of the resurrection of Jesus does not make a person a Christian, but it can be a giant step in the correct direction. Let me provide seven possibly helpful comments (help from Steve Brown cheerfully acknowledged):

A. If Jesus remained dead, how can one explain the exuberant statements of His closest friends? Forty days after Jesus' death, people hear His friends' shouts of excitement, "We've seen a dead man walking!"

B. If Jesus remained dead, how can a person explain the faithfulness of Jesus' closest friends to the testimony of the resurrection, even in the face of their own deaths? Of the eleven apostles, only one died of old age—John—and he was exiled to Patmos, a gruesome island work camp. Jesus' followers died as martyrs, with the truth of the resurrection on their lips. The simple statement "It did not happen" would have spared their lives.

C. If Jesus remained dead, why did 500 people say they saw Him alive (see I Corinthians 15:6)?

D. If Jesus remained dead, how would one explain the credibility of the witnesses? In the first century, countless individuals questioned the firsthand witnesses repeatedly, and their unified yet independent accounts were never disproved.

E. If Jesus remained dead, how does a person explain the inability of the first century skeptics to deal with the resurrection via an alternative explanation? The political power of Rome and the religious establishment in Jerusalem were arrayed to stop the Christian faith. All these powerful forces needed to do was to excavate the grave and triumphantly present the corpse. They were utterly unsuccessful.

F. If Jesus remained dead, how can you explain the reality of the Christian church and its phenomenal growth in the first three centuries of the Christian era? The church of Jesus covered the Western world by the fourth century. A religious movement built on a lie, and with no military or financial resources, could not have accomplished such a remarkable result.

G. If Jesus did not rise from the dead, his closest friends were an extraordinarily compulsive group of liars. This charge does not fit well with the ethical caliber of the writings of Jesus' disciples. Virtually all religions now concede that the writings of the apostles represent a very high level of moral character.

8. Who is Jesus?

I think the best brief answer to this is given by C.S. Lewis in his masterpiece *Mere Christianity*. This book should be required reading for anyone with the faintest interest in the life of the mind. Lewis begins with a statement that most of us have heard, perhaps frequently: "I'm ready to accept Jesus as a great moral teacher, but I don't accept his claim to be God." Lewis argues that the above statement is intellectually indefensible. He writes: "That is the one thing we must not say. A man who was merely a man and said the sort of things Jesus said would not be a great moral teacher. He would either be a lunatic—on a level with the man who says he is a poached egg—or else he would be the devil of hell. You must take your choice. Either this man was, and is, the Son of God; or else a madman or something worse. You can shut him up for a fool, you can spit at Him and kill Him as a demon, or you can fall at His feet and call Him Lord and God. But let us not come with any patronizing nonsense about his being a great human teacher. He has not left that open to us. He did not intend to."

9. Why do bad things happen to good people?

For many people this is the biggest question of all. The best simple answer I have seen was scrawled on the side of a vacant, burned out building in Berkeley, California. This was probably the site of some drug war or other nefarious activity. As one approaches the building, one sees in large, very distinct letters the words "Most people want to serve God." The first time I saw these words I was genuinely surprised, as my 18 years as a professor at the university had actually inclined me to the opposite opinion. However, my puzzlement was dissolved when I drove closer and saw in smaller print the words of explanation: "Usually in an advisory capacity."

In his 1955 lecture to the Oxford Socratic Club, C.S. Lewis expressed the same truth in more sophisticated language: "If human life is in fact ordered by a beneficent being whose knowledge of our real needs and of the way in which they can be satisfied infinitely exceeds our own, we must expect *a priori* that his operations will often appear to us far from beneficent and far from wise, and that it will be our highest prudence to give him our confidence in spite of this." James Packer adds to Lewis's insights: "A god whom we could understand exhaustively, and whose revelation of himself confronted us with no mysteries whatsoever, would be a god in man's image, and therefore an imaginary god."

Human arrogance tends to believe that if we had been in charge of creation we would have done it better. With a little more care about the details, we would have kept the beauty of sunsets, but eliminated cancer and heart disease. The more we understand the processes of the world, however, the less likely does it seem that this would be possible. The fine tuning of our universe is perhaps its most remarkable characteristic. As finite human beings we should not claim to know God's will exhaustively. But it is clear that God did not intend to create an enormous machine whose sole purpose was the elimination of human suffering. Suffering is very much a part of God's plan for our brief sojourn upon this planet.

As John MacArthur has discussed, the major reality of the book of Job, one of the oldest books in the Hebrew Bible, is the inscrutable mystery of innocent suffering. God ordains that His children walk in sorrow and pain, sometimes because of sin, sometimes for chastening, sometimes for strengthening, and sometimes to give opportunity to reveal His comfort and grace. But there are times when the compelling issue in human suffering is unknowable, because it is for a heavenly purpose that those on earth cannot discern. Stephen Curtis Chapman has well written in a popular song: "God is God and I am not. I can only see a part of the picture He's painting." Moreover, it is unwise, as well as uncharitable, to conclude that the sufferings of others are specifically punitive. The concept of karma (punishment for sins in an imaginary prior life) has no role in the Christian faith.

Why do bad things happen to good people? A humorous variant of this important question goes something like this: "God would have a lot more friends if He treated the ones He already has better." The response to this critique seems obvious: if God rescued from every problem those who are true to Jesus, Christians would not need faith. Their religion would be a great big insurance policy, and there would be lines of selfish people ready to sign up.

10. Doesn't the uneven geographical distribution of Christianity around the globe prove that it must not be a universal truth?

No more than the uneven distribution of the understanding of calculus around the world proves that calculus is untrue. Very closely related questions may be expressed in several different ways, but this one captures the essence of the problem. The critical issue must be one of truth, rather than geographical distribution.

11. What about other religions?

This is an important but potentially contentious question, with the capacity to produce more heat than light. My intention is to seek the latter rather than the former. One of the more even-handed ways to compare different religions is in terms of the words and lives of their founders. C. S. Lewis made some helpful comments in this regard, recorded in the anthology *A Mind Awake*, edited by Clyde Kilby. Therein Lewis writes: If you had gone to Buddha and asked him, "Are you the son of Brahma?" he would have said, "My son, you are still in the veil of illusion." If you had gone to Socrates and asked, "Are you Zeus?" he would have laughed at you. If you had gone to Mohammed and asked, "Are you Allah?" he would first have rent his clothes and then cut your head off. If you had asked Confucius, "Are you heaven?" I think he would have probably replied, "Remarks that are not in accordance with nature are in bad taste." The idea of a great moral teacher saying what Christ said (that He is God Almighty, the one through whom the universe was created) is out of the question. In my opinion, the only person who can say that sort of thing is either God or a complete lunatic suffering from that form of delusion which undermines the whole mind of man. He was never regarded as a mere moral teacher. Jesus did not produce that effect on any of the people who actually met Him. He produced mainly three effects: hatred, terror, and adoration.

12. Question from a student at the University of Arizona, February 21, 2001:
"I know I'm not perfect, but I'm not a big sinner. Does God really care about my sins?"

Obviously, before a large public audience of University of Arizona students and faculty, no matter how strong the temptation, this was not the time for me to inquire about that person's particular failures to serve God. But I was able to share from my own experience that my sins are not minor. My sin runs too deep: the way I hurt people, my unloving attitude, my tendency to judge others, my refusal to trust God in all circumstances, my inability to get sinful thoughts out of my mind and heart (and the list could go on and on) cause me to tremble in God's presence. Pride and selfishness are an integral part of the human condition, and they are not "minor" sins. Pride and selfishness are the essence of man's rebellion against God. Credit to Steve Brown.

13. Will not God accept those of other religions who are sincere?

Let us begin another potentially contentious discussion by noting that all other religions are diametrically opposed to Christianity on the most crucial question: "Who is Jesus Christ?" These worldviews deny that Jesus is God, that He rose again after dying on the cross, and that because of His death, all who trust in Him exclusively can have a full and complete forgiveness of their sins.

Given these essential differences, what is one to conclude about the question of sincerity? No one should doubt the sincerity and intensity of faith of a Hindu holy man, a Sadhu, wandering through India with absolutely nothing to his name but a begging bowl. Such a person is not into religion for the big bucks! But sincerity or intensity of faith does not create truth. Faith is no more valid than the object in which it is placed. The critical point should be, "What is true?" I always encourage my friends to read the four original accounts and see what Jesus claimed about Himself. Not every religion can be true. Most are mutually contradictory. Either one is true and the others are false, or they are all false. Either Christ is who He said He is or He is not. If He is not, then He was lying, He was sincerely deluded, or the stories were all made up about Him. If Jesus is who He said He is, then Christianity is true, and He is the only mediator between God and human beings.

14. Hasn't the overall influence of Christianity been negative?

A balanced response to this old question has been given by Dr. Kenneth Scott Latourette, Sterling Professor, Yale University: Christianity has been the means of reducing more languages to writing than have all other factors combined. It has created more schools, more theories of education, and more systems than has any other one force. More than any other power in history it has impelled men to fight suffering, whether that suffering has come from disease, war, or natural disasters. The Christian faith has built thousands of hospitals, inspired the emergence of the nursing and medical professions, and furthered countless movements for public health and for the relief and prevention of famine. Although explorations and conquests which were in part its outgrowth led to the enslavement of African people for the plantations of the Americas, men and women whose consciences were awakened by Christianity and whose wills it nerved (e.g., William Wilberforce) brought about the abolition of slavery (in England and America). Men and women who were similarly moved and sustained wrote into the laws of Spain and Portugal provisions to alleviate the ruthless exploitation of indigenous peoples in Central and South America.

Wars have often been waged in the name of Christianity. They have attained colossal dimensions through weapons and large scale organization initiated in (nominal) Christendom. Yet from no other source have there come as many and as strong movements to eliminate or regulate war and to ease the suffering brought by war. From its first centuries, the Christian faith has caused many of its adherents to be uneasy about war. It has led minorities to refuse to have any part in it. It has impelled others to seek to limit war by defining what, in their judgment, from the Christian standpoint is a "just war." In the turbulent Middle Ages of Europe it gave rise to the Truce of God and the Peace of God. In a later era it was the main impulse in the formulation of international law. But for it, the League of Nations and the United Nations would not have been. By its name and symbol, the most extensive organization ever created for the relief of the suffering caused by war, the Red Cross, bears witness to its Christian origin. The list might go on indefinitely. It includes many other humanitarian projects and movements, ideals in government, the reform of prisons and the emergence of criminology, great art and architecture, music, and outstanding literature.

Atheism has in fact engendered greater carnage than "Christendom" in its politicized exploits. But when atheism

> **Finally, it may be noted that just three atheists—Adolf Hitler, Josef Stalin, and Mao Zedong—were responsible for more deaths than those reported in all the wars of recorded history.**

worked its way into violence and sensuality, it was the logical outworking of some of its assumptions. When politicized Christendom did its evil, it was in violation of the teaching and the very person of Jesus Christ. That is a primary difference in the two worldviews. Finally, it may be noted that just three atheists—Adolf Hitler, Josef Stalin, and Mao Zedong—were responsible for more deaths than those reported in all the wars of recorded history.

15. How can a loving God send people to Hell?

The premise to this question is correct. God loves us. But His love is strong, rather than weak and permissive. The question might equally well be, "How can a perfectly righteous God let self-centered people into heaven?" It betrays a lack of balance to presume upon God's love and ignore His holiness.

No one but God is worthy enough to enter heaven. But because of His love, God wants us to be with Him. Therefore, Jesus' death on the cross, where He paid the penalty for all that those trusting Him exclusively have done wrong, was God's way of simultaneously satisfying His holiness and demonstrating His love.

Consider that sacrifice: God has done everything necessary to rescue people from an eternity separated from Him. What have you done about Jesus' provision? Are you choosing hell rather than heaven?

16. What about people who have never heard even the name of Jesus?

Many people have carefully considered this question over the past two millennia. Few thoughtful persons claim to understand God exhaustively. If I did, I would be God, a possibility to which I assign a probability of absolutely zero. But we do know the Bible says God will judge the world with justice. It also says God has made His presence known to all people through nature and through our consciences, so we all find ourselves without excuse (Romans 1:19,20).

The world can be divided into two groups: those who are familiar with the message of Jesus, and those who have not heard yet. I have confidence that God will take care of the latter group with perfect justice. Part of God's provision in that regard is Jesus' explicit command for His followers to go to every nation and people group with His message of eternal life. Many who have not yet heard will hear. But because everyone reading these words has heard, you will need to make a personal decision about the free gift that Jesus offers.

17. Why are there so many hypocrites in the church?

Again, the premise is correct. Yes, there are people in the institutional church who do not live the life in Christ they profess. God hates such pretense as much as you do. But businesses, social clubs and other religions all have their hypocrites as well. Regrettably, hypocrisy is a part of the human condition.

My challenge to the reader is to look at Christ and who He claimed to be, rather than focusing on the fallible footsteps of those who follow, or profess to follow, Him. Christianity stands or falls on the life of Christ, not on the performance of His followers. Anything in life that is genuine will inspire counterfeits. The deplorable hypocrisy of some who falsely claim to be Christians has little bearing on the central truth claims of Christianity. John Warwick Montgomery once quipped "If Albert Einstein were arrested for shoplifting, would it make the theory of relativity wrong?"

Jesus Christ's claims are true, and He was not a hypocrite. Will you follow Him? Don't miss out on knowing Jesus because of someone else's failures.

18. Won't a good moral life get a person to heaven?

Living a good life cannot get a man or woman into heaven, because God's standard for "good enough" is perfection. In this context, Jesus said "You must be perfect, just as your Father in heaven is perfect." If God allowed anything imperfect into heaven, heaven would be marred. So who can get to heaven on his or her own merit? No one but Jesus, because only He lived a perfect life.

So how can any ordinary person get there? We cannot live a sinless life, nor can we make up for our wrongs. But Jesus did both. God offers a relationship with Him on this earth and eternity with Him in heaven. What one needs to do is trust in Jesus' death on the cross as the penalty for our sins, paid in full.

19. Many people are offended by the "exclusiveness" of Christianity. Can anything be said in response?

A. Christianity is "universal" in the sense that Jesus invites all people everywhere to receive the gift of eternal life made possible by the death on the cross.

B. Since many basic tenets of different religions are contradictory, someone has to be wrong.

C. Exclusivity seems unavoidable. Who wants to board a commercial airplane on which the pilot is not exclusively committed to a safe landing? Does the pluralist not believe exclusively that several religions provide acceptable paths to God? The exclusion of exclusivity is also exclusive.

D. Christianity's uniqueness arises not from the narrow-mindedness of individual Christians, but from the extraordinary claims of Jesus Christ, attested by those who were eyewitnesses of His life, death, and resurrection.

20. What should one make of all the different denominations within Christianity?

Let me focus my answer in stating that under the umbrella of "denominations" I would include the Roman Catholic Church, the Roman Catholic Church Eastern Rite (Uniates), the different branches of Eastern Orthodoxy, and the many forms of Protestantism. Something like one-third of the world's population has at least nominal adherence to one of the above branches of Christianity. My discussion below is not intended to include Mormonism, Jehovah's Witnesses, Christian Science, the Unity School of Christianity, the Boston Church of Christ, Scientology, the Unification Church, and several smaller groups that grossly deviate from the central truths of the Christian faith. I regret having to be explicit here, but I do not want to be misunderstood by the unsuspecting.

I am an advocate of the Ice Cream Theory of denominations. Although I am currently on a low fat diet, I love ice cream. In fact, I love virtually all flavors of ice cream. I readily admit that when a choice of all flavors is available, I always choose Oregon Mountain Blackberry ice cream. This attitude reflects my view of denominations. I am not embarrassed to say that I am a Presbyterian, having regularly attended the same church for the past 15 years, beginning when I moved from Berkeley to Georgia. However, I have worshipped Christ in many parts of the world where there was no Presbyterian church—at Catholic, Orthodox, or several varieties of Protestant churches. Further, I would express my opinion that the different denominations can be helpful, in causing Christians to think deeply and indeed meditate on just what it is that they believe. Firm convictions need not necessarily, indeed should not, lead to rancor among Christians. While we may disagree on the details, we agree on the big picture, which is well expressed in the words of a contemporary song: "It was all about a Man; it was all about a cross; it was all about the blood that He shed so I would not be lost."

21. OK, professor. You promised us ten questions

and you delivered twenty. Now let's cut to the chase. How does a person become a Christian?

God exercises tremendous creativity in the countless mechanisms from which he chooses to draw a person into a relationship with Himself through Jesus. Two perspectives on my own experience ("From Berkeley Professor to Christian" and "The Way of Discovery") may be found elsewhere in the present book. In striking contrast, for a mentally handicapped twelve-year-old child to say in complete earnestness "I love you Jesus" may well be sufficient. So I would not be one to limit the way in which a person comes to Christ to a particular formula. That stated, there would seem to be a logical flow of the response to the offer of eternal life that Jesus gives freely to those willing to listen. Humanly speaking, what needs to be done?

A. Repent. There should first be an admission that I have been living as my own master, driven by selfishness, worshipping the wrong things, violating God's loving laws. Repentance means to ask God for forgiveness and to turn from my self-absorption with a willingness to live for Christ and center on Him.

B. Believe. Faith is transferring my trust from my own efforts to the efforts of Christ. I was relying on other things to make myself acceptable, but now I consciously begin to rely on what Jesus did to achieve my acceptance with God. Nothing else is needed for me to be right with God. If I still think "God owes me something for all the good things I have done," I have completely misunderstood the teaching of Jesus.

C. Approach God in prayer in a manner perhaps like this: "I now understand that I am more flawed and sinful than I ever dared to believe. At the very same time, however, I see that I am much more loved and accepted than I ever dared hope. I turn from my old way of living for myself. I have nothing in my record to merit your approval. But I now rest in what Jesus did, and I ask to be accepted into God's family for His sake." When a person genuinely enters into this transaction, two things happen: (i) that person's accounts are cleared, his or her sins wiped out permanently, and the person is adopted into God's family; and (ii) the Holy Spirit enters one's heart and begins to change that person into the character of Jesus.

D. Follow through. Tell a Christian friend about your new commitment to Jesus. Begin to engage in the basic Christian disciplines of prayer, worship, Bible study, and fellowship with other Christians.

From Berkeley Professor to Christian

9

I was raised in a wonderful family that attended the Episcopal Church (the branch of the Anglican Church in the USA) regularly. My mother and father showed consistent love and concern for me from the day I was born until the month 43 years later in which they both died, first my mother of a heart attack and then my father of a broken heart, followed by pneumonia. But as far as religion was concerned, I might just as well have grown up in a devout Hindu environment in Delhi or an observant Muslim community in Tehran. In short, without having the slightest idea what was happening in this regard, I received a remarkably effective inoculation against Christianity. The churches I grew up in taught that the Bible was good and wholesome and largely mythological. I did not fully appreciate this situation until I became a Christian in 1973. I called my dad on the telephone and tried to share with him the most important event in my life: "Dad, I've become a Christian!" There was a long pause at the other end of the line, followed by "Well, that's interesting, Son. What were you before—a pagan?" The correct answer was "yes," but this insight was beyond my comprehension at the time.

I had glimpses that the family's Christianity was less than vibrant, beginning in September 1965. At that time my brother Ted (after whom my older son is named), the youngest of the three children, left the family home for his studies at Colgate University. From that point on, my parents' church attendance fell off significantly. I think Mom and Dad honestly felt they had done all that God could reasonably expect by being faithful in church attendance while their children were living at home. Moreover, I clearly remember a conversation with my dad about 20 years ago, in which we were discussing a publicly-debated issue of morality. I attempted to bolster my position by noting that the Bible agreed with me. Without a pause, my dad replied "Well, Son, in that case the Bible is wrong."

I would not want to leave any reader with the impression that my parents were bad. Such a conclusion would be utterly wrong. In fact, my beloved parents were very, very good, as the world counts people to be good. And the truth is that I am deeply grateful to God for the loving Mom and Dad that He gave to me. But the fact is that I grew up in a non-Christian American family, and without this understanding, little that I am going to share with you will make sense. I should note that before her death my mother was able to affirm the Christian faith of her youth (spent in Elmira, New York), but my father was always uncomfortable with the spiritual decision I made in 1973.

I was born in Grand Rapids, Michigan in 1944. At age one, the family moved to Syracuse, New York, where I attended kindergarten, first, and second grades at the Cherry Road School. At age 8 the family moved to the promised land, California. We lived in Menlo Park, immediately adjacent to the beautiful campus of Stanford University. I attended grades three through seven at the Hillview School, just two blocks from home. At age 13, the family moved back to my father's ancestral home, Grand Rapids, Michigan, when Dad received a major promotion at the American Seating Company, at the time the largest corporation in Grand Rapids (subsequently passed in size by the home sales giant Amway Corporation).

My father was a remarkable person, and not only in the devotion he showed to his family. Dad grew up in central Grand Rapids, two houses away from Gerald R. Ford, later to become the thirty-seventh President of the USA. Dad went off to the University of Michigan one year ahead of Jerry Ford, but they remained friends for life. The church we attended in Grand Rapids (Grace Episcopal Church) was socially prominent, and not a bad starting place if one aspired to membership in the Kent Country Club, the center of power in Western Michigan. My father eventually rose to become the second or third highest ranking person at the American Seating Company. But in 1968, when James Vermeulen retired as president of the company, my dad lost the battle for the presidency and took early retirement. Interestingly, the son of the man to whom my dad lost the presidency went on to become Dean of the Law School at the University of California at Berkeley, where I served for 18 years as a professor of chemistry.

My father was a strong believer in hard work. When he graduated from the University of Michigan in 1933 in civil engineering, the depression was in full force. Finding no jobs available in engineering, Dad returned to the family home in Grand Rapids and took a job sweeping the factory at the American Seating Company. He crept up the ladder of success, and with the approach of World War II, finally became an engineer, designing seats for U.S. combat airplanes. Following the war Dad continued to progress in the company, eventually reaching the position described in the previous paragraph. The effect of this history on me was that dad expected me to work. I had my first paper route at age 10, and moved up to a better paying position two years later, selling newspapers after school at the Safeway store on the El Camino Real in Menlo Park. In Grand Rapids, my first job was at Lakeside Foods, where I worked every Saturday for $0.75 per hour. My first full time job was during the summer of 1961 at the State Plating Company, located in a rather dangerous part of Grand Rapids. The work involved attaching small automobile parts to an assembly line and then removing them two hours later after the electroplating process was completed. The ambient temperature was about 120 degrees Fahrenheit, my pay was $1.50 per hour, and this was truly an introduction to the real world.

Halfway through the summer of 1961, my body became covered with red spots. I was sent to the family physician, Dr. Joseph Whinery, a good friend of my dad. Dr. Whinery examined the red spots, inquired of my summer activities, and intoned in the most serious manner "Son, I am afraid you are going to have to resign from your job at the plating factory." It was difficult to restrain my exhilaration, but realizing the potential results of the doctor's report to my father, I did my best to feign brokenness. Outside Dr. Whinery's office, I was positively jubilant, knowing that this late in the summer it would be impossible to find another job. So there I was, blissfully unemployed, the world at my feet. We lived on beautiful Fisk Lake in Grand Rapids, and I liked nothing better on a warm day than to swim in the lake and bask in the sun on our raft. The freedom of having nothing to do was fantastic— for about two weeks. At that point I realized that I was experiencing something entirely new to me, namely boredom.

Some sort of adventure was necessary to battle this unexpected malaise. So I decided to travel around Lake Michigan, one of the great inland lakes of the world, on my 125 cc Lambretta motor scooter. This 600 mile journey was indeed memorable and was completed in a week. However, the condition of boredom quickly returned, indeed with a greater intensity. It is a sobering experience, at the age of 17, to have everything you ever wanted (in my case, complete independence and freedom from work) and still be bored. In such a dilemma, heavy questions come to mind, such as "Is there any meaning or import to life?" I remember clearly one particular evening trying to get to sleep and feeling as if the ceiling in my bedroom was a hundred feet high (it was actually the standard height of eight feet). Normally I fall asleep within minutes of climbing into bed. That night, in August of 1961, I knew instinctively that sleep would not be possible. So I went upstairs to my parents' library, knowing that I could expect to find a good book there. The book I found was titled *The Prince of Life*, published by the Episcopal Church. It was a book about Jesus, and I read it from cover to cover that night, finishing at 5 AM. I did not become a Christian that night. I was not even convinced that there was significance to be found in life. But I did conclude that if the universe held purpose, it was somehow connected to the life of that man Jesus. And I made a decision that morning to read a chapter from the Bible every day, a habit that continued until the critical event of my life twelve years later.

With my father's recommendation, I went off to the Massachusetts Institute of Technology, adjacent to Boston, for my undergraduate studies. I quickly located one of the largest churches in Boston, Holy Trinity Episcopal, and embarked on four years of regular attendance. Therein, my inoculation against Christianity continued, indeed accelerated. The senior minister,

Theodore Ferris, was a theist and a warmhearted, elderly gentleman, who it was impossible not to like. However, the spirit of the church was embodied in the agnostic theology of the German academic Rudolf Bultmann, the Anglican bishop John A.T. Robinson, and Harvard Professor Paul Tillich. The latter liked to speak of a god who was "the ground of all being," Tillich and his admirers imagining this to be a profound thought. Some years later, while lecturing at the national meeting of the American Chemical Society, I was delighted to stay in a hotel right next to Holy Trinity Episcopal Church. Between scientific sessions one afternoon, I went into the magnificent sanctuary, hoping to find some evidence of spiritual life. Among materials the church offered gratis to visitors, I seized upon an eight page booklet entitled *The Foundation of Holy Trinity Episcopal Church*. "Aha," I thought: although I seemed to be going nowhere spiritually during my years at M.I.T., perhaps I was absorbing some important ideas. Taking the booklet back to my hotel, I found the opening sentence to read "The foundation of Holy Trinity Episcopal Church is constructed upon 1074 piers drilled deep into the Back Bay of Boston." The booklet continued for eight pages to describe the structural details of the building, considered by many to be the foremost wonder of American church architecture.

Following my freshman year at M.I.T., it was back to the plating factory. Actually, this was an upscale plating factory, the Keeler Brass Company. My salary was elevated to $2.50 per hour and my fellow employees were of a more stable sort. I made it through the summer without an allergic reaction to the chemicals. Instead of one huge assembly line, Keeler Brass functioned with perhaps twenty smaller assembly lines. Each of these was operated by two persons, one senior and one junior. It quickly became apparent to me that I had been assigned to a person who was head and shoulders above the rest of the employees in ethical character. For example, my boss did not follow the widespread practice of inflating his machine's production figures. This man was about 25 years old and a student at the Grand Rapids Bible College, working the night shift to support his family of five. Now you need to know that in the socio-economic circle in which I was raised, the word "Baptist" had some pretty frightening connotations. Perhaps you have seen the scenically spectacular

Robert Redford movie *A River Runs Through It*. The father of the two main characters is a Presbyterian minister in Bozeman, Montana. One of the sons falls in love with a young woman who is a Methodist. When the son asks his father "What is a Methodist?" the father replies "A Methodist is a Baptist who can read." I must sheepishly admit

When the son asks his father "What is a Methodist?" the father replies "A Methodist is a Baptist who can read." that this was my opinion of Baptists in the summer of 1963. But the man I worked for reflected a quality of life I had never before observed, and my views about Baptists changed significantly over the summer.

During the 1963-64 academic year I took the full dose of organic chemistry laboratory. This was before the age of federal safety standards, and we students could work in the laboratory at essentially any hour of the day or night. This was a gift from heaven for me, since I seemed to take at least twice as long as the other students to complete the assigned organic preparations. One night after most of the other students had finished their lab work, the teaching assistant (TA) John Sheats (now a Professor of Chemistry at Ryder College near Princeton) came by to see what was taking me so long. John Sheats was a truly outstanding TA, infinitely patient and always helpful to the students. After making some desperately needed lab suggestions, John told me that at my age a young man sometimes gave consideration to three things, namely his future occupation, his future life partner, and his relationship with God. After a good discussion of the first two topics, he proceeded to share with me how to become a Christian. I would continue to resist God for another nine years, so I politely declined, but I have never forgotten our conversation. Incidentally, John Sheats was part of a student group called Campus Crusade for Christ. My pagan friends and I called them the "God Squad," but I never felt the same about them after that evening's discussion with my favorite teaching assistant.

During the summer of 1964, I took second-year German (then required for a chemistry major) back in Grand Rapids at Calvin College. Calvin College was and is a Christian institution, so as a part of the application procedures, I had to write a brief essay on my spiritual condition. I explained glibly that although people once believed the Bible to have historical value, modern intellectuals such as I knew better now. Obviously, they were willing to accept a few non-Christians, at least for the summer term. The remarkable thing about my German class at Calvin College was that the professor began each class with prayer. This confirmed all I had picked up during my high school years in Grand Rapids about the religious fanatics who made up perhaps 30% of the city's population and had Dutch last names. But I honestly was not too offended by the prayers before German class. My parents had little sympathy for the religious views of the Grand Rapids Christians of Dutch descent, but Mom and Dad recognized them to be hard working, honest people who made good neighbors.

I had been infatuated with a girl named Karen Rasmussen since my junior year at East Grand Rapids High School. I used to sit a few rows in front of her in a large study hall of perhaps 150 students. I still remember that when she went to the front of the auditorium to sharpen her pencil, my heartbeat would rapidly accelerate. I lived for those moments. And not without reason, as Karen went on to become Homecoming Queen of her senior class, one year behind me. We had a few dates in high school, but my interest was only reciprocated in friendship. But while I was home for the summer of 1964, taking German at Calvin College, the opportunity of a lifetime presented itself. Karen's brother Eric was taking calculus at the local junior college that summer, to fulfill a requirement for medical school (he went on to become a distinguished ear, nose, and throat physician near Seattle). Having taken no mathematics course during the previous four years, Eric was not doing well. So, who was called to the rescue, but Karen's nerd friend from M.I.T., yours truly. Of course, it would have been awkward to throw the tutor out of the house after his calculus duties were completed, so I hung around for an hour or so every evening to talk with Karen. Karen must have found something about me that was better than she had seen in high school, because shortly after we both went back to college at the end of the summer, she was wearing my SAE fraternity pin. Incidentally, Eric got the grade of "B" he needed in the calculus class, and Karen's dad, the renowned thoracic surgeon of Western Michigan, paid me $75 for my tutoring efforts.

Karen's family attended the East Congregational Church in Grand Rapids. It was slightly less prestigious than my church socially, but the absence of Christian belief was comparable. So we well understood each other when we conversed about spiritual things. Karen actually became a religion minor (her major was in art history) as an undergraduate at Wells College (founded by Henry Wells of Wells-Fargo fame), which is 25 miles up the road from Cornell University on Lake Cayuga in upstate New York. She related one story to me from Professor Litzenburg's New Testament course that ended up having a profound influence on both of us. Examining the book of Acts in the New Testament, Dr. Litzenburg asked Karen's class how they could explain the boldness of Jesus' friends six weeks after his death. This boldness was particularly surprising, since these same men had been cowering in a locked room immediately following Jesus' death. Dr. Litzenburg noted that perhaps, just perhaps, these men were radically changed by something remarkable that they might have seen with their own eyes—a dead man walking.

Every senior at M.I.T. must submit a research thesis in order to graduate. I wanted to be a spectroscopist, but I couldn't get up the nerve to ask Professor Richard Lord if I could work in his lab. The course advisor for all the M.I.T. seniors in chemistry was Professor Walter Thorson, and eventually he asked me why I was taking so long to find a lab in which to do my thesis research. Sensing my dilemma, Dr. Thorson appealed to vanity: "Schaefer, you seem to be the best chemistry student in the senior class, why don't you do theoretical chemistry with me?" Walter Thorson was voted the most popular chemistry professor at M.I.T. by the undergraduates that year, so I was happy to work for him. The Thorson research group included four Ph.D. students and me, so we got to know each other reasonably well. Professor Thorson somehow learned that I had a vague interest in spiritual things, and he one day asked me "Would you like to know the best reason I believe in God?" Being an obedient research student, I answered in the affirmative. His rejoinder was "Because I talk to Him every day." That was an eerie response to me, strongly reminiscent of the frightening paranormal television series *The Twilight Zone*, quite popular at the time. In hindsight Dr. Thorson was trying to explain to me the nature of prayer, but this was far beyond me at the time. Despite that uneasy exchange, I respected Walter

Thorson enormously, and it was clear to me that his Christianity was genuine.

On September 2, 1966 I married the woman of my dreams, and Karen and I spent our honeymoon driving 2000 miles from Michigan to California, where we would both be students at Stanford University. Karen would complete her undergraduate degree in art history, and I began my doctoral studies in chemical physics. We began to attend St. Mark's Episcopal Church in Palo Alto, although our first Sunday's experience was a bit of a shock. Arriving too early for the church service, we were directed to a Sunday School class taught by the senior minister, Leonard P. Wittlinger. Rev. Wittlinger spent 45 minutes describing Mao Zedong as one of the most outstanding examples of Christianity in the 20th century. With Mao's Cultural Revolution in full bloom, this was hard to swallow. But we met a wonderful couple, Jim and Nan Hobson, after church, and they invited us to their cozy home for lunch. Jim worked for the Hoover Institution, a conservative think tank at Stanford, and he and Nan were from the South, in fact the first southerners we had ever known. The Hobsons' friendship kept us at St. Mark's for more than a year, despite the political orientation of the minister. However, on a fateful Sunday morning the Reverend Wittlinger stated in his sermon that a survey of the congregation had been made, and a large fraction of the congregation was uncertain of its belief in God. Not to worry, said the minister, because he has not sure if he believed in God a large fraction of the time. We never returned to St. Mark's Episcopal Church. As a postscript, Leonard Wittlinger left the ministry a year or so later and became a wealthy man selling real estate in Palo Alto.

The next stop on our spiritual journey was the First United Methodist Church in downtown Palo Alto. The minister was a silver-haired, grandfatherly person whose sermons primarily concerned the war in Vietnam. Should this seem a bit strange, the reader should be reminded that the year was 1968. We were living 30 miles south of San Francisco; drugs, sex, and political protest were as described in the movie *Forrest Gump*. After hearing all we cared to about the Vietnamese War, we tried a few other churches before settling in at St. Bede's Episcopal Church, just across Sand Hill Road from the Stanford Linear Accelerator. This church is a jewel of contemporary California architecture, constructed almost entirely of native redwood. The minister was an Englishman, Father John Burns. Father Burns was highly intelligent, believed in God, and did not think that the only reasonable sermon material was the tragic situation in Vietnam. Professor Harold Bacon of the mathematics department at Stanford was a member at St. Bede's, and he and his wife were legendary in opening their home to students. The lunches we had at their welcoming home on the Stanford campus were truly memorable. Harold Bacon believed in God.

The opening words of Father Burns' sermon at St. Bede's Episcopal Church still ring in my ears. He began "This whole business of Christianity is a sham if Jesus did not rise from the dead."

The most remarkable church experience of my life occurred on Easter Sunday 1969. The opening words of Father Burns' sermon at St. Bede's Episcopal Church still ring in my ears. He began "This whole business of Christianity is a sham if Jesus did not rise from the dead." After the church service I went to Father Burns and told him that I had been struck by his first sentence. He asked if I believed in the resurrection of Christ. I responded that I hadn't thought much about it, although it was a possibility that Karen's religion professor had raised four years earlier. John Burns challenged me to consider the historical evidence for the resurrection of Jesus.

The timing was perfect because my agnostic and atheist friends were all excited at the time about a book titled *The Passover Plot*. The latter book read like a fast-paced novel, a real page turner. The story line in *The Passover Plot* went something like this. Jesus was whipped to a degree which, in and of itself, killed a significant fraction of its victims. Then he carried the cross up the hill outside Jerusalem until he collapsed and was relieved by a curious passerby. Jesus was crucified, hung on the cross for six hours, and was finally pierced in the side with a large spear, water and blood gushing forth. Jesus' body was then placed in a burial cave. Following this factual description, the author of *The Passover Plot* concludes irrationally that the coolness of the cave revived Jesus, and a couple of days later he knocked the socks off his closest friends by appearing in perfect health. My response to this conclusion was utter and complete incredulity. Scientifically, the probability that Jesus did not die was so close to zero as to be immeasurable. Indeed, it was the implausibility of *The Passover Plot* that caused me to seriously begin to investigate the historical evidence for the resurrection of Jesus.

My examination of the historical evidence for the resurrection of Christ continued for nearly three years. In time I became convinced from the evidence not only that Jesus rose from the dead, but that this certainty is one of the best attested facts of ancient history. A widely accessible book that addresses this subject is Frank Morrison's *Who Moved the Stone?* Significantly weightier is University of Manchester Professor F. F. Bruce's brilliant *The New Testament Documents: Are They Reliable?* For those requiring a more purely scholarly work, I recommend Wolfhart Pannenberg's classic 1977 treatise *Jesus—God and Man*. The masterly intellectual treatment of this subject for the early twenty-first century has just appeared in print (Fortress Press, 2003). This is Dr. N. T. Wright's 817 page opus entitled *The Resurrection of the Son of God*.

It might be nice if I could report that I became a Christian once I was prevailed upon intellectually to conclude that Jesus rose from the dead. However, such was not the case, and other parts of my rescue need to be acknowledged.

In December of 1968 I accepted a faculty position at the University of California at Berkeley as assistant professor. It was unusual to do so at age 24 and without research experience beyond the Ph.D. More importantly, it was providential, because the job market for young scholars went very sour shortly thereafter, and many of my gifted classmates had challenges to find suitable positions from which to launch their independent scientific careers. From Stanford, Karen and I moved 40 miles north to the bucolic little town of Orinda, just over the coastal hills from Berkeley. Karen accepted a great job teaching fourth graders (10-year olds) in the adjacent hamlet of Moraga, and I traveled eight miles a day into Berkeley. Our lives were simple: we both worked about 80 hours each week and spent the rest of the time with each other.

For our first week in Orinda, we chose the local Episcopal

church, St. Stephen's. All was well until our third Sunday in attendance. On that day the church took up a second collection of money, this time for the legal defense of a woman named Angela Davis. Angela Davis was an assistant professor of philosophy at the University of California at Los Angeles (UCLA). It had recently become known that Ms. Davis was a high-ranking officer of the U.S. Communist Party, and she had been dismissed from the UCLA faculty. So the Episcopal Church was coming to the rescue of the Communist Party, a bit reminiscent of Rev. Leonard Wittlinger's defense of Mao Zedong, the purported model Christian. Although I have never been a Marxist, my objection to Angela Davis came from a different source. The first thing one did upon joining the faculty of any campus of the University of California was to sign "the oath." In the oath one made a legally binding statement that he or she had never, and did not now, belong to any organization that advocated the violent overthrow of the U.S. government, or worse yet, the government of the State of California. My grievance against Angela Davis was that she had deliberately lied when she took the oath. Being a communist was one thing, but lying was much worse in my bourgeois code of ethics. We did not contribute financially to the Angela Davis defense fund that day and never returned to St. Stephen's Episcopal Church.

By this time, Karen and I had tried the Episcopal Church, the Congregational Church and the Methodist Church. Reflecting on my German and Karen's Danish heritage, we decided to try something new, the Lutheran Church (Parenthetical note: my German credentials are a bit weak: my ancestors fled from Germany as draft dodgers or political radicals way back in 1852). So we drove five miles east to Our Savior's Lutheran Church in the neighboring town of Lafayette. This was a remarkable church. The people were very friendly. They sang the hymns as if they meant them, not just to give themselves a chance to stand up and relieve the boredom of the service. But again the third Sunday presented a crisis. The minister, Al Rommereim, gave a sermon about hell and the devil. Far worse, he spoke as if hell were a real place and the devil a real person. Well, that was over the top, irrespective of the attractiveness of the church. Karen and I were willing to countenance the concept of the devil as the metaphorical personification of evil. But the notion that the devil was a real person was surely a remnant of the dark ages. It went against everything we had been taught growing up. And thus, we never returned to Our Savior's Lutheran Church.

In contemplating our diminishing religious options, Karen and I concluded that we were a bit more distant from the communists than from those who believed in the devil. So we tried another Lutheran church, this one ten miles from home in the larger town of Walnut Creek. Trinity Lutheran Church was another welcoming church, and the pastor, Paul Meyer, did not give any sermons about hell and the devil for our first few years there. In fact, on our fifth Sunday at the church, Dr. Meyer asked if we would be willing to work with the church's high school students. In retrospect, this was not a sensible move for the church. Unbeknownst to Dr. Meyer, Karen and I could not yet affirm any of the central truths of the Christian faith. However, Karen and I were young and energetic, and we possessed a significant asset for the church—a brand new fire engine red 1969 Chevrolet Suburban, capable of carrying 20 teenagers in the age before seatbelt laws.

Our first assignment with Trinity Lutheran's high school students was to transport them to a barbecue and kite-flying event on the slopes of nearby Mt. Diablo. Following an afternoon of fun, the group of perhaps 20 gathered in a circle and held hands. That was a decidedly uncomfortable undertaking for me, as I had never enjoyed holding anyone's hand except Karen's. Then the teenagers said they were going to pray. Now my own experience of prayer was primarily a matter of opening the Episcopal Church's *Book of Common Prayer* and reading from the appropriate place in the book. In striking contrast, several of these high school students appeared to be conversing in a natural way with someone; and they thought that someone was God! Perhaps most surprising was the fact that the ones who were praying appeared to be normal, healthy, vibrant high school students. It was an experience I shall never forget.

Assignment #2 from the church turned out to be rather frightening. We were to transport 25 of the youth group to the Oakland Civic Center to hear a man named David Wilkerson. I was told that Mr. Wilkerson had written a book entitled *The Cross and the Switchblade* that several of the high school students had read and found compelling. Karen and I got them all to the auditorium safely and positioned the group in the balcony, to be a little distant from the action. Wilkerson seemed to me a very stern person that evening; he bluntly insisted that anyone who wanted to whisper during his presentation leave the building. It became very quiet. Moreover, Wilkerson was using a vocabulary that was completely alien to me: terms like "give your life to Christ," "get saved," "born again," "accept Jesus," and many others. About two-thirds of the way through the meeting, he asked all the kids who wanted "to do business with God" to come down to the front. This sounded OK to me, until half of our charges proceeded to walk downstairs. My immediate concern was that I would be unable to regather our students in the Suburban, and that several would be murdered in the dangerous part of Oakland surrounding the Civic Center. With perhaps 2000 students down on the floor of the Civic Center, David Wilkerson told them that before they "Did business with God," there was some other business that had to be accomplished. When Wilkerson asked the teenagers to deposit all their drugs and drug paraphernalia in front of him, I thought he was joking. The kids on the floor looked pretty clean cut to me. It is hard to express the astonishment I felt when the pile of drugs became three feet tall. Furthermore, I could not be certain that the kids from Trinity Lutheran had not contributed to the pile. I cannot remember what David Wilkerson said after he collected the drugs. It must have been more about doing business with God. But his collection had a tremendous impact on me. Karen and I had never done drugs, and we were in agreement that drugs were a terrible thing. Whatever Wilkinson was up to, we had to admire him for apparently reducing the drug usage in the San Francisco Bay Area. We did manage to reassemble our high school students that night and return them all safely to the church. Equally important, God was slowly dissolving the inoculation we had received against genuine Christianity.

Some time later, we conveyed the high school students from Trinity Lutheran to a Billy Graham campaign in Sacramento, 80 miles northeast of Walnut Creek. Billy Graham made me a lot more comfortable than David Wilkerson, but I had to admit that the basic message was about the same. I was becoming more sympathetic to Christianity (this was the period in which I was considering the evidence for the resurrection of Jesus), but still quietly resisting the threat of turning over my life to someone else, namely Christ. One particular student at Trinity Lutheran seemed remarkable to me. Craig Mechler was one of the stars of the Ygnacio Valley High School football team. This was a public high school of perhaps 2000 students, and the football players were "big men on campus." The interesting thing was that Craig Mechler had been at best a mediocre football player in his first year or so at the high school, occupying his spare time doing drugs. But then he became a Christian, and everything changed, including his performance on the football field. Craig Mechler was very straightforward in telling all who were interested about the change Jesus had made in his life.

Summoning my vast resources of ignorance and unbelief, I explained that although modern people knew the Bible to be full of errors and contradictions, there were great practical principles to be drawn from the study of a book like Exodus.

About this time, Paul Meyer, the pastor, asked if I would teach a Sunday School Class for the high school students. I figured that if I could teach chemistry to university students at Berkeley, I would surely be adequate in Sunday School, where the students were typically four years younger. The assignment was Exodus, the second book of the Bible. My first lesson was a sweeping introduction not just to Exodus but to the whole Bible. Summoning my vast resources of ignorance and unbelief, I explained that although modern people knew the Bible to be full of errors and contradictions, there were great practical principles to be drawn from the study of a book like Exodus. The famous skeptics Rudolf Bultmann and Paul Tillich could not have done better! As I recall, my scholarly discourse that morning was not well received by Craig Mechler. I think Craig may even have suggested that if I didn't believe the Bible, he would ask Pastor Meyer to have someone else teach the Sunday School class. Following a few days of cogitation, a helpful analogy occurred to me. In freshman chemistry, to lessen confusion on the part of the embattled students, we sometimes simplify the material in ways that are not entirely truthful. This is what I would do with the Sunday School class! I would teach the book of Exodus as if it were true.

In my role as teacher, I quickly became aware that several of my students knew a great deal more about the Bible than I. Therefore, to avoid embarrassment, I adopted a Socratic style of teaching. One of the high school students would read a few sentences from the Bible, and I would ask the class what it meant. This allowed me to keep my heretical ideas to myself, at least until the students established the correct meaning of the text. These Sunday School classes went on for several years, progressing through a number of books of the Bible. A moment of truth arrived in 1973 (I know not the exact date) during my teaching of the first letter from the apostle John, the closest friend of Jesus. In the thirteenth verse of chapter five, St. John states "These things have I written, that you may know that you have eternal life, you that believe in the Son of God (I John 5:13)." I was honestly puzzled by the verse, so I asked the students what it meant. The brightest of the group immediately answered "That's easy! It means you can know you're going to heaven if you know Jesus." I did not think her conclusion so easy, as I had gone 28 years without knowing Jesus and without a clue to my eternal destiny. In fact, three years earlier, if someone had told me she knew she was going to heaven, I would have considered it arrogance in the extreme. Karen and I discussed this verse later in the day. I checked my Bible in the evening, and the verse had not disappeared. The same result was found the next morning.

Know you're going to heaven? That was the assurance the young woman in Sunday School class had acknowledged. It was a remarkable thought to me. It went against everything I had learned growing up. This view from my past was explicitly confirmed in a discussion with my dad two years later. I asked Dad if he had confidence that he would end up in heaven. He said "Of course not, Son. No one could know such a thing with certainty." Then my father proceeded to explain the procedure by which he thought God would determine who was going to heaven. He said "Son, you ought to be able to understand this. It's just like the analytical balance I used at the University of Michigan when I studied chemistry. God is going to put all the good things you've done in life on one side of the balance, and all the bad things on the other side of the balance. If there is a little more of the good, you're on your way to heaven. Otherwise, it could be a long time in a hot place." I realized that my dad had expressed rather graphically the opinion I held for the first 25 years of my life.

But I had always wondered just what was the instrument God used to weigh the good stuff against the bad. How did something pretty good that I did get related to something really bad? During my first four years as a professor at Berkeley I had learned a number of things about Jesus that were quite new to me. One of them hit me particularly hard. Many people of various religions or no religion at all are familiar with Jesus' famous "Sermon on the Mount." Toward the end, Jesus sets out a standard of behavior well beyond the reach of anyone I have met: "Love your enemies, bless those who curse you, do good to those who hate you, pray for those who persecute you." Immediately thereafter, Jesus gives us the standard for admission to heaven: "You must be perfect, even as your Father in heaven is perfect."

Within the next few days, the pieces of the puzzle came together. I realized that I could know that I am going to heaven, but not because of any adequacy of my own. For those who want to enter heaven on their own merits, the standard is perfection. And I knew that my life did not even measure up to my own standards, not to mention the standards of an all-holy God. But Jesus did live that perfect life. And he died on the cross for all who put their exclusive trust in him. Jesus took the punishment for my sins, which are many. By trusting exclusively in Christ, I will be able to stand in the presence of the God of the universe.

There was no one with me to lead me in a prayer of submission to Jesus. But in the course of a few days of reflection at age 28, a young Berkeley chemistry professor realized that he had become a Christian. And I knew that my life would never be the same. I hope you can see that God was trying to get my attention for a very long time. So many cobwebs had to be knocked out of my attic, as it were. Perhaps the same may be true of your own life.

Although much more could be said, perhaps only one thing further is necessary. You will surely note above that I did not have confidence in the veracity of the Bible when I became a Christian. I had become convinced by the historical evidence that Jesus had risen from the dead in a manner unprecedented in human experience. But it would be several more years before I became convinced of the truthfulness of the Bible. The spurious notion that the Bible was full of errors was strongly impressed upon me as a young person, and that false impression was not easily removed. Following the conversion experience I have described here, I began to study the Bible more earnestly. I would examine each one of the supposed problems, in much the same way a scientist approaches a problem in the natural world. Gradually, I discovered that each of these so-called errors could be explained in terms of history, the context of the passage, or the correct use of the original language. Fortunately, you do not need to work as hard at this as I did. In 1982 the polymath Professor Gleason L. Archer published his landmark volume entitled the *Encyclopedia of Bible Difficulties*. Therein, Archer systematically goes through the collection of purported errors and destroys them one by one. With Dr. Archer's assistance, you can learn that the Bible is true much more rapidly than I did.

The Way of Discovery*   10

I would like to take as my theme this evening the title of a biography of Michael Polanyi. The book, written by Richard Gelwick (1976), is called *The Way of Discovery*. I consider Michael Polanyi to be one of the most interesting figures in twentieth century intellectual history. Michael Polanyi was born into a Jewish family in Budapest in 1891. Polanyi was a brilliant physical chemistry professor in England who later became even better known as a philosopher. Interestingly, about the time his scholarly work began to turn in a philosophical direction, Polanyi joined the Roman Catholic Church. I have known Michael Polanyi's son John, Professor of Chemistry at the University of Toronto, for thirty years. In the early years, perhaps 1971, I had an occasion to introduce John Polanyi for a lecture at Berkeley, and I noted that all in the audience were familiar with the outstanding research of his famous father. But that became less necessary in October 1986, when the son, John Polanyi, received the Nobel Prize in Chemistry. But, under the assumption that one size fits all, I now contend that the son's greatness speaks well for the father!

My opinion is that Michael Polanyi's contributions to the philosophy of science are among the most profound of the twentieth century. Many of these may be viewed in his short but challenging book *Personal Knowledge* (1958). Although the work of Thomas Kuhn (especially his 1962 book *The Structure of Scientific Revolutions*) is perhaps better known, an honest assessment of Kuhn's work reveals significant aspects that are derivative of Michael Polanyi's earlier analysis. Polanyi makes the point in *Personal Knowledge* and elsewhere that scientists are not robots, mechanically filling up notebooks with data and coming to inevitable conclusions. To put it another way, science is not just an advanced exercise in logical positivism. Rather, Polanyi argues, there is much of the artist in the good scientist, and he or she

*An address presented originally at the All-Campus Worship Service, University of California, Berkeley, California on September 29, 1985. This address has gradually evolved over the years, but the outline is essentially unchanged.

approaches the laboratory with a wealth of presuppositions and intuition about how things should be.

I can confirm Polanyi's thesis with an example from my own research. In 1978 one of the most distinguished organic chemists in the world, UCLA Professor Orville Chapman, suggested that it was just a matter of time before the cyclopropyne molecule would be made. Since cyclopropyne would contain a carbon-carbon triple bond in a three-membered ring, my own chemical intuition was very skeptical about such a suggestion. Guided by this presupposition, we were able to demonstrate that cyclopropyne does not involve a triple bond.

One can find pieces of Michael Polanyi's thesis scattered throughout the philosophy of science. For example, none other than Albert Einstein wrote in 1938 that "Physical concepts are free creations of the human mind and are not, however it may seem, uniquely determined by the physical world." So intuition and presupposition in science are by no means harmful, as long as they are continually refined in the dialogue with observation. A colossal example of a failure to refine one's intuition via experiment is Einstein's lifelong distaste for quantum mechanics. Einstein strongly objected to the probabilistic interpretation of quantum mechanics. He argued that while quantum mechanics might be useful, it was at best an incomplete theory. Einstein dreamed of a theory that was, from a human perspective, fully causal and deterministic. At a conference in the late 1920's, Einstein was asked to explain his objections to quantum mechanics. His response, as usual, was that "God does not play dice with the universe." The moderator immediately turned to Einstein's nemesis in this regard, Niels Bohr, with the question "Professor Bohr, would you care to comment?" To which Bohr responded "Albert, stop telling God what He can do!" In 1979 I spent an hour talking with John Wheeler, one of Einstein's closest colleagues at Princeton, on this very matter. I asked Wheeler for a fuller explanation of Einstein's hostility to quantum mechanics. Wheeler stated, "The whole problem was that Einstein did not believe the Genesis story – he never accepted the Big Bang Theory."

Intuition and presupposition are necessary ingredients to discovery. I am a theoretical chemist by profession. Prior to my first involvement with Freshman Chemistry in 1984, I had spent most of my first 14 years on the Berkeley faculty doing research in theoretical chemistry. My research consists of using mathematical equations and computers to understand the electronic structure of molecules. More specifically, we attempt to predict the shapes of molecules, their energetics, their spectra, and how they react with other molecules.

As Polanyi points out, the real excitement of science is the excitement of discovery. To observe things that no human being has ever seen. To discover a new and potentially important molecule or a new type of chemical reaction. If you were to ask the average Ph.D. chemist on the street what my most important discovery was, he or she would probably say "the structure of methylene". From time to time, people actually do ask me "What is your most important discovery?" And I respond that the most important discovery in my life occurred during my fourth year on the faculty at Berkeley. Although I was still an assistant professor I had been told that the chemistry department was going to recommend my promotion to tenure. So this was not a time of professional turbulence, since I had already been married for seven years to the most wonderful woman in the world. Karen and I celebrated our 35th anniversary in Rome, nine days before the events of September 11. At the time of this discovery, my students and I were doing some very interesting theoretical work on the identification of the interstellar molecules hydrogen isocyanide and protonated carbon monoxide.

(1) But the most important discovery of my life was my discovery of Jesus Christ. In 1973 I discovered the real Jesus, the Jesus of history, the Jesus whose life is described on the pages of the New Testament. The Jesus I discovered 35 years ago was rather different from the one I had heard of in church as a boy. That Jesus was a well-intentioned, infinitely tolerant person who laid down some simple moral rules which all religions now embrace. The real Jesus bore some resemblance to the Jesus of my youth, but not very much. In particular the real Jesus sharply challenged the religious leaders of His time. And He claimed to be the only way to heaven, stating that all who declared otherwise were thieves, robbers, and false prophets. The real Jesus was a very controversial person. As C. S. Lewis has well said, there were primarily three responses to Jesus in His own lifetime: hatred, terror, and adoration.

(2) I discovered that on a Sunday morning 1980 years ago Jesus rose physically from the dead. I discovered that the resurrection of Jesus is not only historically true, but that it is one of the best attested facts in all of ancient history. If you have not made this discovery yet, I would strongly encourage you to examine the evidence carefully. A good introductory discussion of the evidence for the resurrection is given in Frank Morrison's book *Who Moved the Stone?* A more challenging exposition is Wolfhart Pannenberg's 1977 but already classic *Jesus – God and Man*. The definitive statement for the early twentieth century is N. T. Wright's 817 page (Fortress Press, 2003) *The Resurrection of the Son of God*.

(3) I discovered that when the apostles spoke of Jesus being the Son of God, they didn't mean that God was His Father in some vague and undefinable way. Jesus closest companions meant that He was God the Son. Jesus Christ, the carpenter from Nazareth, was and is God almighty. As the *Westminster Confession* states "In the unity of the Godhead, there are three persons, of one substance, power, and eternity."

(4) I discovered that I could know for certain that I am going to heaven. Now this may strike some of you as a terribly arrogant statement. And it would be if it were based on anything I had done. But I'm going to heaven not because of anything I have done, but in spite of everything I've done. I'm going to heaven because Jesus died on the cross for my rebelliousness and disobedience.

(5) I discovered that the New Testament is a reliable historical document. When I became a Christian in 1973 I was not sure of this, but a book by the British classics scholar F. F. Bruce changed my thinking in this regard. And as time went by I came to a deep respect for the Old Testament as well, because I discovered that Jesus personally spoke for the authenticity of that book. I want to emphasize here that a belief in the complete truthfulness of the Bible need not carry with it a wooden or unnaturally literalistic understanding of every verse. To quote a statement of conviction (the Chicago inerrancy statement of 1977) that I

like very much, "We affirm that God in His work of inspiration (of the Bible, that is) utilized the distinctive personalities and literary styles of the writers whom He had chosen and prepared." In this context, my personal opinion is that the universe probably is 13-15 billion years old. And I am convinced that such a view is completely consistent with the teaching of the first chapter of *Genesis*. For those of you who want to go into this matter in depth, I recommend James Montgomery Boice's commentary on the first eleven chapters of *Genesis*.

(6) I discovered that I could share my new-found faith in Jesus with friends and with strangers. I discovered that most of the questions that people have about Christianity boil down to about ten distinct questions, and that there are intellectually sound answers to all ten. One of my most interesting experiences in sharing Christ occurred in California in 1979. My wife Karen and I and a friend paid a visit on a husband and wife who had visited our church. We should have expected something unusual because this couple was only about 25 years old and they lived in a $500,000 house. Furthermore, the man who answered the door was about 6'8" tall. As we sat around getting acquainted I asked Tom where he and Susie had come from, to find that they had just moved up from Los Angeles. When I asked what kind of work Tom did, he replied that he was in professional sports. I was still oblivious to all this and so was Karen, but fortunately the third member of our party recognized that we were talking to the starting forward for the Golden State Warriors and blurted out "Oh, so you're that Tom Abernathy!" But the best part of that evening was the ending. Two hours after that awkward introduction, Tom and Susie Abernathy received Jesus Christ as Savior and Lord.

(7) I discovered that there is no problem too heavy for Jesus to deal with. Twenty-nine years ago I spent several months at the University of Texas. I would have two weeks in Texas, then come home to Berkeley for a couple of weeks and so on. On a Sunday morning (December 9, 1979, to be exact) I had just returned from church and was tidying up a few

things in my office in Austin. My wife called and told me that our five-month old son Pierre had just died of crib death, or sudden infant death syndrome. Whatever illusions I had that life was just a bowl of cherries disappeared forever in that instant of time. Without going into the details, I can stand here tonight and tell you that never before or since have I been so overwhelmed with the certainty of the love of my heavenly Father. There is no problem in your life that Jesus can't bring you through.

(8) I discovered that life with Jesus begins at the moment of conversion, continues to the moment of my physical death, and then on to eternity. Jesus is not only interested in extracting a prayer of submission from me. He wants to change my whole life. And that is a tremendous and ongoing challenge. Three times during the past two decades I have led Bible studies on the book of *Revelation*. It is always exciting! One of the fringe benefits of studying *Revelation* is that it allows you to understand what Bob Dylan has been saying (for example, his song *When the Night Comes Falling from the Sky*) in his music for the last twenty years. Something I found in Chapter 14 of *Revelation* was a real challenge to me, and I hope it will be to you. *Revelation* 14:1 states "The believers in Jesus had His name and His Father's name written on their foreheads." And three verses later we read "They follow the Lamb wherever He goes." Have you openly identified yourself as a follower of Jesus Christ? Do you endeavor to follow Jesus wherever He goes?

(9) Finally, I discovered that the intellectual challenge to fully understand the riches of the Christian faith is quite comparable to that required to plumb the depths of molecular quantum mechanics. I've been at the former in earnest for a quarter century and haven't come close to exhausting the wealth of even 20th century Christian intellectual writing. My scholarly hero for the period through 1940 is Princeton Professor J. Gresham Machen. Machen's great books *The Origin of Paul's Religion* and *Christianity and Liberalism* are holding up extremely well in the first years of the twenty-first century. Almost anything

written by C.S. Lewis is good – my advice is to read it all. If you want to understand existentialism, read Francis Schaeffer. An excellent book to start with is *The God Who Is There*. I think that Francis Schaeffer's early writings, including *Escape from Reason* and *He is There and He is Not Silent* get better with each passing year. If you like biography and history, as I do, read Arnold Dallimore's two volumes on the great English evangelist George Whitefield. I've read many biographies and Dallimore's Whitefield is the best; I have read it four times. If you want to concentrate on Bible study and have gone through the lighter commentaries, check out Martin Lloyd-Jones' eight volumes on the Apostle Paul's Letter to the Romans. Lloyd-Jones speaks with authority to both the intellect and the heart. And finally, if your passion is theology, make an investment in Carl Henry's six volumes of *God, Revelation, and Authority*. I think Carl Henry is one of the most outstanding theologians of this generation. His wisdom overflows each of these volumes.

I would like to close this address with a series of four questions that Francis Schaeffer (no relation to me) asked to a young woman who had come to Switzerland searching for truth.

(a) He asked her, first, did she believe that God existed - God as clearly revealed in the Bible, who is infinite and yet can be known personally?

(b) Second, did she recognize that she was a sinner in light of God's perfect standards? Or was she just comparing herself to other sinners in order to get a passing grade?

(c) Third, did she believe that Jesus Christ truly came in space, time, and history?

(d) And fourth, would she bow to Him and accept what He, Christ, did for her individually by taking her deserved punishment on the cross?

If you are searching for truth in the universe, my earnest desire is that you will seriously consider these four questions.

180   *The Way of Discovery*

About the Author

enry F. Schaefer III was born in Grand Rapids, Michigan in 1944. He attended public schools in Syracuse (New York), Menlo Park (California), and Grand Rapids (Michigan), graduating from East Grand Rapids High School in 1962. He received his B.S. degree in chemical physics from the Massachusetts Institute of Technology (1966) and Ph.D. degree in chemical physics from Stanford University (1969). For 18 years (1969-1987) he served as a professor of chemistry at the University of California, Berkeley. During the 1979-1980 academic year he was also Wilfred T. Doherty Professor of Chemistry and inaugural Director of the Institute for Theoretical Chemistry at the University of Texas, Austin. Since 1987 Dr. Schaefer has been Graham Perdue Professor of Chemistry and Director of the Center for Computational Chemistry at the University of Georgia. In 2004 he became Professor of Chemistry, Emeritus, at the University of California at Berkeley. His other academic appointments include Professeur d'Echange at the University of Paris (1977), Gastprofessur at the Eidgenossische Technische Hochshule (ETH), Zurich (1994, 1995, 1997, 2000, 2002, 2004, 2006, 2008), and David P. Craig Visiting Professor at the Australian National University (1999). He is the author of more than 1150 scientific publications, the majority appearing in the Journal of Chemical Physics or the Journal of the American Chemical Society. A total of 300 scientists from 35 countries gathered in Gyeongju, Korea for a six-day conference in February, 2004 with the title "Theory and Applications of Computational Chemistry: A Celebration of 1000 Papers of Professor Henry F. Schaefer III."

Critical to Professor Schaefer's scientific success has been a brilliant array of students and coworkers; including 54 undergraduate researchers who have published papers with him, 88 successful Ph.D. students, 44 postdoctoral researchers, and 62 visiting professors who have spent substantial time in the Schaefer group. A number of his students have gone on to positions of distinction in industry (Accelrys, Allstate Insurance,

American Cyanamid, AstraZeneca, AT&T, Avaya, Bicerano and Associates, Chemical Abstracts, Clariant, Computational Geosciences, DeNovaMed, Deutsche Bank, Dow Chemical, ELANTAS, Electronic Arts, Endress-Hauser, GAUSSIAN, Goodrich, Henkel, Hewlett-Packard, Hughes Aircraft, IBM, Komag, Lehman Brothers, Locus Pharmaceuticals, Mobil Research, Molecular Simulations, Monsanto, OpenEye, OSI Software, Pharmaceutical Research Associates, Polaroid, Proctor & Gamble, Q-CHEM, Reagens Deutschland, Ricoh, Schroedinger, SciCo, Sugen, and WaveSplitter Technologies). Four of his graduated Ph.D.s have successfully started their own companies. Several have gone on to successful careers in government laboratories, including the Australian National University Supercomputer Center, Joint Institute for Laboratory Astrophysics (JILA), Lawrence Livermore National Laboratory, NASA Ames, National Cancer Institute, National Center for Disease Control, National Institutes of Health (Bethesda), Naval Research Laboratory, Oak Ridge National Laboratory, Pacific Northwest National Laboratory, Pittsburgh Supercomputing Center, and Sandia National Laboratories. Charles Blahous went directly from his Ph.D. studies with Dr. Schaefer to the position of American Physical Society Congressional Scientist Fellow, and eventually to positions of significant importance in the U.S. political system (chief of staff for Senator Alan Simpson of Wyoming and later Senator Judd Gregg of New Hampshire; and chief strategist for President George W. Bush's initiative to reform social security; see Wall Street Journal article April 22, 2005).

Many of Dr. Schaefer's students have accepted professorships in universities, including the University of Alabama at Birmingham, University of Arizona, Budapest University (Hungary), University of California at Merced, City University of New York, Fatih University (Istanbul, Turkey), Georgia Tech, University of Georgia, University of Giessen (Germany), University of Girona (Spain), University of Grenoble (France), University of Guelph (Ontario), University of Illinois-Chicago, University of Illinois-Urbana, Johns Hopkins University, Indiana University-Purdue University at Indianapolis, Indian Association for the Cultivation of Science (Kolkata), University of Kentucky, University of Manchester (England), University of Marburg (Germany),

University of Massachusetts, University of Michigan, University of Mississippi, National Tsing Hua University (Taiwan), University of North Dakota, Ohio State University, Osaka University (Japan), University of Paris – Sud (France), Pohang Institute of Science and Technology (Korea), Portland State University, Pennsylvania State University, Rice University, Rikkyo University (Tokyo), Scripps Research Institute, St. Andrew's University (Scotland), Stanford University, University of Stirling (Scotland), University of Stockholm (Sweden), University of Tasmania (Australia), Technical University of Munich (Germany), Texas A&M University, the University of Texas at Arlington, University of Trondheim (Norway), University of Tubingen (Germany), and Virginia Tech.

Dr. Schaefer has been invited to present plenary lectures at more than 220 national or international scientific conferences. He has delivered endowed or named lectures or lecture series at more than 40 major universities, including the 1998 Kenneth S. Pitzer Memorial Lecture at Berkeley, the 2001 Israel Pollak Distinguished Lectures at the Technion - Israel Institute of Technology, Haifa, the 2007 C. V. Raman Memorial Lecture in Calcutta, India, and the 2007 Per-Olov Lowdin Lectures at the University of Uppsala, Sweden. He is the recipient of eighteen honorary degrees. He was the longest serving Editor-in-Chief of the London-based journal Molecular Physics (1995-2005). He was also the longest serving President of the World Association of Theoretical and Computational Chemists, from 1996 to 2005. His service to the chemical community includes the chairmanship of the American Chemical Society's Subdivision of Theoretical Chemistry (1982) and Division of Physical Chemistry (1992). At the 228th National Meeting of the American Chemical Society (Philadelphia, August, 2004) the Division of Computers in Chemistry and the Division of Physical Chemistry co-sponsored a four-day symposium in honor of Dr. Schaefer.

Professor Schaefer's major awards include the American Chemical Society Award in Pure Chemistry (1979, "for the development of computational quantum chemistry into a reliable quantitative field of chemistry and for prolific exemplary calculations of broad chemical interest"); the American Chemical Society Leo Hendrik Baekeland Award (1983, "for his contributions to computational quantum chemistry and for outstanding applications of this technique to a wide range of chemical problems"); the Schrödinger Medal (1990); the Centenary Medal of the Royal Society of Chemistry (London, 1992, as "the first theoretical chemist successfully to challenge the accepted conclusions of a distinguished experimental group for a polyatomic molecule, namely methylene"); the American Chemical Society Award in Theoretical Chemistry (2003, "for his development of novel and powerful computational methods of electronic structure theory, and their innovative use to solve a host of important chemical problems"). In 2003 he also received the annual American Chemical Society Ira Remsen Award, named after the first chemistry research professor in North America. The Remsen Award citation reads "For work that resulted in more than one hundred distinct, critical theoretical predictions that were subsequently confirmed by experiment and for work that provided a watershed in the field of quantum chemistry, not by reproducing experiment, but using state-of-the-art theory to make new chemical discoveries and, when necessary, to challenge experiment." The Journal of Physical Chemistry published a special issue in honor of Dr. Schaefer on April 15, 2004. He was elected a Fellow of the American Academy of Arts and Sciences in 2004. He was named the recipient of the prestigious Joseph O. Hirschfelder Prize of the University of Wisconsin for the academic year 2005-2006. He became a Fellow of the Royal Society of Chemistry (London) in 2005.

During the comprehensive period 1981 – 1997 Professor Schaefer was the sixth most highly cited chemist in the world; out of a total of 628,000 chemists whose research was cited. The Science Citation Index reports that by December 31, 2007 his research had been cited more than 40,000 times. Professor Schaefer's Wikipedia h-index is 96. His research involves the use of state-of-the-art computational hardware and theoretical methods to solve important problems in molecular quantum mechanics.

Professor Schaefer is also well known as a student of the relationship between science and religion. One or more of the lectures in his popular lecture series on this important topic have been presented at most major universities in North America, including Harvard, Stanford, Berkeley, M.I.T., Yale, Princeton, and the Universities of Alberta and Toronto. Dr. Schaefer has also presented these lectures in many universities abroad, including those in Ankara, Bangalore, Beijing, Berlin, Bern, Bratislava, Brisbane, Budapest, Cajamarca (Peru), Canberra, Cape Town, Chengdu, Chennai (Madras), Christchurch, Cluj-Napoca, Kochi (Cochin), Delhi, Durban, Goa, Guangzhou, Hong Kong, Hyderabad, Istanbul, Kanpur, Kolkata (Calcutta), Krakow, Kunming, Lanzhou, Lausanne, Leipzig, London, Lucknow, Mumbai (Bombay), Paris, Prague, Sarajevo, Seoul, Shanghai, Singapore, Sofia, Split, St. Petersburg, Sydney, Szeged, Taipei, Tokyo, Trivandrum, Urumqi, Warsaw, Wuxi, Xiamen, Zagreb, and Zurich. His continuously evolving lecture "The Big Bang, Stephen Hawking, and God" appears in many locations and in several languages on the worldwide web. This lecture has been one of the most popular articles about science on the web in recent years, as discussed in Michael White and John Gribbin's best selling biography of Professor Hawking (pages 314-315 of the 2002 edition). On April 24, 2002 Dr. Schaefer received the Erick Bogseth Nilson Award, given to an outstanding university professor in North America, by the organization Christian Leadership. In May 2005 Dr. Schaefer was elected a Corresponding Member of the Catholic Academy of Sciences in the USA. A brief spiritual biography (through 1991, written by Dr. David Fisher) of Professor Schaefer may be found on pages 323 - 326 of the book "More Than Conquerors", edited by John Woodbridge (Moody Press, Chicago, 1992). At the University of Georgia Professor Schaefer teaches a popular two credit freshman seminar each year entitled "Science and Christianity: Conflict or Coherence?" Dr. Schaefer's book with the same title had its fifth printing (with additions) in May 2008. The book reached position #84 on the best-selling list of Amazon.com in March 2004.

About the Lectures

The Introduction to the book *Science and Christianity: Conflict or Coherence?* gives a brief history of the origin of these lectures at the University of California at Berkeley. Audience sizes have ranged from 5 students at the University of Kansas (1986) to 1300 at the University of Michigan (1995). The typical university audience has been about 200, including perhaps 120 undergraduates, 60 graduate students, and 20 faculty. More than 500 have been in attendance at each of the three premier Ivy League universities (Harvard, Yale, and Princeton). The dates and locations of the lectures follow.

1. University of California, Berkeley, California, April 1984.
2. Brown University, Providence, Rhode Island, April 1985.
3. University of California, Berkeley, California, September 1985.
4. University of Canterbury, Christchurch, New Zealand, March 1986.
5. Stanford University, Palo Alto, California, April 1986.
6. University of Kansas, Lawrence, Kansas, April 1986.
7. University of Georgia, Athens, Georgia, October 1987.
8. University of Virginia, Charlottesville, Virginia, January 1988.
9. Emory University, Atlanta, Georgia, February 1988.
10. Baylor University, Waco, Texas, March 1988.
11. University of Alabama, Tuscaloosa, Alabama, April 1988.
12. Florida State University, Tallahassee, Florida, October 1988.
13. Georgia Institute of Technology, Atlanta, Georgia, April 1989.
14. Texas A & M University, College Station, Texas, April 1989.
15. Thomas F. Staley Lectures, Huntington College, Huntington, Indiana, November 1990.
16. Leningrad Institute of Technology, Leningrad, USSR, April 1991.
17. Leningrad State University, Leningrad, USSR, April 1991.
18. John Marks Templeton Lecture, Case Western Reserve University, Cleveland, Ohio, April 1992.
19. Stanford University, Palo Alto, California, April 1992.
20. St. Petersburg State University, St. Petersburg, Russia, May 1992.
21. Australian National University, Canberra, Australia, December 1992.

22. University of Florida, Gainesville, Florida, February 1993.
23. Kansas State University, Manhattan, Kansas, April 1993.
24. University of Pennsylvania, Philadelphia, Pennsylvania, November 1993.
25. Princeton University, Princeton, New Jersey, November 1993.
26. Rutgers University, New Brunswick, New Jersey, November 1993.
27. Clemson University, Clemson, South Carolina, March 1994.
28. University of South Carolina, Columbia, South Carolina, March 1994.
29. University of Minnesota, Minneapolis, Minnesota, April 1994.
30. University of Colorado, Denver, Colorado, April 1994.
31. U. S. Air Force Academy, Colorado Springs, Colorado, April 1994.
32. University of Sofia, Sofia, Bulgaria, May 1994.
33. Western Kentucky University, Bowling Green, Kentucky, September.
34. Southern Methodist University, Dallas, Texas, September 1994.
35. North Texas State University, Denton, Texas, September 1994.
36. Nanyang Technological University, Singapore, Singapore, September 1994.
37. Purdue University, West Lafayette, Indiana, November 1994.
38. Australian National University, Canberra, Australia, December 1994.
39. The Francis A. Schaeffer Lectures, Washington University, St. Louis, March 1995.
40. University of Kentucky, Lexington, Kentucky, September 1995.
41. Morehead State University, Morehead, Kentucky, September 1995.
42. Veritas Forum, University of Michigan, Ann Arbor, Michigan, October 1995.
43. Veritas Forum, Texas A & M University, College Station, Texas, October 1995.
44. Union University, Jackson, Tennessee, November 1995.
45. Vanderbilt University, Nashville, Tennessee, November 1995.
46. University of Tokyo, Tokyo, Japan, December 1995.
47. Veritas Forum, Yale University, New Haven, Connecticut, January 1996.
48. National Taiwan University, Taipei, Taiwan, January 1996.
49. Appalachian State University, Boone, North Carolina, March 1996.
50. Virginia Polytechnic Institute, Blacksburg, Virginia, March 1996.

51. Veritas Forum, Ohio State University, Columbus, Ohio, March 1996.
52. George Mason University, Fairfax, Virginia, March 1996.
53. University of Paris, Paris, France, April, 1996
54. University of Alabama, Birmingham, Alabama, September 1996.
55. Veritas Forum, University of North Carolina, Asheville, North Carolina, October 1996.
56. Clemson University, Clemson, South Carolina, October 1996.
57. Veritas Forum, University of Louisville, Louisville, Kentucky, November 1996.
58. Biola University, La Mirada, California, November 1996.
59. University of Hawaii, Honolulu, Hawaii, November 1996.
60. University of Hyderabad, Hyderabad, India, December 1996.
61. Indian Institute of Technology, Madras, India, December 1996.
62. Australian National University, Canberra, Australia, February 1997.
63. University of New South Wales, Sydney, Australia, February 1997.
64. Vanderbilt University, Nashville, Tennessee, March 1997.
65. Veritas Forum, Ball State University, Muncie, Indiana, March 1997.
66. C. S. Lewis Lecture, University of Tennessee, Chattanooga, Tennessee, April 1997.
67. University of North Dakota, Grand Forks, North Dakota, April 1997.
68. University of Zagreb, Zagreb, Croatia, May 1997.
69. University of Alberta, Edmonton, Alberta, Canada, July 1997.
70. L'Abri Fellowship, Huemoz, Switzerland, July & August, 1997.
71. National University of Singapore, September 1997.
72. Nanyang Technological University, Singapore, Singapore, September 1997.
73. John Marks Templeton Lecture, Colgate University, Hamilton, New York, October 1997.
74. Veritas Forum, University of Iowa, Iowa City, Iowa, October 1997.
75. Beijing Peoples University, Beijing, China, November, 1997
76. Veritas Lecture, Indiana University, Bloomington, Indiana, December, 1997.
77. The YMCA, Pune, India, January 1998.
78. Rashtriye Vidyalaya College of Engineering, Bangalore University, Bangalore, India, January 1998.

79. Indian Institute of Science, Bangalore, India, January 1998.
80. Veritas Forum, University of California, Santa Barbara, California, February 1998.
81. Hong Kong University of Science and Technology, Hong Kong, March 1998.
82. Chinese University of Hong Kong, Shatin, Hong Kong, March 1998.
83. University of Hong Kong, Hong Kong, March 1998.
84. City Polytechnic of Hong Kong, Hong Kong, March 1998.
85. University of Plovdiv, Plovdiv, Bulgaria, May 1998.
86. University of Sofia, Sofia, Bulgaria, May 1998.
87. Coastal Georgia College, Brunswick, Georgia, September 1998.
88. The Medical School, Emory University, Atlanta, Georgia, October 1998.
89. University of Georgia, Athens, Georgia, November 1998.
90. Kennesaw State University, Marietta, Georgia, December 1998.
91. University of Capetown, Capetown, South Africa, January 1999.
92. The Swiss Hotel, Istanbul, Turkey, February 1999.
93. The Turkish-American Association, Ankara, Turkey, February 1999.
94. The Aegean University, Izmir, Turkey, February 1999.
95. Montana State University, Bozeman, Montana, March 1999.
96. Comenius University, Bratislava, Slovakia, April 1999.
97. Slovak Technical University, Bratislava, Slovakia, April 1999.
98. University of Zilina, Slovakia, April 1999.
99. Georgia Southern University, Statesboro, Georgia, April 1999.
100. University of Toronto, Ontario, Canada, April 1999.
101. University of Guelph, Ontario, Canada, April 1999.
102. University of Waterloo, Ontario, Canada, April 1999.
103. Eidgenossische Technische Hochschule (ETH), Swiss Federal Institute of Technology, Zürich, Switzerland, May 1999.
104. University of Sofia, Sofia, Bulgaria, May 1999.
105. University of Plovdiv, Plovdiv, Bulgaria, May 1999.
106. Southeastern U. S. Conference for Doctoral Students, Intervarsity Christian Fellowship, Jasper, Georgia, May 1999.
107. Charles University, Prague, Czech Republic, June 1999.
108. Czech Technical University, Prague, Czech Republic, June 1999.
109. Czech Republic Academy of Sciences, Prague, Czech Republic, June 1999.

110. Book City, Peking University, Beijing, China, September 1999.
111. Tsinghua University, Beijing, China, September 1999.
112. Huntington College, Huntington, Indiana, September 1999.
113. Conference "By Chance or Design," Georgia Institute of Technology, Atlanta, Georgia, November 1999.
114. Australian National University, Canberra, Australia, December 1999.
115. Delhi University, Delhi, India, January 2000.
116. Indian Institute of Technology, New Delhi, India, January 2000.
117. National Physical Laboratory, New Delhi, India, January 2000.
118. Seventy-Fifth Anniversary Lecture, Valparaiso University, Indiana, January 2000.
119. Mercer University, Macon, Georgia, February 2000.
120. University of Hong Kong, China, February 2000.
121. Hong Kong University of Science and Technology, Hong Kong, China, February 2000.
122. Hong Kong Polytechnic University, China, February 2000.
123. University of Natal, Durban, South Africa, March 2000.
124. University of Durban Westville, Durban, South Africa, March 2000.
125. University of Rochester, Rochester, New York, March 2000.
126. University of Kansas, Lawrence, Kansas, April 2000.
127. Interaction with Steven Weinberg, Baylor University, Waco, Texas, April 2000.
128. Imperial College, London, England, May 2000.
129. Eotvos Lorand University, Budapest, Hungary, May 2000.
130. Eidgenossische Technische Hochschule (ETH), Swiss Federal of Technology, Zürich, Switzerland, June and July 2000.
131. University of Bern, Switzerland, June 2000.
132. L'Abri Fellowship, Huemoz, Switzerland, June 2000.
133. The Donald Frederick Othmer Lectures, Tokyo, Japan, September 2000.
134. University of Florida, Gainesville, Florida, October 2000.
135. Calcutta University, Park Street, Calcutta, India, January 2001.
136. The Demosthenian Literary Society, University of Georgia, February 2001.
137. University of Arizona, Tucson, Arizona, February 2001.
138. Institute for Christian Studies, Austin, Texas, March 2001.
139. University of Texas, Austin, Texas, March 2001.
140. Southwest State Texas University, San Marcos, Texas, March 2001.

141. University of Tokyo, Tokyo, Japan, March 2001.
142. Veritas Forum, Harvard University, Cambridge, Massachusetts, April 2001.
143. Babes-Bolyai University, Cluj, Romania, April 2001.
144. Eotvos Lorand University, Budapest, Hungary, April 2001.
145. Imperial College of Science and Technology, University of London, England, May 2001.
146. University of Southern Queensland, Toowoomba, Queensland, Australia, July 2001.
147. The Cranach Institute, Concordia University, Mequon, Wisconsin, September 2001.
148. University of California, Davis, California, October 2001.
149. Southern Methodists University, Dallas, Texas, October 2001.
150. University of Texas, Artlington, Texas, October 2001.
151. Louisiana State University, Baton Rouge, Louisiana, November 2001.
152. East China Normal University, Shanghai, China, November 2001.
153. Fudan University, Shanghai, China, November 2001.
154. Shanghai University, Shanghai, China, November 2001.
155. Georgia Institute of Technology, Atlanta, Georgia, November 2001.
156. K. J. Somaiya College of Science and Commerce, University of Mumbai, Bombay, India, January 2002.
157. St. Xavier's College, Bombay University, Mumbai, India, January 2002.
158. Bhabha Atomic Research Centre (BARC), Mumbai, India, January 2002.
159. King's College, New York City, February 2002.
160. Veritas Forum, Rice University, Houston, Texas, February 2002.
161. Eotvos Lorand University, Budapest, Hungary, March 2002.
162. University of Szeged, Szeged, Hungary, March 2002.
163. Clemson University, Clemson, South Carolina, April 2002.
164. Stanford University, Palo Alto, California, April 2002.
165. Bosnian Academy of Arts and Sciences, Sarajevo, Bosnia, April 2002.
166. Sarajevo University, Sarajevo, Bosnia, April 2002.
167. Commencement Address and Honorary Doctorate, Huntington College, Huntington, Indiana, May 2002.
168. Ecole Polytechnique Federale de Lausanne (EPFL), Lausanne, Switzerland, June 2002.
169. Eidgenossische Technische Hochschule, ETH Zentrum, Zürich, Switzerland, June 2002.

170. Swiss Federal Institute of Technology, ETH Hönggerberg, Switzerland, June 2002.
171. University of Minnesota, Minneapolis, Minnesota, October 2002.
172. Kunming University of Science and Technology, Kunming, China, October 2002.
173. Yunnan University, Kunming, China. October 2002.
174. The Open University, Zagreb, Croatia, November 2002.
175. Veritas Forum, Texas A&M University, College Station, Texas, January 2003.
176. University of Lucknow, Lucknow, India, January 2003.
177. Isabella Thoburn College, Lucknow, India, January 2003.
178. University of Kanpur, Kanpur, India, January 2003.
179. Indian Institute of Technology, Kanpur, India January 2003.
180. Calcutta University, Park Street, Kolkata, India, January 2003.
181. Veritas Forum, Oglethorpe University, Atlanta, Georgia, January 2003.
182. The Bar Association of the City of New York, New York, March 2003.
183. University of Massachusetts, Amherst, Massachusetts, March 2003.
184. Emory University, Atlanta, Georgia, April 2003.
185. University of Split, Split, Croatia, April 2003.
186. The Multi-Media Cultural Center, Split, Croatia, April 2003.
187. The Technical University, Berlin, Germany, May 2003.
188. Waynesburg College, Waynesburg, Pennsylvania, August 2003.
189. University of Georgia, Athens, Georgia, August 2003.
190. Guangxi Normal University, Guilin, China, September 2003.
191. Honorary Degree, University of Chengdu, Chengdu, China, September 2003.
192. The Brenzier and Wilhelmina Price Lectures, Wingate University, Wingate, North Carolina, October 2003.
193. University of California, Davis, California, November 2003.
194. University of Houston, Houston, Texas, December 2003
195. University of North Florida, Jacksonville, Florida, January 2004.
196. Chung-Ang University, Seoul, Korea, February 2004.
197. Seoul National University, Seoul, Korea, February 2004.
198. Clemson University, Clemson, South Carolina, February 2004.
199. John M. Templeton Lecture, Princeton University, Princeton, New Jersey, March 2004.

200. John M. Templeton Lecture, Carnegie - Mellon University, Pittsburgh, Pennsylvania, March 2004.
201. The Sigma Zeta Lectures, Asbury College, Wilmore, Kentucky, April 2004.
202. Rochester Institute of Technology, Rochester, New York, April 2004.
203. Biola University, La Mirada, California, April 2004.
204. Eidgenössische Technische Hochschule, ETH Zentrum, Zürich, Switzerland, June 2004.
205. Ecole Polytechnique Federale de Lausanne, Lausanne, Switzerland, June 2004.
206. University of Bern, Bern, Switzerland, June 2004.
207. University of Zürich, Zürich, Switzerland, June 2004.
208. Massachusetts Institute of Technology, Cambridge Massachusetts, September 2004.
209. Honorary Degree Ceremony, Xinjiang University, Urumqi, China, September 2004.
210. Honors Luncheon, University of Georgia, Athens, Georgia, September 2004.
211. The 2004 New College Lectures, University of New South Wales, Sydney. Australia, October 2004.
212. The Metanexus Lecture, Valley Forge College, Valley Forge, Pennsylvania, October 2004.
213. Erskine College, Due West, South Carolina, October 2004.
214. The Pew Foundation Lectures, Union University, Jackson, Tennessee, October 2004.
215. Open Forum, Ravi Zacharias International, Hyderabad, India, February 2005.
216. Osmania University, Hyderabad, India, February 2005.
217. Indian Institute of Science, Bangalore, India, February 2005.
218. University of Madras, Chennai, India, February 2005.
219. Veritas Forum, University of California, Santa Cruz, California, March 2005.
220. Augusta State University, Augusta, Georgia, March 2005.
221. Duquesne University, Pittsburgh, Pennsylvania, April 2005.
222. University of Illinois, Urbana, Illinois, April 2005.
223. Conference, "Science - Ethics - Faith", Wisla, Poland, May 2005
224. Krakow University of Science and Technology, Krakow, Poland, May 2005.
225. University of Warsaw, Warsaw, Poland, May 2005.
226. Technical University of Berlin, Berlin, Germany, June 2005.
227. University of Chemnitz, Chemnitz, Germany, June 2005.

228. University of Halle, Halle, Germany, June 2005.
229. University of Queensland, Brisbane, Australia, June 2005.
230 Xiamen University, Amoy, China, September 2005.
231. Sichuan University, Chengdu, China, September 2005.
232. Southwestern University of Finance and Economics, Chengdu, China, September 2005.
233. Oklahoma State University, Stillwater, Oklahoma, October 2005.
234. University of Wisconsin, Madison, Wisconsin, October 2005.
235. University of Georgia, Athens, Georgia, November 2005.
236. University of Goa, Goa, India, February 2006.
237. Southeastern College, Lakeland, Florida, February 2006.
238. University of Mississippi, Oxford Mississippi, March 2006.
239 Mississippi State University, Starkville, Mississippi, March 2006.
240. Idaho State University, Pocatello, Idaho, April 2006.
241. University of Sofia, Sofia, Bulgaria, May 2006.
242. University of Plovdiv, Plovdiv, Bulgaria, May 2006.
243. Eidgenössische Technische Hochschule (ETH), Zürich, Switzerland, June 2006.
244. University of Karlsruhe, Karlsruhe, Germany, June 2006.
245. Groupes Bibliques Universitaires de France, Strasbourg, France, July 2006.
246. University of California, Berkeley, California, September 2006.
247. University of Georgia, Athens, Georgia, September 2006.
248. Lanzhou University, Lanzhou, China, September 2006.
249. Lanzhou University, Yuzhong, China, September 2006.
250. University of Chicago, Chicago, Illinois, November 2006.
251. Open Forum, Bombay Central, Mumbai, India, January 2007.
252. Calcutta University, Kolkata, India, January 2007.
253. Central University of Hyderabad, Hyderabad, India, January 2007.
254. Delhi University, Delhi, India, January 2007.
255. Medical College of Georgia, Augusta, Georgia, March 2007.
256. Veritas Forum, Georgia Institute of Technology, Atlanta, Georgia, April 2007.
257. Huntington University, Huntington, Indiana, April 2007.
258. Taylor University, Upland, Indiana, April 2007.
259. University of Chemnitz, Chemnitz, Germany, May 2007.
260. University of Leipzig, Leipzig, Germany, May 2007.
261. University of Halle, Halle, Germany, May 2007.
262. University of Cajamarca, Cajamarca, Peru, June 2007.

263. The Case for Faith Symposium, Atlanta, Georgia, September 2007.
264. Uppsala University, Uppsala, Sweden, October 2007.
265. Johns Hopkins University, Baltimore, Maryland, October 2007.
266. South China Normal University, Guangzhou, China, November 2007.
267. Southern Yangtze University, Wuxi, China, November 2007.
268. Medical College of Georgia, Augusta, Georgia, January 2008.
269. Plenary Lecture, Techfest, Indian Institute of Technology, Bombay, Mumbai, India, January 2008.
270. St. Albert's College, Mahatma Gandhi University, Ernakulam, India, January 2008.
271. Distinguished Lecture Series, Rajagiri School of Engineering and Technology, Kochi, India, January 2008.
272. Rajiv Gandhi Centre for Biotechnology, Trivandrum, India, January 2008.
273. Veritas Forum, University of California, Santa Barbara, California, February 2008.
274. Univerity of Georgia, Athens, Georgia, March 2008.
275. The King's College, New York City, March 2008.
276. Herman Hotz Lecture, University of Arkansas, Fayetteville, Arkansas, March 2008.
277. Marquette University, Milwaukee, Wisconsin, April 2008.
278. European Scientific Network, Eger, Hungary, May 2008.
279. University of Vienna, Vienna, Austria, June 2008.
280. University of Queensland, Brisbane, Australia, September 2008.
281. North-Eastern Hill University, Shillong, India, October 2008.

Index

Noteworthy Comments on
SCIENCE AND CHRISTIANITY:
CONFLICT OR COHERENCE?

"Dr. Schaefer has addressed many important issues concerning science and Christianity. This work is thorough as well as insightful. It is scholarly, yet written in a style that is entertaining and a joy to read. A great reference for those exploring the issues."

Dr. Michael Atchison
Professor of Biochemistry
University of Pennsylvania
Philadelphia, Pennsylvania

"While talking to a colleague the other day, I learned about this new book and immediately ordered it. It was absolutely delightful. This is a wonderful contribution, not the least of which is the author's personal experience."

Dr. Nathan L. Bauld
Professor of Chemistry
University of Texas
Austin, Texas

"The best kept secret of science is how strongly it points toward a creator and dovetails with Christianity. In this marvelously lucid book, the eminent physical chemist Henry Schaefer unfolds the secret."

Dr. Michael J. Behe
Professor of Biology
Lehigh University
Bethlehem, Pennsylvania
Author of *Darwin's Black Box*

"Using the statements and experiences of numerous past and present, well-known scientists, in addition to his own profound Christian testimony, Professor Schaefer convincingly dispels the surprisingly still often-held view that a personal Christian faith and science are incompatible. In so doing, this important book persuasively affirms that it is only in Christ that all things hold together. This is a "must read" book for all thoughtful people in the twenty-first century and beyond."

Dr. Christopher E. Brion
Professor of Chemistry
University of British Columbia
Fellow, Royal Society of Canada

206

"What a dynamite book! If you've ever believed the propaganda about the ongoing conflict between science and Christianity (or for that matter, between thoughtful, rational, intelligent people and Christianity) this book will forever disabuse you of that notion. Dr. Schaefer, with great wit, power, insight and skill, sets the record straight. Read this book! You'll thank me for recommending it to you."

Dr. Steve Brown
Professor of Practical Theology
Reformed Theological Seminary
Orlando, Florida
Teacher, Key Life Radio Program

"A thought provoking book that will encourage those who take for granted that science and Christianity are incompatible to look more closely at important issues."

Dr. Tucker Carrington, Jr.
Professor of Chemistry
University of Montreal
Quebec, Canada

"In *Science and Christianity: Conflict or Coherence?* Schaefer demolishes the common notion that science and Christianity are incompatible. He weaves together an abundance of documentation to make his case, and does so with a good natured, personal style that takes good advantage of his personal acquaintance with hosts of leading scientists. The book has the solid ring of authenticity. I recommend it for scientists and non-scientists, Christians and non-Christians."

Dr. R. David Cole
Professor Emeritus of Molecular and Cell Biology
University of California, Berkeley
Berkeley, California

"I couldn't put this book down. Dr Schaefer has shown us how he is a faithful traditional Christian and a hard-working scientist -- and how he's still one person! There is so much intelligence and clear thought here, and a warm and winning personality to boot. I will recommend this book to friends in the sciences, and to young Christians thinking about the sciences. I will also give it to people who think the sciences keep them from being Christians. I can't wait to show it to people I know."

Dr. Jack Collins
Professor of Old Testament
Covenant Theological Seminary
St Louis, Missouri

"This is a great book by one of the Christian world's premier thinkers and one of America's eminent scientists. It is an invaluable contribution to the intelligent design debate."

Charles W. Colson
Founder, Prison Fellowship
Recipient of the 1993 Templeton Prize

This book was featured on Mr. Colson's radio program Breakpoint on January 5, March 8, and March 9, 2004. See Breakpoint.org.

"This is an impressive book that is both professional and personal. It handles a wide range of topics, from cosmology and evolution to postmodernism and intellectual questions about Christianity. With this book as well as with the story of his own life, Schaefer compellingly demonstrates that, contrary to popular thinking, it is entirely well possible to be one person that is at the same time a dedicated scientist and a dedicated disciple of Jesus Christ. I have hardly ever read a book with ideas on the science/faith and evolution/creation debate that matches my own opinions so closely."

Dr. Cees Dekker
Professor of Molecular Biophysics
Delft University of Technology
The Netherlands
Recipient, 2003 Spinoza Prize

"Schaefer is a world-class scientist and a thoroughly orthodox Christian. For years now he has been giving popular lectures on the consonance of Christian truth and science. This book distills those lectures and also provides a very personal look at Schaefer's life and faith."

Dr. William A. Dembski
Carl F. H. Henry Professor of Science and Theology
Southern Seminary, Louisville, Kentucky
Author of *The Design Inference* (Cambridge University Press)

"This is one of those rare books that combines solid substance with understandable style, spiced with humor. I read some books for amusement, others to stretch my mind. This book does both."

Dr. David Fisher
Editor, *Newsletter* of the American Scientific Affiliation
September, 2003

"Professor Schaefer's book is an inspiring contribution that is backed with solid arguments, which in turn make you reflect very seriously about your own position on the issue. This is not only a wonderful reaffirmation of the coherence between science and religion, but also a warm and optimistic story of the random walk the author took toward the most important discovery he ever made. I really hope the reader considers and meditates carefully on the questions that this stellar and distinguished scientist poses and the answers he provides. Within is a hidden treasure to be found indeed. This is a book that ends with a very positive message; one that will make you stop and reflect on where your life is heading."

Professor Roberto A. Garza-López
Department of Chemistry
Pomona College
Claremont, California

"Dr. Schaefer's new book will serve as an inspiring introduction for thoughtful people who are seriously interested in understanding the origin, function and future of our universe. But the book is not a cold compendium of facts and figures. It is highly personal, drawing on the author's own experiences and surveying, with characteristic good humor, the breadth and depth of Christian belief in scientists across the ages. This is a book to inform the mind, warm the heart, and inspire the evangelical lifestyle that has always been the hallmark of true Christianity."

Dr. Peter M. W. Gill
Professor of Chemistry
University of Nottingham
Nottingham, England

"These personal stories are excellent to reach our postmodern generation - this work will enlighten the mind and penetrate the heart."

Derwin "Dewey" Gray
1995 - 1996 Team Captain, Indianapolis Colts
One Heart at a Time Ministries

"The strength of the lectures is their clarity, the way they draw from a wide range of commentators -- from both sides of the debate, the open-hearted and good-natured approach, and the measured presentation of a perspective of firm but reasoned conviction. These are just the sorts of things that the science and faith discussion most needs. And they go to make up a powerful and helpful book of Christian apologetic that I can heartily recommend. I particularly enjoyed the personal testimony chapter which resonated greatly with my own experience."

Professor Ian Hutchinson
Chair, Department of Nuclear Engineering
Massachusetts Institute of Technology
Cambridge, Massachusetts

"Professor Schaefer makes a lucid and persuasive case for why it is 'natural' for a natural scientist to believe in God. He reminds us of the historical origins of modern science among people of faith, and shows himself to be an heir to their tradition as a first-rate scientist with a deep commitment to the eternal truths revealed by our Creator."

Dr. Robert Kaita
Principal Research Physicist, Plasma Physics Laboratory
Princeton University
Princeton, New Jersey

"Professor Schaefer is one of the most highly cited chemists in the world. His book is the easiest to read of those I recommend on science and Christianity. It is full of interesting quotes and anecdotes and includes the story of how he became a Christian as a professor at Berkeley."

Dr. Adriaan A. Louis,
Royal Society University Research Fellow
Cambridge University
England

"This book is a great testimony to God's power in a scientist's life."

Dr. Christopher W. Macosko
Professor of Materials Science
University of Minnesota
Member, National Academy of Engineering

"Professor Schaefer's book is like the author himself... outrageous and fascinating and funny and very serious and hard to put down. Neither author nor book needs a 'put-down' because both are completely genuine and unpretentious creations. The title is just right. Although he's quite convinced himself that Christianity is 'right' he knows it can't be 'proved right'. So instead of knockouts or put-downs, he goes for the infinitely superior 'please consider this', which is the closing sentence of the book. It's also what gives the rest of the book such appeal."

Professor Eric Magnusson
School of Physical, Environmental, and Mathematical Sciences
University College
University of New South Wales
Canberra, Australia

"A very valuable and reliable and inspiring contribution to the literature on science and religion."

Dr. Norman March
Coulson Professor of Theoretical Chemistry
Oxford University
Oxford University, England

"I enjoyed *Science and Christianity* very much and am recommending it to my students. There is a real absence of books which take a thoughtful approach to the subject without an obvious underlying agenda."

Professor Todd Martinez
School of Chemical Sciences
University of Illinois
Urbana-Champaign, Illinois
Recipient, 2005 MacArthur Foundation Genius Award

"*Science and Christianity: Conflict or Coherence* is a thought-provoking and inspiring book. In his very readable book, Dr Schaefer presents the case for God in creation and the very natural sequence of Christ in the Christian. Both of these concepts are life changing. That one can be a scientist of renown and a practicing Christian is demonstrated many times over in the examples he quotes and in the story of his own life. Reading this book will be a tremendously rewarding experience for serious students who are still grappling with the intellectual challenge of the Creation versus Evolution debate and also to those who have formed their opinions but who are still open to responsible argument."

Dr. Murray McEwan
Professor of Chemistry
University of Canterbury
Christchurch New Zealand

"In this book, prolific quantum chemist Henry (Fritz) Schaefer explores, as the title suggests, the relationship between Christianity and science, giving many personal anecdotes and reflecting on a wide range of writers in a long history of discourse on the subject. This is a highly recommended read for both Christians and non-Christians."

Review by Dr. J. Terence Morrison
Fall 2003 *University Faculty Newsletter*
InterVarsity Christian Fellowship

"Because of the philosophical pronouncements of some scientists and non-scientists, many people today assume that there is a conflict between science and Christianity. But the eminent physical chemist and Christian Henry Schaefer shows in *Science and Christianity: Conflict or Coherence?* that there need be no conflict. This delightful set of essays, arising out of lectures that Professor Schaefer has delivered at hundreds of leading academic institutions around the world, answers many questions that people have about the relationship between science and Christianity and also gives examples of many leading scientists that are Christians."

Dr. Don Page
Professor of Physics
University of Alberta
Edmonton, Canada
Long time collaborator with Stephen Hawking

"In *Science and Christianity: Conflict or Coherence?* an internationally distinguished chemical physicist and one of the principal architects of modern quantum chemistry, Professor Henry F. Schaefer, has accomplished a remarkable feat. The book is based on countless lectures that he has courageously presented all over the world and touches on everything from the deepest secrets of Creation to postmodernism, while providing a fascinating and unequalled insight into the scientific mind that is brought to life by both personal and historical anecdotes, skillfully and entertainingly woven into the text. This is a very captivating and personally highly engaging work, bringing the philosophical and theistic attitudes of various scientists to a general audience without causing offense to anyone. A very engrossing piece of work for its breadth, its thought-provoking, witty and whimsical - yet compelling and highly winsome - narrative, always lucid, very readable and richly rewarding to an attentive reader. Last but not least, a marvelous treasure trove of references and of their critical assessment. A book to treasure, to savor and to re-read."

Dr. Josef Paldus
Professor of Applied Mathematics
University of Waterloo
Waterloo, Ontario, Canada
Fellow, Royal Society of Canada

"This is an intensely personal book. It should be required reading for all scientists who are willing to identify themselves as Christians. The book is also recommended for all people interested in an honest exploration of the interaction of science with Christianity."

Dr. Gary D. Patterson
Professor of Chemical Physics and Polymer Science
Carnegie-Mellon University
Pittsburgh, Pennsylvania

"This is a wonderful book, and I read through it immediately. The liveliness of the lectures shines through in the printed word."

Dr. Martin Quack
Professor of Physical Chemistry
ETH Zürich, Switzerland
1988 Hinshelwood Lecturer, Oxford University, England

"*Science and Christianity: Conflict or Coherence?* is beautifully written, and accessible to non-scientists. Each chapter can be read independently. Schaefer writes with humor and personality, and shows great respect for those who believe differently, while making no apologies for his own viewpoints. The serious scholar of science and religion will likely be frustrated by the poor referencing throughout the book (a point acknowledged by the author) and the lack of in-depth discussion of certain topics. Yet all who read this book will be touched by the coherence of science and Christianity in the life of Professor Henry Schaefer. Indeed, anyone who feels that science and Christianity are fundamentally at odds will find much to ponder as this book provides a compelling case for the contrary."

Dr. Jonathon C. Rienstra-Kiracofe
Review in *Books and Culture,* February 23, 2004
Named *Christianity Today* "Book of the Week"

"During a recent trip to Spain, where I was invited to receive an award of the Spanish Chemical Society, I discovered Henry Schaefer's book *Science and Christianity*, and I read it with great interest."

Professor Jean-Louis Rivail
Laboratoire de Chimie Theorique
Université Henri Poincaré
Nancy, France

"Having heard Professor Schaefer give one of the lectures that have been collected into this book, I was anxious to read it as soon as it came out. Schaefer tackles the question of the coherence between Christianity and science with refreshing honesty and the intellectual rigor of a first class physical scientist -- applying it equally to scientific evidence and Biblical interpretations in a way that will help students of science think through these issues for themselves. The book manages to capture the electricity of Schaefer's public lectures to a university lecture hall packed full of students. It is a 'must read' for those interested in the relation between science and Christianity."

Dr. Thomas R. Rizzo
Professor of Chemistry
Ecole Polytechnique Federale de Lausanne
Lausanne, Switzerland

"*Science and Christianity* by Professor Henry Schaefer is a fascinating read worthy of careful study. He presents his personal convictions and supports them with carefully crafted arguments, all in the context of the views of other scientists from Isaac Newton and Charles Townes to Francis Crick and Stephen Weinberg. The result is a rare combination: a scholarly treatise which is fun to read."

Dr. Marlan O. Scully
Burgess Distinguished Professor
Director of the Institute for Quantum Studies
Texas A&M University
College Station, Texas
Member, U. S. National Academy of Sciences

"It is not often I read a book with which I find so much accord."

Dr. Phillip S. Skell
Evan Pugh Emeritus Professor
Pennsylvania State University
Department of Chemistry
University Park, Pennsylvania
Member, U. S. National Academy of Sciences

"Professor Schaefer's book is a great book for anyone who is interested in how a world-class scientist can also be a Bible believing Christian. I deliberately did NOT say how he can "reconcile" his faith and his science, since the whole point of this book is that there isn't anything to reconcile. An intelligent reading of the Bible, even when it is considered to be the inerrant word of God, does not produce any conflict with solid science. There are some open questions and mysteries to be sure, but no real conflicts. Read Dr. Schaefer's book to see!"

Dr. Richard Spencer
Professor of Electrical Engineering
University of California at Davis
Davis, California

"*Science and Christianity: Conflict or Coherence* is a delightful read that is sure to quench some fires and ignite others! As in Schaefer's lectures, though the content is deep, he distills down the meanings so that we can all enjoy. I have long felt that the perceived division between scientists and Christianity was more in the minds of the rookies than inherent within the halls of the academy. Indeed, this book underscores the fact that there are many scientists that love God, honor Him and delight in His creation. Within these pages is fuel for thought and discussions."

Dr. James M. Tour
Chao Professor of Chemistry
Computer Science, Mechanical Engineering, and Materials Science
Rice University
Houston, Texas

214

"Dr. Henry Schaefer is arguably among the top twenty living research chemists in the world. He is also a deeply committed Christian."

Professor Robert Vergenz
Department of Chemistry and Physics
University of North Florida
Jacksonville, Florida

"A most readable book drawn from years of popular lectures on the subject, this is a highly recommended reading. Treating questions of origins and related oft-debated questions, Schaefer illustrates with good humor, taste and balance how the Christian faith and the natural sciences are coherent."

Dr. J. Michael White
Robert A. Welch Professor of Chemistry
University of Texas
Austin, Texas

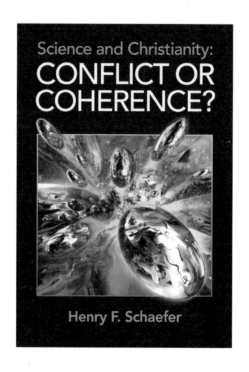

Available at

Amazon.com

or

Amazon.co.uk